D0084314

RELIGION TODAY: TRADITION, MODERNITY AND CHANGE

PERSPECTIVES ON CIVIL RELIGION

Religion Today: Tradition, Modernity and Change – an Open University/Ashgate series

The five textbooks and Reader that make up this series are:

- *From Sacred Text to Internet* edited by Gwilym Beckerlegge
- *Religion and Social Transformations* edited by David Herbert
- *Perspectives on Civil Religion* by Gerald Parsons
- *Global Religious Movements in Regional Context* edited by John Wolffe
- *Belief Beyond Boundaries* edited by Joanne Pearson
- *Religion Today: A Reader* edited by Susan Mumm

Each textbook includes:

- an introduction to the issues and controversies relevant to the topic under discussion
- a series of detailed case studies, which allow readers to see the theories and debates at work today in the experience of religious practitioners from various parts of the world
- extracts from other publications, which address the same issue from different perspectives (except *Perspectives on Civil Religion*)
- extensive references to other published material on the same topics
- supporting colour and black-and-white illustrations

The series offers an in-depth introduction to contemporary themes and challenges in religious studies. The contents highlight the central issues and ideas that are shaping religion today – and will continue to do so tomorrow. The textbooks contain plentiful contemporary case studies spanning many countries and religions, and integrate methods of analysis and theoretical perspectives. They work to ensure that readers will understand the relevance of methodologies to lived experience and gain the ability to transfer analytic skills and explanatory devices to the study of religion in context. The textbooks focus on the following key issues in contemporary religious studies: representation and interpretation; modernity and social change; civil religion; the impact of globalization on religion; and the growth of alternative religion.

The accompanying Reader presents primary and secondary source material structured around these core themes. It will serve as an invaluable resource book, whether used to accompany the textbooks in the series or not.

Cover: (clockwise from top left) photo of boots left at 'The Wall' (Vietnam Veterans Memorial Fund); detail from *Madonna degli occhi grossi*, Museo dell'Opera del Duomo, Siena (Foto Lensini, Siena); headstone of an unknown soldier (Commonwealth Graves Commission. Photo: Marcus Taylor); detail from the *drappellone* for the Palio of 16 August 1996 (Foto Lensini, Siena); Remembrance Day poppy (photo: Mike Levers); detail from the *drappellone* for the Palio of 16 August 2000 (Foto Lensini, Siena).

RELIGION TODAY: TRADITION, MODERNITY AND CHANGE

PERSPECTIVES ON CIVIL RELIGION

GERALD PARSONS

Ashgate

Aldershot • Burlington USA • Singapore • Sydney

in association with

The Open
University

This publication forms part of an Open University course AD317 *Religion Today: Tradition, Modernity and Change*. Details of this and other Open University courses can be obtained from the Call Centre, PO Box 724, The Open University, Milton Keynes MK7 6ZS, United Kingdom: tel. +44 (0)1908 653231, e-mail ces-gen@open.ac.uk

Alternatively, you may visit the Open University web site at http://www.open.ac.uk where you can learn more about the wide range of courses and packs offered at all levels by the Open University.

To purchase this publication or other components of Open University courses, contact Open University Worldwide Ltd, The Berrill Building, Walton Hall, Milton Keynes MK7 6AA, United Kingdom: tel. +44 (0)1908 858785; fax +44 (0)1908 858787; e-mail ouwenq@open.ac.uk; web site http://www.ouw.co.uk

British Library Cataloguing in Publication Data

Perspectives on civil religion. (Religion today : tradition, modernity and change; v.3)
 1. Relgions   2. Civil religion
 I. Title   II. Open University
 291.1'7

Library of Congress Control Number: 2001053652

Co-published by

The Open University	Ashgate Publishing Ltd	Ashgate Publishing Company
Walton Hall	Gower House, Croft Road	Burlington, VT 05401-5600
Milton Keynes MK7 6AA	Aldershot, Hants GU11 3HR	USA

Ashgate web site: http://www.ashgate.com

First published 2002.

Copyright © 2002 The Open University

All rights reserved. No part of this publication may be reproduced, stored in a retrieval system, transmitted or utilized in any form or by any means, electronic, mechanical, photocopying, recording or otherwise, without written permission from the publisher or a licence from the Copyright Licensing Agency Ltd. Details of such licences (for reprographic reproduction) may be obtained from the Copyright Licensing Agency Ltd of 90 Tottenham Court Road, London W1P 0LP.

Edited, designed and typeset by The Open University.

Printed and bound in the United Kingdom by The Bath Press, Bath.

ISBN 0 7546 0746 1 (hbk)
ISBN 0 7546 0818 2 (pbk)

1.1

23843B/ad317b3prelimsi1.1

Contents

Preface

Perspectives on Civil Religion is the third of a five-volume series entitled *Religion Today: Tradition, Modernity and Change*, published by Ashgate Publishing Ltd in association with The Open University. Like all the volumes in the series, *Perspectives on Civil Religion* has been compiled primarily with the needs of Open University undergraduate students in mind. However, it is hoped that the contents of the volume will also be of interest and value to other readers who would like to know more about the place of religion in the world today.

The author has benefited greatly from the careful and constructive comments on the first drafts of his chapters by Professor Kim Knott of the University of Leeds (external assessor), Professor Ken Thompson of the Faculty of Social Sciences at The Open University (reader) and Dr Claire Disbrey (tutor consultant). Any inaccuracies or questionable judgements are the responsibilities of the author alone.

The author wishes to acknowledge the contribution made to the production of this volume by: Adrian Roberts (course manager), Julie Bennett, Kate Clements and Peter Wright (editors), Paul Smith (picture researcher), Richard Hoyle (designer) and Pip Harris (compositor).

The author of the volume is:

- Gerald Parsons, Department of Religious Studies at The Open University

Introduction: the concept of civil religion

In 1967, the American sociologist Robert N. Bellah published an article in the journal *Daedalus* entitled 'Civil religion in America'. The article claimed that, alongside the churches and official religious bodies of the modern USA, there also existed 'an elaborate and well-institutionalized civil religion in America' (Bellah, 1967, p.1). This 'civil religion', Bellah argued, was rooted in American history and in a concept of America as, in some sense, a chosen nation with a mission to uphold certain God-given principles and values. Such a concept, he suggested, was already to be found in the Declaration of Independence of 1776, and had received powerful contemporary re-expression in the mid-twentieth century in the inaugural address of President John F. Kennedy, delivered in January 1961.

Bellah suggested that, a hundred years earlier, in the mid-nineteenth century, American civil religion had experienced a period of profound trial and testing, as the American Civil War raised the very deepest questions about national identity, values and meaning. Out of this experience came new emphases on the significance of death, sacrifice and rebirth within American civil religion. These themes were symbolized above all by the life and death of President Abraham Lincoln, by the Gettysburg Address, and by the setting up of the Gettysburg and Arlington National Cemeteries. The latter site, Bellah asserted, had subsequently become the most hallowed monument of American civil religion, with a section set aside for the dead of the defeated South as well as the dead of the victorious North, and with the subsequent reception of the dead of each of America's later wars, including the Tombs of America's Unknown Soldiers. Similarly, Memorial Day – an event that also grew out of the Civil War – provided an annual opportunity for remembrance of the dead and their sacrifice, for renewal of dedication to the American vision, and for local communities to associate themselves with the national expression of such civil religious values.

American civil religion could thus be said to possess 'sacred texts', such as the Declaration of Independence, the Constitution, and President Lincoln's Gettysburg Address; 'sacred places', such as the

Gettysburg and Arlington National Cemeteries; an annual ritual calendar of 'holy days', such as Memorial Day, Veterans Day, Thanksgiving and the Fourth of July; and symbolic 'sacrificial martyrs', such as the assassinated Presidents Lincoln and John F. Kennedy – the grave and the eternal flame for the latter also being located in Arlington National Cemetery. Therefore, according to Bellah, American civil religion possessed a seriousness and integrity that deserved both respect and careful understanding, just like any other religion. At its best, he asserted, American civil religion amounted to a 'genuine apprehension of universal and transcendent religious reality as seen in or, one could almost say, as revealed through the experience of the American people', and it constituted 'a heritage of moral and religious experience' from which America might learn and on which it might draw in facing contemporary and future crises and decisions (Bellah, 1967, pp.12 and 19).

But now, Bellah argued, in the mid- to late 1960s, both America and American civil religion faced a new time of trial. America's role in the world, its status as a major power, and its relationship with other nations and contemporary revolutionary movements, posed acute moral and ethical questions. In particular, American involvement in the war in Vietnam presented a moment of intense crisis. The war divided America, and civil disobedience in opposition to the American military involvement in Vietnam was added to the civil disobedience of the civil rights movement – itself arguably an attempt to complete the task begun with the abolition of slavery during the Civil War a hundred years earlier. Out of this new trial of American civil religion, Bellah now hoped, there might emerge a new version of American civil religion – one that incorporated international symbolism and values and thereby became 'one part of a new civil religion of the world' (Bellah, 1967, p.19).

As Bellah acknowledged, in framing his description of 'American civil religion' he had drawn on a variety of precedents and earlier ideas. Thus, he took the phrase 'civil religion' from the eighteenth-century French philosopher Jean-Jacques Rousseau, who had used it in his seminal work of political philosophy *The Social Contract*, first published in 1762. Similarly, he acknowledged the significance of the observations on Americans, and their almost mystical understanding of themselves and their history, by the early nineteenth-century French historian, Alexis de Tocqueville, in his study of *Democracy in America*, first published in 1835. Meanwhile, from the late nineteenth- and early twentieth-century sociologist, Emile Durkheim, Bellah drew the idea that any human group – in Bellah's case, the American people – may possess a religious dimension, in which a system of 'sacred' beliefs and practices will unite all those who share them into one community. Finally, in advancing his particular concept of an 'American civil religion', Bellah clearly also stood in succession to the earlier and highly influential study of the role of religion in American life by Will Herberg. In his book, *Protestant, Catholic, Jew,* first published in 1955, Herberg had argued that successive generations of immigrants to the USA had come to share – above and beyond their particular religious identities and beliefs – in a broader collective commitment to the values and beliefs of 'the American way of life'.[1]

Bellah's article proved to be the catalyst for a series of sustained and sometimes fierce debates over the definition, the nature and the significance of 'American civil religion' that have continued to the present day. The academic and scholarly debates over the concept crossed disciplinary boundaries and involved historians, sociologists, students of religion and political scientists. At the same time, broader cultural discussions also involved political and religious leaders and pressure groups in attempts to claim and define 'American civil religion' in terms of their own particular values and ideological positions. In the course of these debates, a variety of questions were raised about 'American civil religion'. Was it, in fact, little more than an uncritical and even idolatrous devotion to American interests and values? Was it at heart 'liberal' or 'conservative' in nature and influence? Was its content clearly agreed and understood? Was it essentially a celebration of American power and, especially, of the memory of America's past wars, and the justification of present military involvements? Was it essentially a beneficial phenomenon or a harmful one?

Few – if any – of these questions received answers that were clear, unambiguous or uncontested. On the contrary, both the concept of 'American civil religion' and the deployment of the concept in American cultural and political debates remain highly controversial and contested issues, even to the present. It is clear, for example, that there are different versions of 'American civil religion' and that the concept can, in principle, be deployed by representatives of sharply contrasting political views. Thus a series of commentators have distinguished between two broad – and opposing – versions of 'American civil religion', defining them as 'prophetic' and 'liberal' on the one hand, and as 'priestly' and 'conservative' on the other. The 'liberal' or 'prophetic' version of 'American civil religion' tends to emphasize America's commitment to broad values such as justice and liberty, to focus on issues such as civil rights, disarmament and

---

[1] For the original sources see Rousseau (1950); de Tocqueville (1969); Durkheim (1915); and Herberg (1955).

ecology, and understands 'American civil religion' to have a vital role in judging America itself and recalling the nation to its own highest standards. The 'priestly' or 'conservative' version of 'American civil religion', by contrast, is inclined to celebrate and affirm the belief that America has a divinely appointed role in the world, is more likely to uphold 'traditional' moral values, and appeals to a generally uncritical acceptance of the correctness and goodness of American values and their influence in the world (Marty, 1974; Wuthnow, 1988a, pp.244–57, 266–7; 1988b; Pierard and Linder, 1988, pp.284–96; Mathisen, 1989, p.140; Davis, 1997, pp.415–17). It is also clear that, especially during the 1980s and early 1990s, there was a concerted attempt by conservative political groups in America to annex the concept of 'American civil religion' firmly to their cause. These included the Republican Presidents Ronald Reagan and George Bush and their politically militant supporters among America's large and influential evangelical community (Coleman, 1996). Indeed, for some among the 'new Christian Right' within recent and contemporary American politics, the concept of an American civil religion has been deployed as part of a campaign to create and sustain a distinctively 'Christian America'.[2] Conversely, it has been argued that during the mid- and late 1990s, President Bill Clinton deliberately appealed to a much broader version of American civil religion, one that emphasized the themes of peace, justice and community and sought to locate these ideals within the context of a 'worldwide civil religion' (Linder, 1996, pp.742–9).

Bellah, meanwhile, after participating for over a decade in the debates to which his original article gave rise, withdrew from the discussion and even ceased to use the term – although he has never in fact gone back on his original argument and position. He stopped partly because he grew weary of the seemingly endless discussion of definitional issues, and partly because he became tired of replying to – and arguing against – those who insisted on understanding 'civil religion' only and inevitably as the idolatrous worship of the state (Bellah, 1989). For Bellah, this must have been a particularly ironic and frustrating, if not distressing, experience. It is clear from his original article that he always intended to show that 'American civil religion' possessed a critical, prophetic dimension as well as being a means of integrating and uniting the American people through shared historical memories, symbols and rituals (Aldridge, 2000, p.144). Indeed, as Bellah subsequently observed, his original article

---

[2] For a brief discussion of the 'new Christian Right' and its place within the wider context of American evangelicalism, see *Global Religious Movements in Regional Context* (Wolffe, 2001), Book 4 in this series, chapter 1.

'was an effort to argue that the civil religion required *opposition* to the Vietnam War, not support for it' (Bellah, 1989). It was, moreover, the importance of the critical and prophetic dimension of 'American civil religion' that Bellah emphasized even more strongly in his later writings on the subject (Bellah, 1974; 1975; 1976).[3]

If Bellah has withdrawn from the debate over 'American civil religion', however, his original article has nevertheless continued to stimulate discussion – and not only in the American context. Indeed, Bellah's original article has some claim to have become a seminal text for the consideration of the concept of civil religion in general. Thus, for example, at the level of the nation-state, it has been cited as a key text in discussions of civil religion – or the absence of it – in the United Kingdom, Australia, Canada and eastern Europe.[4] Below the level of the nation-state, Bellah's concept of civil religion has been used to explore the relationship between religion, ethnicity and the creation and maintenance of communal identities among Protestants in Northern Ireland and among Afrikaners in South Africa (Aldridge, 2000, pp.148–52; Fawcett, 2000, especially pp.10–11, chapter 4 and pp.181–3).

Bellah's ideas have also prompted some scholars to attempt to define the broad characteristics of 'civil religion' understood as a phenomenon that may occur in a variety of contexts. Thus, Richard Pierard and Robert Linder have suggested that a civil religion may be said to have the following five characteristics. First, it will refer to the widespread acceptance by a people of a shared sense of their nation's history and destiny. Second, it will relate their society to a realm of absolute meaning. Third, it will enable them to look at their society and community as in some sense special. Fourth, it will provide a vision which ties the nation together as an integrated whole. And

---

[3] The debate over 'American civil religion' has generated an immense literature. For surveys of the debate at different stages, together with extensive references to the literature, see Richey and Jones (1974); Bourg (1976); Hammond (1976); Mathisen (1989); and Hammond *et al.* (1994). For an example of extended and ongoing engagement with the issue over several decades, see the *Journal of Church and State* from the early 1970s onwards, in which articles and editorials have regularly returned to the subject. It is notable that, despite the acknowledged uncertainty, conflict and ambiguity that continues to surround the subject, there is substantial agreement that 'American civil religion' will continue to be a significant concept and phenomenon at least for the foreseeable future.

[4] For the UK see, for example, Bocock (1985) and Aldridge (2000, pp.144–6); for Australia, Crouter (1990); for Canada, Kim (1993); and for eastern Europe, Mestrovic (1993, chapter 6). This list does not claim to be complete, but merely provides a number of examples of discussions of civil religion in these particular contexts that are directly related to, or inspired by, Bellah's work on this subject.

fifth, it will provide a collection of beliefs, values, rites, ceremonies and symbols which, taken together, give sacred meaning to the life of the community and thus provide an overarching sense of unity that transcends internal conflicts and differences (Pierard and Linder, 1988, pp.22–3).

Pierard and Linder first presented their five-fold characterization of 'civil religion' as a broad phenomenon in the introduction to their detailed analysis of specifically American civil religion, particularly in relation to the institution of the presidency in the USA. Subsequently, Pierard then deployed the same definition in an article devoted to the history and development of the concept of civil religion in a variety of particular historical and geographical contexts (Pierard, 1999). It has, moreover, proved to be a general definition of the characteristics of 'civil religion' that has commended itself to other scholars working in very different national or local contexts, including both the modern United Kingdom (Wolffe, 1993, pp.317–27; 1994, p.267; 2000, p.7) and modern Siena (Parsons, 1997). This book is primarily concerned with aspects of civil religion in the USA, in the UK and in Siena, and the five-fold characterization offered by Pierard and Linder is also, therefore, adopted as an analytical tool in this context.

In the first three chapters of this book, the five-fold characterization is applied to the particular theme of the remembrance of those killed in war in modern and contemporary America and Britain. These chapters will explore how far the concept of civil religion may be used to elucidate and interpret the significance of American and British rituals and traditions of remembrance and memorial. They will thus examine aspects of civil religion in two particular contexts, each of which is *national, modern* and predominantly, though by no means exclusively, both *Anglo-Saxon* and *culturally Protestant* by historical tradition. None of these categorizations is, of course, simple, straightforward or unambiguous. Each is at best only a partial characterization of the two countries in question. Thus, in the USA, despite the proposed unifying influence of 'American civil religion', profound divisions exist between ethnic, cultural and religious groups – divisions which, in the intensity of the controversies to which they give rise, may even be said to constitute a challenge to the very concept of 'American civil religion'. In the UK, meanwhile, both the growth of ethnic and religious diversity and the assertion of distinctive Scottish, Welsh and Irish identities present profound and serious challenges to conventional assumptions concerning the identity and status of 'Britain' and the 'British'. Such important qualifications notwithstanding, however, both the USA and the UK remain national in that, so far at least, they both continue to be commonly recognized political entities. Similarly, despite the intense debates that surround the concept of 'modernity', both the contemporary USA and the contemporary UK are 'nations' that trace their 'modern' forms broadly to the eighteenth century. Both are also predominantly Anglo-Saxon and culturally Protestant in ethos, in the sense that English-speaking and Protestant majorities have historically shaped and dominated their key institutions, traditions and cultures. In examining the rituals and traditions of remembrance of these two societies, various questions will be addressed. How far do such rituals and traditions constitute expressions of 'civil religion'? How successful are they in fulfilling the unifying function that civil religions are supposed to supply? How far do they reflect the predominantly Anglo-Saxon and Protestant traditions of the societies from which they have emerged? How far do they answer both personal needs and collective, communal needs in relation to the remembrance and commemoration of those killed in war?

By deliberate contrast, in the second part of the book Pierard and Linder's five-fold definition of civil religion is applied to a very different and even more specific test-case that is *local*, culturally *Latin* and *Catholic*, and that also has roots in a much older tradition of civil religion dating back to the *medieval* and *renaissance* periods. The concept of civil religion – as defined by Pierard and Linder – is here used to analyse and interpret various Sienese expressions of civil religion, especially, but by no means only, in relation to the famous Sienese festival of the Palio. As recent scholarship has emphasized, the distinctive identities and particular values of individual Italian city-states of the medieval and renaissance eras were frequently expressed in civic rituals that amounted to a form of civil religion. Characteristically, such rituals were associated especially with the annual festivals of the city's patron saints, with the celebration of the Virgin Mary as a particular protectress of the city, or with other religious festivals that were adopted as the focus of civic identity and devotion. Usually, such celebrations culminated in elaborate civic processions in which the various constituent parts of the community honoured the designated heavenly protector and patron with gifts of candles and banners. Such ceremonies and rituals were also, in most cases, an important annual reassertion and reconfirmation of the intimate relationship that existed between a late medieval Italian city-state and the subject towns and communities of its surrounding territory and possessions.

From the late sixteenth century onwards, however, the Italian city-states were gradually absorbed into larger regional political entities, while the Catholic Church sought to reassert the specifically religious – as opposed to civil – significance of the annual festivals dedicated to the Virgin and to other patron saints. As a result of these two processes, both the traditional relationship between a city and its surrounding territories, and the civic rituals in which that relationship was annually celebrated and confirmed, tended to decline, even to the point at which some civic festivals disappeared altogether. In other cases, civic rituals survived, even if in modified and reduced form, into the modern era. The Tuscan city of Siena provides a particularly striking case of such survival and, moreover, an example of the integration of surviving elements of medieval and renaissance Sienese civil religion with later traditions and rituals that may plausibly be interpreted as a modern version of Sienese civil religion. In the present context, Siena thus provides an opportunity to ask how far it is appropriate and reasonable to speak of continuity between medieval and modern versions of civil religion.

Other issues and questions concerning civil religion occur throughout the book. One such issue is the relationship – and potential conflict – between 'official' and 'unofficial', 'institutional' and 'popular', attitudes to, and interpretations of, the examples of civil religion that are discussed. What, for example, is the relationship between 'official' and 'civil' religion? Are there 'official' and 'popular' approaches to civil religion? How do public and private responses to war memorials and rituals of remembrance coexist or conflict? Or, in the Sienese case, how do official church understandings and perceptions of Sienese devotion to the Virgin, and the religious rituals of the Palio and Sienese civil religion, relate to popular Sienese attitudes towards these activities, and understandings of them? Such questions, in turn, help to test the value of the very concept of 'civil religion'. Is the concept of 'civil religion' – according to the evidence of these particular case studies – one that genuinely helps us to understand the phenomena in question? Is 'civil religion' a genuinely religious phenomenon? And does 'civil religion' – to borrow Bellah's terminology – indeed possess the seriousness and integrity of other religions, and therefore deserve to be treated with similar respect and understanding?

Finally, the three concepts that form the subtitle of the series of which this volume is a part – tradition, modernity and change – run throughout the book. The first three chapters examine the ways in which the experience of modern warfare caused two modern nation-states to invent traditions of memorial and remembrance, and look at how such 'invented traditions' subsequently evolved and changed – and continue to do so. The remaining chapters examine the way in which local traditions of civil religion, some of which stretch back as many as seven hundred years, have not only survived into the modern period, but have changed and developed into a modern and contemporary expression of the civil religion of a particular city and community.

References

Aldridge, A. (2000) *Religion in the Contemporary World: A Sociological Introduction*, Cambridge: Polity Press.

Bellah, R. (1967) 'Civil religion in America', *Daedalus*, 96, pp.1–21.

Bellah, R. (1974) 'American civil religion in the 1970s', in R. Richey and D. Jones (eds), pp.255–72.

Bellah, R. (1975) *The Broken Covenant: American Civil Religion in Time of Trial*, New York: Seabury Press.

Bellah, R. (1976) 'Response to the panel on civil religion', *Sociological Analysis*, 37, pp.153–9.

Bellah, R. (1989) 'Comment', *Sociological Analysis*, 50, p.147.

Bocock, R. (1985) 'Religion in modern Britain', in R. Bocock and K. Thompson (eds) *Religion ad Ideology*, Manchester: Manchester University Press, pp.207–33.

Bourg, C. (1976) 'A symposium on civil religion', *Sociological Analysis*, 37, pp.141–9.

Coleman, S. (1996) 'Conservative Protestantism in the United States', in D. Westerlund (ed.) *Questioning the Secular State: The Worldwide Resurgence of Religion in Politics*, London: Hurst, pp.24–47.

Crouter, R. (1990) 'Beyond Bellah: American civil religion and the Australian experience', *Australian Journal of Politics and History*, 36, pp.154–65.

Davis, D. (1997) 'Law, morals, and civil religion in America', *Journal of Church and State*, 39, pp.411–25.

Durkheim, E. (1915) *The Elementary Forms of the Religious Life: A Study in Religious Sociology*, London: Allen & Unwin.

Fawcett, L. (2000) *Religion, Ethnicity and Social Change*, London: Macmillan.

Hammond, P. (1976) 'The sociology of American civil religion: a bibliographic essay', *Sociological Analysis*, 37, pp.169–82.

Hammond, P., Porterfield, A., Moseley, J. and Sarna, J. (1994) 'American civil religion revisited', *Religion and American Culture*, 4, pp.1–23.

Herberg, W. (1955) *Protestant, Catholic, Jew: an Essay in American Religious Sociology*, Garden City, New York: Anchor.

Kim, A. (1993) 'The absence of Pan-Canadian civil religion: plurality, duality, and conflict in symbols of Canadian culture', *Sociology of Religion*, 54, pp.257–75.

Linder, R. (1996) 'Universal pastor: President Bill Clinton's civil religion', *Journal of Church and State*, 38, pp.733–49.

Marty, M. (1974) 'Two kinds of two kinds of civil religion', in R. Richey and D. Jones (eds), pp.139–57.

Mathisen, J. (1989) 'Twenty years after Bellah: whatever happened to American civil religion?', *Sociological Analysis*, 50, pp.129–46.

Mestrovic, S. (1993) *The Road from Paradise: Prospects for Democracy in Eastern Europe*, Lexington, Kentucky: University Press of Kentucky.

Parsons, G. (1997) '"Unità nella diversità": civil religion and the Palio of Siena', *The Italianist*, 17, pp.176–203.

Pierard, R. and Linder, R. (1988) *Civil Religion and the American Presidency*, Grand Rapids, Michigan: Zondervan.

Pierard, R. (1999) 'Civil religion', in *Encyclopedia of Christianity*, Grand Rapids, Michigan: Wm. B. Eerdmans/Leiden, Netherlands: Brill, pp.583–8.

Richey, R. and Jones, D. (eds) (1974) *American Civil Religion*, New York: Harper & Row.

Rousseau, J. (1950) *The Social Contract and Discourses*, New York: Dutton.

Tocqueville, A. de (1969) *Democracy in America, Volume 1*, New York: Doubleday.

Wolffe, J. (1993) 'The religions of the silent majority', in G. Parsons (ed.) *The Growth of Religious Diversity: Britain from 1945, Vol.1, Traditions*, London and New York: Routledge, pp.305–46.

Wolffe, J. (1994) *God and Greater Britain: Religion and National Life in Britain and Ireland 1843–1945*, London and New York: Routledge.

Wolffe, J. (2000) *Great Deaths: Grieving, Religion, and Nationhood in Victorian and Edwardian Britain*, Oxford: Oxford University Press and The British Academy.

Wolffe, J. (2001) *Global Religious Movements in Regional Context*, Aldershot: Ashgate/Milton Keynes: The Open University.

Wuthnow, R. (1988a) *The Restructuring of American Religion: Society and Faith since World War II*, New Jersey: Princeton University Press.

Wuthnow, R. (1988b) 'Divided we fall: America's two civil religions', *Christian Century*, 115, pp.395–9.

CHAPTER I

'Lest we forget': British and American rituals of remembrance as civil religion

In any attempt to summarize the elements that make up the 'civil religions' of the UK and the USA, the rituals associated with the remembrance of those killed in war must surely occupy a prominent position. In the UK, the events and ceremonies that surround the annual celebration of Remembrance Sunday – the Sunday falling closest each year to 11 November, the anniversary of the armistice that ended the First World War in 1918 – arguably constitute the most widespread and visible expression of British civil religion. On that Sunday, in literally thousands of cities, towns and villages across the UK, representatives of local communities gather at local war memorials to remember and to honour members of those communities killed in Britain's wars since the First World War. And in so doing, they function as so many local expressions of the national focus of remembrance, led by the royal family, that takes place at 11 a.m. on that same Sunday at the Cenotaph in Whitehall, London.

Similarly, public ceremonies, including the observance of a moment of silence, take place in the USA every year on Veterans Day, 11 November, to honour and commemorate the dead of that nation's wars. These ceremonies too provide widely diffused and localized expressions of an official national ceremony – the focal point of which is the laying of a presidential wreath – which takes place at 11 a.m. that day at the Tomb of the Unknown Soldiers in Arlington National Cemetery in Washington, DC. Together with similar ceremonies for the remembrance of the dead of all of America's wars held on Memorial Day (another and historically earlier focus for commemoration, stemming from the American Civil War and celebrated in most states on 30 May), Veterans Day, like the British Remembrance Sunday, provides a highly visible annual reaffirmation of national recollection of the war dead and their sacrifice for America.

In neither the UK nor the USA are such rituals the only, or even arguably the predominant, expression of 'civil religion'. In the UK, the symbolic role of the monarchy in national life is another major element in civil religion (Bocock, 1985, pp.213–18; Wolffe, 1993, pp.318–27). And in the USA the celebrations of the Fourth of July and of Thanksgiving[1] provide further annual festivals of American civil religion with somewhat different emphases, while the institution of the presidency remains an important focus for American civil religious sentiments and reflections (Pierard and Linder, 1988; Linder, 1996). Nevertheless, it is clear that rituals of remembrance and commemoration play a central part in the construction of civil religion in both countries. Indeed, one recent and hostile critic of Robert Bellah's seminal formulation of American civil religion (Bellah, 1967) has complained that 'the holidays of American civil religion seem predominantly militant', and that Bellah's use of the concept of civil religion in the American context is restricted to militant expressions of the values involved (Mestrovic, 1993, pp.130–1). It is by no means clear that this criticism of Bellah's description of American civil religion is either fair or adequate. For example, it seriously neglects the self-critical and prophetic role that Bellah included in his understanding of American civil religion (Bellah, 1967, pp.16–19; 1974; 1975), and it fails to distinguish between American civil religion as understood by Bellah himself and the militant – and indeed military – uses to which the concept has subsequently been put by others. It also fails to consider whether acts of remembrance of those killed in war must *necessarily* in themselves be understood to be militaristic in nature or uncritically celebratory in relation to the wars whose dead they commemorate. However, the criticism at least serves to confirm that the association between civil religion and the remembrance of those killed in war is one that is both intimate and complex.

The rest of this chapter will explore aspects of that complexity. It will do so in two main sections. The first will review the origins and broad development of the principal rituals of remembrance in both the UK and the USA. The second will consider the preceding section in the light of Richard Pierard's and Robert Linder's five-part definition of the nature and function of a 'civil religion', and will

---

[1] The Fourth of July is the anniversary of the adoption of the Declaration of Independence in 1776. Thanksgiving is the holiday on the fourth Thursday in November commemorating the thanksgiving to God for the annual harvest by the first colonists in America.

also explore some of the ambiguities and unresolved tensions raised by the relationship between rituals of remembrance and civil religion in both the UK and USA.

Inventing remembrance

The origins of American rituals of commemoration

The emergence – 'invention' is arguably an even better word – of national rituals of remembrance of those who died in war began at significantly different points in British and American history. For both nations, the traumatic experience of the First World War – between 1914 and 1918 for the UK, between 1917 and 1918 for the USA – was to prove a crucial moment in the development of such rituals. Indeed, in the UK this experience was the origin and inspiration of all of the principal elements in the still continuing traditions of remembrance that are characteristic of British civil religion. In the USA, by contrast, some of the most important rituals and symbols of what was to become the national understanding of remembrance had begun to take shape some 50 years earlier in the aftermath of the American Civil War.

As Bellah argued in his seminal essay on American civil religion, the Civil War in the mid-nineteenth century was a moment of severe trial and crisis in the history of the American nation and in the development of its civil religion. Between 1861 and 1865, the Civil War tested the ideals and values of the American people and threatened the very existence of America as a single, unified nation. It also resulted in the addition of a number of new and powerful elements to the stock of traditions, values and rituals, derived from the American Revolution of the late eighteenth century, that had already come to constitute an American civil religion. The Revolution had given American civil religion the 'sacred text' of the Declaration of Independence, the annual ritual of the Fourth of July, and a core of beliefs about the newly independent nation, including the belief in a God that had a special interest in America and its destiny (Bellah, 1967, pp.5–9). The Civil War – one of the bloodiest wars of the nineteenth century and one which, by definition, divided the American people and tested their collective identity to the point of potential destruction – added new themes, new sacred texts, new rituals, and both sacred places and a sacrificial martyr figure to the civil religion of the nation that emerged from the war.

The powerful sacrificial martyr figure was President Lincoln, who was assassinated in April 1865, just as the Civil War was coming to an end. The violent and untimely death of the president who had led the North to victory over the Confederacy in the South – thereby preserving the nation as a single entity – provided a striking symbol of the themes of death, personal sacrifice and rebirth that were so prominent in the wider interpretation of the Civil War and its painful meaning by those who had lived through it and seen so many others die. And such themes were nowhere more dramatically or memorably enshrined than in Lincoln's own most famous attempt to derive meaning from the conflict into which he had led his nation. On 19 November 1863, on the battlefield at Gettysburg in Pennsylvania, where just four and a half months earlier one of the most decisive battles of the Civil War had been fought, Lincoln delivered what became known as the Gettysburg Address. Only 268 words long, the Gettysburg Address encapsulated themes that became central to the Civil War's contribution to the development of American civil religion. Opening with a reference to the founding principles of the nation some 87 years earlier – the belief in liberty and the equality of all – Lincoln explained that they had assembled at Gettysburg to dedicate a part of the battlefield to those who had died there in order that the nation might live. Yet, he continued, in a larger sense it was the sacrifice of those who had died which had already consecrated the ground, while for the living the task was to dedicate themselves to the completion of the work begun by the dead. Thus, Lincoln concluded, the living must now be resolved that 'this nation under God shall have a new birth of freedom' (quoted in Foote, 1997, pp.8–9). Despite – or perhaps because of – its brevity, Lincoln's Gettysburg Address has become one of the sacred texts of American civil religion. Thus, it has been described as 'a symbolic and sacramental act' (Lowell, 1964, pp.88–9, quoted in Bellah, 1967, p.11), and as a 'key sermon of American civil religion, delivered by its principal patron saint' (Sellars and Walter, 1993, p.188). Its status has also been recognized by the fact that the full text of the Gettysburg Address is inscribed on two American national monuments – the Lincoln Memorial in Washington DC and at Gettysburg, where a monument was erected to the Address itself (Hass, 1998, pp.53 and 138).

The Gettysburg Address, Bellah suggested, thus became one of the 'civil scriptures' of American civil religion. Indeed, for Bellah, this addition to the 'civil scriptures' was part of the 'Lincolnian New Testament' of American civil religion which the legacy of the Civil War added to the 'Old Testament' of the civil religion of America's founding fathers. The original civil religion, Bellah argued, had been

'Hebraic', without being in any specific sense 'Jewish'. Thus, the founding fathers of America had seen it as a new 'promised land' to which God had led their predecessors. Similarly, Bellah claimed, in speaking of the dead of Gettysburg as 'those who here gave their lives, so that the nation might live', Lincoln used Christian symbolism and language, yet without equating American civil religion specifically with Christianity or the Christian Church (Bellah, 1967, pp.8–11).

The pivotal role of the Civil War in the construction of American national identity has recently been re-emphasized in historical scholarship (Grant, 1998). It has also been demonstrated dramatically at the popular level by the phenomenal success of a monumental eleven-hour-long television series on the Civil War edited by Ken Burns and first broadcast in the UK in 1990. Moreover, as recent scholarship strikingly demonstrates, the Civil War was not simply a key moment in the development of American identity but is still regarded as a 'salvation-drama of the American nation', and is frequently described or discussed in 'religious' language and terminology. Thus, historians have described it as providing Americans with 'a sense of identity, of resurrection through disintegration'; as a 'war of national redemption'; as 'a struggle over the nation's soul', and as 'America's Holy War', which is consequently 'sacred' to Americans – and in using such language modern historians echo the sentiments of observers and commentators who lived through the war itself (Grant, 1998, pp.163–5). Significantly, it has also been shown that both sides in the Civil War drew on the traditions and ideals associated with the American Revolution and the successful struggle for independence from Britain in the late eighteenth century. The armies of both sides celebrated both the birthday of the first president, George Washington, and the Fourth of July. Both sides also found moral justification for their own cause in the Civil War in the values and heritage of the American Revolution. The earliest stages in the formulation of 'American civil religion' thus provided the resources for both the Union in the North and the Confederacy in the South to develop their own distinctive mythical and mystical understandings of the Civil War some 80-odd years later (Linenthal, 1991, pp.23–5; Grant, 1998, pp.170–1).

In the North, the war came to be seen as a 'holy crusade', a blending of patriotism and religious devotion, in which the ending of slavery was the moral imperative that justified the war and all the sacrifices involved. This was the ideological position of the North that was enshrined in Julia Ward Howe's famous 'Battle Hymn of the Republic', with its defining line, 'as He [Jesus] died to make men holy, let us die to make men free'.[2] Howe thus provided a clear example of the introduction of the language of death and sacrifice into the civil religion of the North – and, because the North won the war, into the civil religion of the post-Civil War nation as whole. In the North, therefore, such language was used to create an understanding of the war as a process of national sacrifice – a 'baptism of blood' that might lead to a moral purification and rebirth of the nation. In the South, meanwhile, the bitter experience of defeat gave rise to a different – but arguably no less mystical – understanding of the war as sacrifice. In the South, however, it was a myth of sacrifice for a tragically lost cause and a celebration of the devotion and heroism of an outnumbered army in the defence of a just but losing cause.[3] Significantly, the concept of a 'baptism of blood' has also been used in relation to the interpretation of the Southern cause, as has the concept of civil religion (Wilson, 1980; Foster, 1987; Grant, 1998, pp.170–3).

The myths of sacrifice created in both the North and the South were, inevitably, partial and in many respects problematic: that of the North conveniently ignored the existence of racism in the North as well as the South, and glossed over the bloody realities of the war with its rhetoric of heroic sacrifice; that of the South similarly ignored the issue of race and slavery, and appealed to a romantic view of the graciousness and elegance of pre-war Southern life that was, in reality, largely mythical. But as a means of integrating the legacy and the memory of the Civil War into the civil religion of post-Civil War America, the theme of sacrifice was invaluable and highly effective. By emphasizing the shared experience of war and sacrifice, and by recognizing the bravery and devotion to their cause of Southern soldiers as well as those of the North, the Civil War could even become a shared experience of national suffering and rebirth. If the war was thus recast as a heroic and painful struggle between brothers, then it was possible to claim that the blood of both sides had ultimately strengthened and purified the newly reborn nation. Thus,

[2] In many hymn books the second half of this line was changed subsequently to 'let us live to make men free', but the original version, published in February 1862, used the verb 'die'. The fact that Lincoln actually died on Good Friday 1865, just as the Civil War was ending, further nurtured both the 'mystical' image of the war and also the association of the suffering of the war with Christian ideas of sacrifice (Grant, 1998, p.176).

[3] While the North understood its cause as a crusade against slavery and the splitting of the nation by the secession of the Southern states, the South understood its cause to be a just defence of its constitutional and legal right to resist the interference of the federal government within the Southern states and to secede if such interference persisted.

the emergence and growth of the 'cult of the Lost Cause', and the celebration of Confederate heroes as part of this 'cult', enabled even the defeated South to contribute to the patriotic mythology of the nation as a whole (Wilson, 1980; Foster, 1987, Linenthal, 1991, pp.93–4; O'Leary, 1994, pp.24–6; Grant, 1998, pp.174–6). It is not surprising, therefore, that it was the Civil War that prompted the emergence of some of the most important and enduring features of the rituals of memorialization and remembrance that are characteristic of modern American civil religion.

Along with literally hundreds of memorials located on the battlefields of the American Civil War and in local courthouse squares and parks (Sellars, 1986), the Civil War gave American civil religion two of its most hallowed and sanctified 'sacred places' and one of its most revered 'holy days'. The two 'sacred places' are both cemeteries; the 'holy day' is the annual day set aside for recalling the dead of America's wars. The Civil War marked a dramatic change in attitudes to the remains of those killed in America's wars, for until then the standard practice had been to bury the dead in mass and unmarked graves. The American dead of the Revolution had been buried in this way in the late eighteenth century. The one marked grave at Valley Forge – of a lieutenant from Rhode Island – was remarkable precisely because it was the only individually marked grave at a place where some 3,000 Americans had died in the winter of 1787–8. Indeed, the practice of mass burial continued in the early stages of the Civil War itself – the dead of both the Union and the Confederacy being buried in unmarked mass graves after the battle of Manassas in 1861.

However, by the time of the Civil War such attitudes were changing. The war was fought by mass armies and in the name of democratic ideals. Advances in military technology, together with the very size of the armies and the inability of medical services and science to keep pace with the efficiency of the new weaponry, resulted in ferocious casualty rates. Of the one and a half million Northerners and one million Southerners who fought, 359,000 and 259,000 respectively were killed (Mayo, 1988, p.170), a fatality rate of 1 in 4, and thus far in excess of fatality rates in America's subsequent wars. Improved communications and photography brought the realities – or at least the grim post-battle evidence – of such casualty rates closer to the rest of the nation. And, in an age before it was standard practice for soldiers to wear identity tags, many soldiers on both sides in the Civil War contrived to fashion their own means of identification – such as a scrap of leather around an ankle or a note placed in a shoe – thereby indicating a personal sense that they should be and wished to be remembered as individuals. Thus, by the end of 1861, the War Department of the Union resolved that commanding officers should have responsibility for the burial of dead soldiers under their command and that they should try to provide names that would enable an individual headboard to be placed at each soldier's grave[4] (Patterson, 1982, pp.317–18; Hass, 1998, pp.36–7 and 43–5).

It was at Gettysburg that such personal and official trends first powerfully came together. After a fierce three-day battle, lasting from 1–3 July 1863, thousands of dead were left on the battlefield. This proved to be the turning point of the war, and in the days that followed the Union bodies became the focus of a concerted attempt to turn the battlefield into a sacred memorial to the men who had died there. And so it was that, in November 1863, Lincoln came to deliver his famous Address at the opening of the National Soldiers Cemetery at Gettysburg. Less than a year later, in June 1864, the North established a second National Soldiers Cemetery at Arlington, across the Potomac river from the nation's capital in Washington. Here, too, soldiers – both Union and Confederate – were buried individually, although for many years the site was officially regarded as only a Union cemetery. In time, however, both cemeteries were to become hallowed ground and shrines to the memory of the Civil War and its dead for both Northerners and Southerners.[5]

The Civil War also gave rise to the first annual days and rituals set aside for the commemoration of America's war dead. The precise origins of Memorial Day remain a matter of debate. As early as 1865, there was a documented example of flowers being placed on the graves of Union soldiers on 30 May (Ahlstrom, 1972, p.689). There is also evidence, however, that even before the end of the Civil War, Southern women had begun the practice of placing flowers on the graves of Confederate soldiers. Certainly, after the end of the Civil War, the annual celebration of a Confederate Memorial Day was a key element in the Southern attempt to come to terms with defeat and to commemorate the heroism and devotion of the Confederate dead.

---

[4] In the present context it is worth noting that the phenomenal success of Ken Burns' television series on the Civil War probably owes much to the way in which the producers chose to focus so much attention on individuals, through the use of letters, diaries, photographs and personal memoirs. It may well be that the popular appeal of the series derived in part from a similar interest in the fate of specific people to that which led the participants in the war and their contemporaries to seek to commemorate the Civil War dead as individuals.

[5] The desire to commemorate individuals was by no means limited to national cemeteries and monuments. Local Civil War monuments were common in both North and South, and had the shared aim of perpetuating the memory of the local men who had fought and died (Savage, 1994, p.129). Moreover, such local Civil War memorials tended to name the dead as individuals.

The graves of soldiers would be decorated and a variety of local customs and rituals would ensue – usually involving, in some form, an address, a religious service, and perhaps a parade. Different communities in the South adopted different dates to celebrate Memorial Day, but the observance itself was extremely widespread. It is even arguable that the North adopted the custom of Memorial Day from the South (Albanese, 1974, p.389; Wilson, 1980, pp.28 and 36; Foster, 1987, pp.42–3, 44–6).

In the North, in 1868, the Grand Army of the Republic – the organization of Union veterans of the war – formally recognized the practice by instituting 'Decoration Day' and calling for the placing of flowers on Civil War graves. Special ceremonies took place at both Gettysburg and Arlington. In 1873, the state of New York made the day a legal holiday, and in the 1880s its title was changed to 'Memorial Day'. It has been argued that Memorial Day was always conceived as a focus for reconciliation, with examples of joint observances at battlefields and the return of captured battle flags. In reality, however, Memorial Day only began to assume such a role somewhat later in its history, as the two sides in the Civil War began to explore the possibility of reconciliation. The first such tentative steps towards the common celebration of Memorial Day occurred in the 1880s. Not surprisingly, however, for many years much of the defeated South staunchly refused to associate itself with a common Memorial Day shared with the victorious North (Ahlstrom, 1972, p.689; Foster, 1987, p.68; Inglis, 1992a, p.16). Only in the twentieth century, and in the light of American participation in the two world wars, did Memorial Day come to be celebrated, as it is today, in almost every state on the last Monday in May (Mayo, 1988, pp.51–2).

If the general acceptance of Memorial Day as a truly national occasion of annual remembrance required the passage of several decades and the experience of American involvement in the trauma of twentieth-century world war, the broader process whereby North and South began to share in the commemoration of the Civil War began much earlier. It was, moreover, at the 'sacred sites' of Gettysburg and Arlington that some of the most enduring symbols of such reconciliation through shared remembrance took place. As early as 1882, and again in 1887, symbolic meetings between Northern and Southern survivors of the battle of Gettysburg took place, while in 1888, on the twenty-fifth anniversary of the battle, both Union and Confederate veterans held a major reunion at Gettysburg and inaugurated a monument to American heroism on the battlefield (Foster, 1987, p.68). Four years later, in 1892, a new monument was dedicated at Gettysburg. Called the 'High Water Mark of the Rebellion Monument', it commemorated 'Pickett's Charge', the fateful climax to the battle of Gettysburg when Southern troops made a final desperate attack on the Union lines. The charge failed, at great cost: the South lost the battle and retreated, never again to threaten the North with invasion. The High Water Mark of the Rebellion Monument was paid for by the Northern states, but significantly it explicitly honoured the soldiers of both sides, listing the names of all the units, both Union and Confederate, that participated in Pickett's Charge and its defeat. The monument thus constituted a major landmark in the transformation of Gettysburg into a shared site of remembrance and commemoration and a genuinely national shrine.

The fiftieth anniversary of the battle saw a further crucial stage in this process. In 1913, over 54,000 veterans of both armies – including many who had not fought at the battle – gathered at Gettysburg for a commemorative act attended by President Woodrow Wilson. One of the veterans suggested to his old comrades that what the battlefield now needed was a monument to peace. The idea was slow to be realized. In 1938, however, on the seventy-fifth anniversary of the battle, the 'Eternal Peace Light Memorial' was dedicated by President Franklin Roosevelt in the presence of 1,800 Civil War veterans, most of whom were by then in their nineties and some of whom were over a hundred years old. Funded by contributions from states on both sides in the Civil War, the monument shows two figures holding a wreath and embracing, and carries the inscription, 'Peace Eternal in a Nation United. An enduring light to guide us in unity and friendship.' At the top of the monument is an eternal flame (Patterson, 1982, pp.329–30; Foster, 1987, pp.193–4; Sellars, 1986; Linenthal, 1991, pp.93–7; Foote, 1997, pp.122–33; Grant, 1998, pp.174–5).

Successive dedications at Gettysburg, it has been argued, thus demonstrated the evolving meaning of this sacred place of American civil religion and shrine to the memory of those who died in the Civil War. The initial dedication of the cemetery in 1863 consecrated the ground to the dead of the Union. The monument to the High Water Mark of the Rebellion celebrated the heroism and sacrifice of both sides in the war. And the Peace Light Memorial dedicated the site of the battle to the ideals of peace, unity and friendship. In so doing, it also gave symbolic expression to the judgement expressed, in 1915, by Joshua Lawrence Chamberlain – himself a famous veteran of the battle of Gettysburg – that the Civil War gave both Northerners and Southerners 'a rushing tide of memories which divided us, yet made us one forever' (Foote, 1997, p.133; Chamberlain quoted in Grant, 1998, p.175). In the light of such language, it is hardly surprising that the history of the reunions held at Gettysburg should have been described as a process whereby 'modest reunions eventually became elaborate rituals of reconciliation', offering the 'opportunity to

Figure 1.1 The High Water Mark of the Rebellion Monument, Gettysburg. National Archives and Records Administration.

Figure 1.2 The Eternal Peace Light Memorial, Gettysburg. National Archives and Records Administration.

dramatize [an] ideology of reconciliation', itself based on the view that the 'sacred causes' of North and South were equally just because of the valour and heartfelt commitment displayed by the soldiers of both sides (Linenthal, 1991, p.93).

At Arlington, meanwhile, a similar – if less dramatic – process had also occurred. Although the Arlington National Cemetery had always contained the graves of Confederate as well as Union dead, for several decades it was officially regarded only as a Union cemetery. The graves of Confederate dead were not allowed to be decorated and entrance to the cemetery was even, at times, denied to relatives of the Southern dead. By the turn of the century, however, circumstances had altered radically. In 1898, America went to war with Spain, in support of the attempts of both Cuba and the Philippines to secure their independence. The Spanish-American War proved to be a turning point in the reconciliation of North and South. The South was swept by a wave of patriotism for the new cause. Southern veterans of the Civil War still young enough to do so volunteered to fight in the war. Veterans too old to fight encouraged a new generation of Southern young men to enlist and emulate the military prowess, dedication and traditions of their elders in the Civil War. Veterans' associations on both sides exploited the war as a further focus for reconciliation. The North as a whole responded by reaffirming its recognition of the courage of Southern soldiers and the place of the South within a reunited nation[6] (Wilson, 1980, pp.162–3; Foster, 1987, chapter 11; O'Leary, 1994, p.25). More specifically, in 1900, the United States Congress authorized the setting aside of a section of Arlington National Cemetery as an official site for the burial of Confederate dead. By the end of 1901, the Confederate dead had been reburied in concentric circles in a section of the cemetery dedicated to them and marked by distinctive headstones. In 1903 the first Confederate Memorial Day celebration at Arlington took place. Other Confederate graves in the North were also now to be cared for out of federal funds. In 1905 Congress also approved the return of captured Confederate battleflags to the South – an idea that had first

[6] A partial precedent had been set earlier in 1876 when, after the defeat of General Custer by the Plains Indians at the battle of the Little Big Horn, Confederate veterans volunteered to fight against the 'new enemy' in the west. The significance of this will be considered further in the third section of this chapter. The process of reconciliation through Southern participation in subsequent American wars was completed in 1917–18 when Southern commitment to the American cause during the First World War confirmed the precedent set in the late 1890s in relation to the Spanish-American War. In the context of the First World War, moreover, it was a further symbol of reconciliation that Woodrow Wilson, the president who took America into the war, was a Southerner (Wilson, 1980, pp.171–82).

been suggested in 1888, but had been dropped in the face of public opposition (Foster, 1987, pp.153–4).

In 1906, it was agreed that a major monument should be erected at Arlington to the Confederate dead. In 1912, the cornerstone of the monument was laid – situated at the centre of the concentric circles of Southern graves – and the finished monument was unveiled on 4 June 1914, the 106th anniversary of the birth of Jefferson Davis, the president of the short-lived Confederacy. At the unveiling, President Woodrow Wilson delivered an address, and Union and Confederate veterans placed wreaths on the graves of former foes. The Confederate Monument was in many ways a remarkable symbol of reconciliation precisely because it celebrated the brief existence and suffering of a defeated state, but in a location in the capital of the larger state and nation that had been victorious over it. In a Latin quotation at its base the monument also explicitly embraced the Southern myth of 'the Lost Cause' (Mayo, 1988, pp.188–9).

It was American involvement in the First World War that brought the next decisive development in American rituals of remembrance. In 1913, it had been agreed by Congress that a Memorial Amphitheatre should be constructed in the Arlington National Cemetery to honour and remember all Americans who had died in war for their country. The cornerstone of the Memorial Amphitheatre was laid in 1915 and the monument was completed and dedicated in May 1920. It thus provided a readymade location for the American Tomb of the Unknown Soldier when it was decided to follow the example set in Europe and bury an unidentified casualty of the First World War as a national symbol of all of America's dead from that conflict.[7] Accordingly, four unknown American dead were exhumed from American cemeteries in France. On Memorial Day 1921, a veteran of the war chose one of these and the casket was transported to America, the other three unknown American soldiers being reburied in France. After lying in state in Washington, the chosen unknown soldier was interred, on 11 November, in a white marble sarcophagus located at the Memorial Amphitheatre, which was inscribed with the words, 'Here rests in honoured glory an American soldier known but

---

[7] It should also be noted, however, that the main memorial to the Union dead of the Civil War at Arlington is the 'Tomb of the Unknown Dead of the War Between the States'. The title of this memorial thus set a precedent for the later Tomb of the Unknown Soldier of the First World War. The origins of this memorial were, however, significantly different, for it contains the remains of over 2,000 Union soldiers killed in the earliest battles of the war and buried in mass graves. While the title of the memorial looks forward to later American rituals of remembrance, its origins look back to the era before the commemoration of individual deaths became a matter of concern.

Figure 1.3 The Confederate Memorial, Arlington National Cemetery. © 1998, Parks and History Association. Photo: Jack Metzler.

Figure 1.4 The Memorial Amphitheatre, Arlington National Cemetery. National Archives and Records Administration.

Figures 1.5 The Tomb of the Unknown American Soldier, Arlington National Cemetery. Associated Press/Wide World Photos.

Figure 1.6 Notice at Arlington National Cemetery announcing that it is sacred ground. Photo: John Wolffe.

to God' (Mayo, 1988, pp.94–5; Hass, 1998, pp.56–7). Subsequently, in 1926, 11 November was officially called Armistice Day, in recollection of the date in 1918 when the First World War ended. Twelve years later, in 1938, the day was officially made a national holiday.

In 1954, the title Armistice Day was officially changed to Veterans Day, and in 1956, after American participation in both the Second World War and the Korean War, it was decided to add the remains of unknown soldiers from both later conflicts to the tomb of the unknown soldier from the First World War. Similarly careful arrangements were made to select an unknown American casualty from each conflict, and the two additional unknown soldiers were interred in front of the existing tomb of the unknown soldier on Memorial Day in 1958. A fourth American unknown soldier – from the Vietnam War – was added to the other three on Memorial Day 1984. In a development that might well be taken as an unintended symbol of America's still unresolved relationship with the Vietnam War, however, the remains interred in the tomb of the unknown soldier of the Vietnam War were subsequently exhumed and identified with the aid of DNA testing. The decision was then made to leave the tomb of the Vietnam unknown soldier empty (Mayo, 1988, pp.192–3 and 205).

The origins of British rituals of commemoration

In the UK, the absence of a comparably traumatic experience of war during the nineteenth century – equivalent to the American experience in the Civil War – meant that the emergence of the characteristic rituals of British remembrance did not take shape until the early twentieth century. Certainly, British history in the nineteenth century did not lack experience of war. The campaigns in Spain against Napoleon in the first decade of the nineteenth century left thousands of British dead – but none are commemorated by name on memorials where they fought. At Waterloo in 1815, 15,000 British soldiers died, but their names – bar a very few – are not individually commemorated. Similarly, in mid-century in the Crimean War, anonymity in death again remained the norm, although it is also possible to perceive a slight, slow increase in the number of individually marked graves. But, even where graves existed, the state did little or nothing either to preserve them or, as the years passed, to prevent their dissolution and disappearance (Laqueur, 1994, pp.150–3).

Only with the Anglo-Boer War of 1899–1902 is it possible to discern the beginning of a significant shift in attitudes and practices towards commemoration of those killed in Britain's wars. For the first time the state made some modest provision for the commemoration of its individual soldiers. Even then, however, the government was prepared to do no more than provide a small iron cross for the grave of each of the British dead in South Africa who were not commemorated by privately financed monuments or memorials. Moreover, the Secretary of State for War resisted the gathering of scattered burial sites into larger locations that might have been preserved with greater order and dignity. Such care of any individual graves fell to a voluntary society – though one favoured with royal patronage (Laqueur, 1994, p.152; Lloyd, 1998, pp.22–3). At the local level, however, there was a widespread trend towards the commem-oration of soldiers killed in the Anglo-Boer War, usually focused on memorials to the dead of county regiments and the many local volunteer units to which the Boer War had given rise. Over 900 such memorials were produced (Borg, 1991, p.ix). Such memorials drew on the precedents set by local civic memorials of the Victorian period – for example, the many local memorials to Queen Victoria's golden and diamond jubilees of 1887 and 1897. Local memorials to casualties of the Anglo-Boer War were, however, characteristically the result of initiatives led by prominent public figures – such as the Lord Lieutenant of the county in question – and relied on voluntary subscriptions that sought to draw contributions from all classes. They thus built on the widespread popular interest that had accompanied the war itself, which had involved the general population to an unusual degree – not least because it had been so extensively reported in the press and because of the large number of volunteer units raised in response to the perceived crisis posed by a series of early British defeats (King, 1998, pp.40–4).

If the Anglo-Boer War marked an extension of the concern for the commemoration and remembrance of individual British soldiers, it nevertheless remained only a modest advance on previous practice. It was the First World War that prompted a massive shift in both official and public attitudes towards commemoration and proved to be the defining moment in the emergence of British rituals of remembrance. It has been pointed out that none of the rituals and symbols that are still most commonly and most closely associated with British remembrance of those killed in war existed in any form before 1919. The national act of remembrance held at the Cenotaph in Whitehall on Remembrance Sunday; the Festival of Remembrance at the Royal Albert Hall the night before, culminating in the emotional intensity of the descent of a million poppy petals on the heads of a new generation of young servicemen and women; the wearing of poppies; the Field of Remembrance at Westminster Abbey; the two minutes' silence; the Cenotaph itself; the Tomb of the Unknown Warrior in Westminster Abbey; and the thousands of local memorials and ceremonies across the UK: none of these existed before 1919. All of them emerged – more or less rapidly – from the traumatic experience of the First World War (Bushaway, 1992, pp.136–7).

As with the American experience of the Civil War half a century earlier, it was the sheer scale of the deaths in the First World War that was the principal cause of the changes that occurred in national attitudes to the commemoration of those killed. The scale of the losses was unprecedented. At the outbreak of war in 1914, the British public had been completely unprepared for the realities of modern mass warfare conducted with military technology of even more lethal sophistication than that which had shocked Americans during their Civil War. By the end of the war, four years later in November 1918, over a million British and Imperial (as the various African, Australasian, Canadian, Indian and Caribbean soldiers were then called) troops were dead – over 700,000 of them from the UK itself. Moreover, again echoing the American experience 50 years earlier, the vast majority of the soldiers who fought in the First World War were not regular soldiers who had chosen the army as a career, but were either volunteers or, from 1916 onwards, conscripts. In this sense, at least, the First World War was not only a 'total war' but also a 'democratic' one. The majority of the dead were men whose families had not accepted the risk of death as a realistic if unfortunate consequence of a military career, but who, on the contrary, regarded such loss and sacrifice as utterly exceptional and demanded recognition of this fact by, at the very least, the existence of an individual grave or similar memorial (Bushaway, 1992, pp.137–40; Moriarty, 1991, pp.63–5).

The demand for such recognition began during the war itself. Commemorative rolls of honour were created by communities and institutions, listing the names of those who had joined the forces. At first, these were intended to be aids to recruitment, honouring those who had joined the services and potentially shaming those who had not into doing so – especially in the energetic recruiting campaigns of 1914 and 1915. Increasingly, however, and inevitably, as casualties mounted inexorably, such commemorative rolls became a focus for the remembrance of those who had been killed. From 1916 onwards street shrines also became increasingly common. Such shrines were originally an initiative by Anglican clergy, in connection with the Church of England's 'National Mission of Repentance and Hope' held in 1916. The idea quickly became popular with clergy of various denominations, however, and also with local communities – especially after a well-publicized visit by the queen in August 1916 to one of the first of such shrines in south Hackney. By the end of 1916, street shrines of standard design were commercially available and continued to be, in increasing degrees of sophistication, throughout the war. As with rolls of honour, from 1915 onwards, street shrines were designed to list the names both of those who were currently serving with the forces (whose continued well-being might be prayed for), and of those who had been killed (whose memory and sacrifice might be remembered and, depending on theological beliefs, whose soul might also be commended to God) (Wilkinson, 1978, pp.67, 170–1; King, 1998, pp.44–61; Lloyd, 1998, p.61; Moriarty, 1991, pp.66–8; Bushaway, 1992, p.140).

The meanings – both intended and actual – of such street shrines were by no means straightforward. For the clergy – especially those of the Church of England in the context of the National Mission of Repentance and Hope – they were part of the process of evangelism and the attempt to reassert the relevance of the message of Christianity in the midst of the war. For others, including many clergy, they were also part of the war effort: they kept alive the spirit of patriotism, helped to maintain morale on the home front, and endorsed the understanding of the war as a holy crusade[8] (King, 1998, pp.54–5). For the laity and for local people who may have had only tenuous or ambiguous links with the churches, the precise meanings and significances of the street shrines are more difficult to assess. For some they were no doubt vehicles for conventional Christian intercessory prayer for the safety of those in the services, and for recollection of, or prayer for the souls of, those who had died. For others such shrines may well have been less 'orthodox' symbols of good luck, a focus for the hopes associated with the living, and perhaps even a perceived point of continuing contact and association with the dead.

That the latter is at least a possibility at the popular level is suggested by the marked growth of interest in spiritualism during the First World War. Unsurprisingly, the sheer number of deaths and the distress caused by them prompted an upsurge in belief in the possibility of contact with the spirits of the dead, and a consequent

---

[8] For discussion and examples of the extent to which the churches in Britain supported the war effort and interpreted the war as a holy crusade see, for example, Matheson (1972); Marrin (1974, especially pp.74–81 and 119–42); Clements (1975); Wilkinson (1978, especially pp.30–9); Hoover (1989, especially chapters 2 and 3); Brown (1994); and Morgan (1997). As all of these scholars acknowledge, although the churches did not adopt a completely uniform response to the First World War, critical attitudes were very much in a minority, while support for the nation's war effort and belief in the definite moral rightness of the British cause were overwhelmingly predominant.

enthusiasm for seances and for literature that provided support for spiritualist beliefs (Cannadine, 1981, pp.227–30; Winter, 1992; 1995, pp.54–77). The churches opposed such unorthodox beliefs and activities, and if popular attitudes to street shrines did include association with spiritualist ideas then that too would have received official disapproval from the clergy. But the history of popular religion would suggest that, whatever churches and clergy may have argued, individuals on the fringes or beyond the periphery of official Christianity would have felt free to associate street shrines with a rich variety of personal beliefs, hopes and convictions. Significantly, after the war there was also a widespread sense that the dead were, in some way, still present – especially at ceremonies and rituals of remembrance or near memorials. The Cenotaph in Whitehall became a particular focus for such beliefs and hopes (Lloyd, 1998, pp.58 and 62–3; King, 1999, p.156).

At the official level, meanwhile, the war prompted a wholly new concern with the commemoration of the individual dead and the identification of their graves. In early 1915, members of Red Cross units were specifically assigned the task of searching for graves, identifying the dead, registering the location and marking the site with a cross. By March 1915, this activity had been taken over by the War Office and reorganized as the Graves Registration Commission, and in 1917 the Imperial War Graves Commission was established to organize and care for the graves of all members of the British, Dominion and Imperial forces who died on active service. In due course, the Commission was to be responsible for the design, construction and maintenance of hundreds of cemeteries where, for the first time, British dead were to be gathered together and reinterred in individually marked graves. The task was a massive one. By 1930, the Commission had overseen the reburial in named graves of over 550,000 British and Empire servicemen (over 450,000 of them from the UK). It had also individually reburied over 180,000 more unidentified bodies, each in a single marked grave. And then, with great irony, despite all the unprecedented effort to recover the body and mark the grave of each individual, there still remained over 330,000 more dead whose remains were simply never found. But they too were commemorated by name, if not by grave, on the walls and panels of monuments and memorials to the missing: almost 34,000 on the Tyne Cot memorial at Passchendale alone; almost 55,000 on the Menin Gate memorial at Ypres; and over 73,000 at Thiepval near the Somme. At other places such memorials recorded 'only' five, ten or twenty thousand names. By 1938, the War Graves Commission had overseen the construction of 1,850 cemeteries, some containing only ten or twenty graves, others with as many as 10,000[9] (Stamp, 1977, pp.8–9; Lacquer, 1994, pp.152–4).

The ending of the First World War in November 1918 was, understandably, a moment of celebration and rejoicing. But by 1919 the pressing question arose of how best and most appropriately the war might be remembered. By the end of 1920 that question had been answered and a number of the principal elements in British rituals of remembrance had been established. In July 1919 an official victory parade was held in London. It had not originally been intended to include remembrance of the dead as part of the parade but – largely as a result of the efforts of the prime minister, Lloyd George, and against considerable opposition – it was agreed that a temporary and non-denominational shrine would be placed in Whitehall, on the route of the parade. It was to be called a 'Cenotaph' – literally an 'empty tomb' – and was to represent the war dead of Britain, the Dominions and the Empire. The public response to this took the authorities by surprise. At the end of the parade many of the public placed wreaths at the Cenotaph and, in the words of its architect, Edwin Lutyens,

> ... the plain fact emerged, and grew stronger by the hour, that the Cenotaph was what the people wanted, and that they wanted to have the wood and plaster original replaced by an identical memorial in lasting stone. It was a mass feeling too deep to express itself more fitly than by the piles of good fresh flowers which loving hands placed at the Cenotaph day by day. Thus it was decided, by the human sentiment of millions, that the Cenotaph should be as it is now.
>
> (Quoted in Cannadine, 1981, p.221)

Within eleven days it had been decided to replace the temporary structure with an identical and permanent one (Cannadine, 1981, pp.219–21; Gregory, 1994, pp.8–9; King, 1998, pp.141–5).

The anniversary of the end of the war in November 1919 presented a further question. The experience of the public response to the Cenotaph suggested that some form of commemoration of this moment might prove popular. But what form should it take? As late as the beginning of November no decision had been reached. A former High Commissioner in South Africa, Percy Fitzpatrick, had suggested the adoption of a practice observed in South Africa during the war – namely, the observation of a period of silence. The Cabinet discussed

---

[9] The significance of this process of naming – whether at a grave or a memorial to the missing – will be explored more closely in the next chapter.

Figure 1.7 The temporary Cenotaph, Whitehall, 1919, with wreaths left by the public. Hulton Getty.

the idea on 5 November and – subject only to the king also approving – accepted the proposal for two minutes' silence at 11 a.m. on 11 November, the anniversary of the exact time of the coming into force of the armistice the previous year. George V duly signalled his agreement and the request for the two minutes of silence was carried in all newspapers on 7 November, with a reminder and many editorials on the subject on the day itself.

It proved to be an immediate and profound success. At the Cenotaph in Whitehall wreaths were laid, including one from the king and queen, and another from the prime minister – although no conventionally religious acts, such as prayers, were performed. Some towns and cities marked the two minutes with public gatherings and ceremonies, sometimes including hymns and the National Anthem as well as the laying of wreaths. Even more striking, however, was the interruption that came over everyday life: shops, trains, stations, factories and other locations fell movingly still and silent. The emotional impact of the silence was recognized to be immense – not least because it intrinsically combined public and private commemoration, leaving individuals to their own thoughts and memories, yet immersing them within a collective act. The public support for it was overwhelming. It was immediately clear that another 'new tradition' had been invented and would be observed regularly (Cannadine, 1981, pp.221–3; Gregory, 1994, pp.8–19).

In 1920, the 'traditions' that had begun to take shape the previous year were at once confirmed and also associated with a third element in the ritual of national remembrance. The celebration of Armistice Day 1920 included the unveiling, by the king, of the permanent version of the Cenotaph in Whitehall. Because the Cenotaph was intended as a commemoration of the dead of the entire empire, and thus of soldiers of varying races and religious beliefs, it was initially thought inappropriate for the unveiling ceremony to include 'any distinctive denominational flavour'. The ceremony was therefore originally planned to include no explicit Christian reference or content. Randall Davidson, the Archbishop of Canterbury, succeeded, however, in securing the inclusion of a modest but specifically Christian element within the ceremony. This consisted of the playing of the National Anthem when the king arrived in Whitehall, the singing of the hymn 'O God our help in ages past', the Lord's Prayer led by the archbishop, the simple unveiling of the permanent Cenotaph by the king, and the observation of the two minutes' silence, followed by the sounding of the 'Last Post' (Bell, 1952, p.1037; Cannadine, 1981, p.223; Bushaway, 1992, p.154; Gregory, 1994, pp.187–8; Lloyd, 1998, pp.69–70; Wolffe, 2000, p.262). Although the ceremony was thus given an overtly Christian character, it is nevertheless significant that the government was still concerned to secure the inclusion of Jewish, Muslim, Sikh and Hindu representatives at this event (Wolffe, 2000, pp.262–3). Moreover, it is also worth noting that the hymn chosen, although Christian in origin, is notably lacking in highly specific Christian references or theological content. Instead, it emphasizes the contrast between the eternal and unchanging nature of God and the fleeting and transitory nature of human existence – themes with an obvious relevance and resonance in the context of the remembrance of the many dead of the First World War. Consider, for example, lines such as 'A thousand ages in thy sight / Are like an evening gone', or 'Time like an ever rolling stream, / Bears all its sons away; / They fly forgotten, as a dream / Dies at the opening day.'

The unveiling of the Cenotaph was followed by a further ceremony. Earlier in 1920, the Dean of Westminster, acting on the suggestion of a wartime chaplain, had suggested the reburial in

Westminster Abbey of the remains of an unidentified British soldier originally buried in France. The king had been unenthusiastic, believing that such a ceremony would reopen wounds that were beginning to heal. However, the prime minister, Lloyd George, supported the proposal, and it was agreed that such a ceremony would take place. In November, a blindfolded officer chose one of six coffins each containing the body of an unknown British soldier. The chosen coffin was transported to London, passing crowds who had gathered at the railway stations and along parts of the track (Lloyd, 1998, pp.63–9). After the unveiling of the permanent Cenotaph, a ceremony of intense and detailed ritual ensued. The coffin – made of oak from a tree at Hampton Court Palace – was transported on a gun carriage from the Cenotaph to Westminster Abbey, with the king as chief mourner. At the abbey, with admirals, field marshals and generals as pallbearers, and before a congregation composed predominantly of war-bereaved, the coffin passed between two lines composed entirely of 100 holders of the Victoria Cross. It was interred in a grave filled with 100 sandbags of French earth and sealed with a slab of marble given by the Belgian people. The Church of England burial service was read at the grave and the hymns 'Lead kindly light' and 'Abide with me' were sung. At the beginning and end of the service, the further hymns, 'O valiant hearts' and 'Recessional', were also sung. Again, the event elicited overwhelming public support. In the following week, between 500,000 and 1,000,000 people paid homage at the tomb, and 100,000 wreaths were left at the new permanent Cenotaph by those who had visited the grave (Cannadine, 1981, pp.223–4; Bushaway, 1992, p.154; Gregory, 1994, pp.24–8; Wolffe, 2000, p.263).

It is clear that the events at the Cenotaph and Westminster Abbey in 1919 and 1920 not only established the elements of a national ritual of remembrance, but also acted as a collective national 'rite of passage'. With the unveiling of a permanent 'empty tomb' and the burial of a specific yet unknown soldier, something approaching the national equivalent of a family funeral had taken place (Lloyd, 1998, pp.81 and 90). The creation of local memorials and the ceremonies that were associated with them performed a similar function in literally thousands of cities, towns and villages. In the necessary absence of a normal family burial – because the bodies of the dead had not been repatriated but buried in official war cemeteries – the unveiling of local war memorials often functioned as 'surrogate funerals', even to the extent of including extracts from the burial service within the ceremonies (Hüppauf, 1985, pp.68–9; Moriarty, 1991, p.66; 1995, p.12; 1997, p.126; Inglis, 1992b, p.599). In due course such local memorials commonly became the sites for annual local Armistice Day

Figure 1.8 The Tomb of the Unknown Warrior, Westminster Abbey, 1920. Press Association.

observances, the rituals of local observance characteristically mirroring those of the national observance at the Cenotaph. Both the memorials and the annual rituals conducted at them served to give public recognition to communal and personal sadness, grief and bereavement and, at the same time, provided a focus for personal and communal rededication to good works and common ideals in the future (Inglis, 1992b, p.602; Gregory, 1994, pp.28–34; Winter, 1995, pp.96–7). Indeed, it has even been suggested that, in suburbs that had grown up without traditional features such as a village green or an old parish church, the memorial to those who died in the First World War could become the focal point of the community (Walter, 1990, pp.211–12).

The national ceremonies at the Cenotaph and Westminster Abbey in 1919 and 1920, together with the many local versions of these events, thus established the principal features of modern British rituals of remembrance of those killed in war. By the end of the 1920s, three other enduring elements of those rituals had also become established. The first was the Haig Poppy Appeal. Inspired by lines from a poem by John McCrae, a Canadian medical officer killed in Flanders in 1915,[10] the British Legion – an organization of ex-servicemen and women – first organized the sale of poppies to raise money for Earl Haig's fund for ex-servicemen in 1921. The practice was immediately popular and successful, becoming both a major annual charitable fundraising event and establishing a further enduring symbol of remembrance. Thus it became the established custom not only to wear an individual poppy but also to place wreaths of poppies, instead of fresh flowers, at war memorials on Armistice Day – a practice endorsed and encouraged by the example of the royal family and other dignitaries at the Cenotaph each November. The manufacture of poppies also provided work for disabled ex-servicemen (Gregory, 1994, chapter 3).

In 1927, the first British Legion Festival of Remembrance was held at the Albert Hall in London on the evening of 11 November. The event emerged out of controversy concerning dances and dinners held in previous years to celebrate Armistice Day. Such events, it was argued, were doubly inappropriate. On the one hand, they were high spirited, jovial occasions, whereas it was widely thought that a more sombre and reflective mood was the appropriate tone for celebration and recollection of the Armistice. On the other hand, they were, by definition, occasions for the wealthy – or at least the comfortably well off – and excluded the many ex-servicemen and their families who lacked the means to participate in such middle- and upper-class social activities. The Festival of Remembrance was designed to overcome these objections. It was to be organized by the British Legion, and it was to be open to all ex-servicemen and women. Places at the Albert Hall were to be allocated by the Legion, but the festival was to be free, and dress was to be 'uniform or day dress', thus avoiding the social distinctions and display of status implicit in evening dress. Any money raised was to go to the British Legion for its charitable work. The Prince of Wales was to attend, along with other political and military figures. The event was also to be broadcast by the BBC to all parts of the empire and dominions. The festival proved to be an immense success – over 50,000 applied for the 10,000 places available – and immediately it became another 'invented tradition' of British remembrance, which has survived to the present day. The structure and content of the festival were also significant and revealing. It was specifically called a 'festival' of 'remembrance', so

[10] 'In Flanders' fields the poppies blow / Between the crosses row on row, / That mark our place, and in the sky / The larks, still bravely singing, fly / Unheard amid the guns below.'

avoiding any suggestion that it was inappropriately celebratory. A central element was to be community singing – of old popular songs from the war, patriotic songs and hymns. The whole event, it has been suggested, was 'hedged round with a semi-religious aura' (Gregory, 1994, pp.77–84).

The Festival of Remembrance proved a popular success and by 1929 had already come to include the defining image of a million poppies falling on those present in the Albert Hall. Each poppy represented a life and, as a contemporary observer commented and others have subsequently agreed, the ritual conveyed the scale of loss of life far more effectively than any mere recitation of figures – however detailed – could do (Bushaway, 1992, p.156). After the Second World War, the broadcasting of the Festival of Remembrance on television as well as radio continued to bring this annual symbolic ritual to a wider audience, as it still does to this day. In 1928, two final pieces were added to the mosaic of British rituals of remembrance. First, the annual Field of Remembrance was initiated at Westminster Abbey, in which small crosses, each adorned with a poppy, were placed in the ground outside the abbey in remembrance of particular individuals. An initiative of the current director of the British Legion poppy factory, this too established a tradition that has lasted to the present day. Second, the ceremony at the Cenotaph was broadcast for the first time. At its centre was the two minutes' silence. The paradox of 'broadcasting silence' was not lost on those who first undertook this task but, as with so many aspects of the emergence and invention of British rituals of remembrance after the First World War, it immediately proved effective and symbolically powerful. The silence that followed the chimes of Big Ben made it possible for those listening on the radio to associate themselves and their own personal observation of the two minutes with the central national act of remembrance in Whitehall (Gregory, 1994, pp.133–8).

The 'invention' of the various traditions that became, and remain, central to British rituals of remembrance of those killed in the nation's wars may reasonably be described as a 'liturgy' of remembrance, or even an example of a 'civil religious liturgy'. The key elements of the 'liturgy' of Armistice Day – or Remembrance Sunday as it became after the Second World War – were already established by the early 1920s. The central act was the ceremony held at the Cenotaph in Whitehall. The nation's remembrance and commemoration was led by the monarch, supported by political and military dignitaries, including representatives of the dominions and colonies. A short religious service was led by a bishop of the Church of England. The two minutes' silence was at the heart of the ceremony. Wreaths of poppies were laid at the Cenotaph. Although there were early examples of confusion in the performance of these rituals – wreaths were laid in the wrong order, for example – the basic ceremony was to prove remarkably resistant to change and innovation. The broadcasting of the ritual on the radio from 1928 onwards increased this conservatism as the ceremony at the Cenotaph became an even more widely significant and immediately accessible ritual beyond the geographical confines of Whitehall (Gregory, 1994, pp.126–7).

By the 1930s, the organization and occupation of the 'sacred space' around the Cenotaph on 11 November had already assumed a basic form that is still readily recognizable to anyone watching the television broadcast of the Remembrance Sunday ceremony at the Cenotaph today. Representatives of the army, navy, air force, marines and merchant navy, together with war veterans in civilian dress, formed a hollow square around the Cenotaph. The bands of the Brigade of Guards played traditional folksongs and laments before the two minutes' silence, which was followed in turn by the 'Last Post'. There was common agreement that it was the silence that was at the heart of the event and the ritual, not least because, in order to 'work', the silence had to be a huge collective act on the part not only of the central actors in the drama but also of the immense crowds that attended in Whitehall, overspilling as far as Trafalgar Square, Pall Mall

Figure 1.9 The Cenotaph on Remembrance Sunday. Press Association.

and the Strand (Gregory, 1994, pp.130–1). At the same time the practice also began of holding memorial services – either in church or at local war memorials – on the Sunday closest to 11 November. As early as 1921, the Archbishop of Canterbury had suggested that such services should be held and the British Legion had supported the idea. After 1923, when Armistice Day fell on a Sunday and church attendances proved particularly large, the custom became widely established (Gregory, 1994, pp.188–90).

During the 1930s there were extensive debates concerning the appropriate meaning of Armistice Day, and the nature and content of the memory of the First World War was highly contested. Earlier and traditional notions of patriotic sacrifice for king, country and empire were challenged by the view that the war had been a monstrous folly. The dead might still be understood to have made a valuable sacrifice, but that sacrifice would be understood differently. On such a view, it was a sacrifice to the failure of humanity to avert such slaughter, and its value lay in the possibility that the lesson of so much suffering might be learnt and war be avoided in the future. Inevitably, therefore, the observance of Armistice Day became bound up in the wider debates of the 1930s concerning national and international politics, the League of Nations, peace, war, pacifism and appeasement. 'Alternative Armistice Days' were held, including the wearing of white poppies to symbolize commitment to peace and the holding of peace rallies. It was even suggested that Armistice Day itself might be discontinued. Although some of those opposed to the traditional Armistice Day called for its abolition – just as there was some hostility from the British Legion to the wearing of white poppies – the more characteristic attitude was one of 'live and let live'. For the most part, supporters of the established rituals accepted that those committed to alternative peace rallies at least recognized and respected the central themes of honouring the dead and respecting the bereaved in the official Armistice Day ceremonies. Significantly, moreover, justifications for the continuance of Armistice Day itself were increasingly couched in terms of the contribution of such rituals to a commitment to the cause of peace (Gregory, 1994, chapters 4 and 5). The editorial in *The Times* for 11 November 1937 summed up such views:

> The heart of today's commemoration lies not in the prayers publicly recited or the hymns sung, but in the two minutes' silence. This in each year anyone is free to employ as they will ... Thoughts will turn this morning to the future rather than to the past; they will concern themselves less with bygone victory than with the hopes of peace to come. Yet to devote the two minutes to silent prayer for peace is certainly not to show forgetfulness for the fallen or ingratitude for their

sacrifices. It is, on the contrary, to commemorate them in just the way they would wish.

(Quoted in Gregory, 1994, p.172)

Such sentiments tend to confirm the judgement of several recent historians that British rituals of remembrance and war memorials were characterized above all by mourning and bereavement, not by patriotism or the celebration of military prowess. Thus, Armistice Day was 'not a festival of homage by the citizens to the state, but a tribute by the living to the dead' (Cannadine, 1981, p.219). The tone of the ceremony at the Cenotaph 'changed from a tribute to the Army and the British victory, to a tribute from the relatives of the bereaved and ex-servicement to the dead' (Lloyd, 1998, p.90). War memorials characteristically represented the achievement of the dead as an 'ethical triumph over evil rather than a military triumph over other people' (King, 1998, p.176). Whereas it has been argued that in some countries rituals of remembrance after the First World War amounted to a 'cult of the fallen soldier', in which traditional virtues of masculine honour and patriotism were affirmed and support was given to a nationalistic civil religion (Mosse, 1990, especially chapter 5), in the UK, it has been suggested, the individual soldier was commemorated as innocent victim. Thus 'the characteristic discussion of the Unknown Soldier stressed ordinariness, rather than heroism, and placed him in a specific individual context, as husband, father, son or comrade' (Gregory, 1994, p.144).

The outbreak of the Second World War in early September 1939 prompted the cancellation of Armistice Day that November – a further indication that it was not a celebration of patriotism and national prowess, for if it had been, then surely cancellation in November 1939 would have been unthinkable (Gregory, 1994, p.172)? Instead, it was decided that, with the country again at war, it would be inappropriate to celebrate Armistice Day. However, it was agreed that the Poppy Day appeal would continue and that Sunday 12 November would still be observed as a day of dedication. Remembrance Sunday, as the Sunday of dedication came to be known, was also celebrated by church services during the years of the Second World War. With the end of the war in 1945, the question arose of whether Armistice Day would be reintroduced or another day established to commemorate the dead of both world wars. Various dates were considered but rejected. In 1945, Armistice Day and Remembrance Sunday fell together on 11 November. A combination of pressure groups, including in particular the churches and the British Legion, argued for the adoption of Remembrance Sunday – understood as the Sunday nearest to 11 November – as the annual date for the nation's collective act of remembrance. On this day the ceremony at the Cenotaph would be held, as would the two minutes' silence. The British Legion moved its annual Festival of Remembrance to the Saturday evening before 'Remembrance Sunday', as the day was now officially called. The new arrangement was officially instituted in 1946, when the Cenotaph was rededicated, having also been newly inscribed with the dates 1939–1945, in addition to the original inscription of the dates 1914–1918 (Gregory, 1994, pp.215–21).

There is no question that, in the period since the Second World War, 'Remembrance Sunday' has never attained the same degree of prominence and significance in British life that 'Armistice Day' had secured in the years between the two world wars. And yet it remains arguably the single most substantial expression of British civil religion – an annual commemoration of the two most traumatic periods in the history of twentieth-century Britain and an annual act of remembrance of all those killed in the nation's wars since 1914. The annual ceremony at the Cenotaph continues to provide a national focus for thousands of local ceremonies, and in the decades since 1945 the broadcasting of the event on television as well as radio has brought the sights as well as the sounds of this annual ritual to a wider audience. In fact, the annual ceremony at the Cenotaph had first been broadcast on television as early as 1937, but it was not until after the Second World War that the ownership of television sets became widespread and thus a significant factor in the diffusion of the Cenotaph ritual to the public (Briggs, 1965, p.611). Subsequently, the televising of both the British Legion Festival of Remembrance on the Saturday evening before Remembrance Sunday and the live broadcast from the Cenotaph itself on the Sunday became firmly fixed as annual events in the BBC calendar. Moreover, despite recurrent discussion of the nature and significance of the rituals and ceremonies, particularly since the majority of the population has no personal recollection of either world war, there continues to be a substantial level of support for the institution of Remembrance Sunday, not least after the experiences of the Falklands War of 1982 and the Gulf War of 1991 (Wolffe, 1993, pp.324–5).

Rituals of remembrance and civil religion: towards an assessment

Sources of unity

As noted in the introduction to this book, the American historians, Richard Pierard and Robert Linder, have argued that a civil religion may appropriately be characterized as fulfilling the following five functions. It will refer to the widespread acceptance by a people of a shared sense of their nation's history and destiny. It will relate their society to a realm of absolute meaning. It will enable them to look at their society and community as in some sense special. It will provide a vision that ties the nation together as an integrated whole. And it will provide a collection of beliefs, values, rites, ceremonies and symbols which, taken together, give sacred meaning to the life of the community and thus provide an overarching sense of unity that transcends internal conflicts and differences (Pierard and Linder, 1988, pp.22–3). It is clear that the gradual invention and subsequent history of the principal rituals of remembrance of those killed in war in both the USA and the UK do, indeed, reflect and express most – if not all – of the characteristics of civil religion identified by Pierard and Linder. At the same time, however, the application of even a modest degree of critical reflection will readily confirm that, in both contexts, these processes are far from being straightforward, unambiguous or uncontested.

In both the USA and the UK, the rituals of remembrance that emerged out of the two nations' experiences of modern war led to the establishment of sacred places and memorials and to the institution of annual rites, symbols and ceremonies that recalled, honoured and commemorated those who had died in the service of their country and its official values. In both contexts the language of sacrifice was commonly used to characterize the meaning of the deaths commemorated. The dead were understood to have sacrificed themselves for the preservation of their communities and the ideals and values associated with those communities. Their sacrifices would impose a debt of remembrance on the living – and also a moral obligation on the living to continue to uphold the values and the commitment to a particular community and nation for which the dead were perceived to have died.

The rituals and traditions of remembrance that are examined briefly in the previous pages supply striking examples of the way in which such remembrance of sacrifice might serve to unite a people in a shared sense of history and destiny, enabling them to understand their community as special and distinctive, and to achieve a unity that transcends internal divisions and conflicts. Indeed, the way in which American rituals of remembrance emerged out of the catastrophic and traumatic *dis*unity of the Civil War provides – at one level – a compelling demonstration of the way in which rituals of remembrance can embody and focus the aims of a civil religion. As the successive stages in the commemoration of the battle of Gettysburg amply illustrate, the remembrance of the Civil War in terms of the sacrifice and suffering of *both* sides provided the basis for a powerful reinterpretation of the war as a moment of *shared* trauma and dedication to opposing, but equally cherished, ideals. The result was the development of an ideology of reconciliation between North and South and the consequent 'rebirth' of a unified American nation. The extent to which the success of this ideology was secured only at the cost of deliberately forgetting and perpetuating other profound divisions within American society is a point which should not be overlooked and which will require attention later in this chapter. In its own terms, however, the ideology of reconciliation expressed in the history of American remembrance of the Civil War was remarkably successful. By the time that the world wars of the twentieth century again presented Americans with the need to invent further traditions of remembrance, they already had a civil religious tradition of commemoration into which new rituals could be fitted. The tombs of the American unknown soldiers and the celebration of Armistice Day could be fitted easily into a tradition and a ritual calendar of remembrance that already included the sacred sites of Gettysburg and Arlington and the annual institution of Memorial Day.

British rituals of remembrance also expressed and fulfilled the civil religious function of providing a focus for national unity, integration, and a sense of both shared history and shared duty. As one recent analyst of the invention and subsequent history of British rituals of remembrance after the First World War has observed, during the inter-war period 'British society witnessed an annual event in which social and political unity was reaffirmed'. A 'language of remembrance' emerged that enshrined the experience of the war, removed it from normal social and political debate, and elevated it 'to a level of spiritual significance from where its memory for peacetime British society was of a special, supranational and sacred quality'. In this way, 'Armistice Day became a point of reference for British society'. The sacrifice of the dead became the centre of remembrance and was symbolically renewed each year in a ceremony led by the king and the established church and in the presence of a spectrum of political leaders. Thus, the culture and rituals of remembrance became symbols and expressions of unity – even in the midst of the profound social, economic and political divisions of the decades between the two world wars that witnessed both the General Strike and the chronic unemployment of the Great Depression (Bushaway, 1992, pp.159–61).

Similarly, another recent historian of British memorials of the First World War, and of the symbolism and politics of remembrance involved in them, deploys strikingly religious concepts in the titles of key chapters in his study – and concepts, moreover, that are suggestive of the central concerns of civil religion. Accordingly, the first chapter is entitled 'The Composition of a National Cult' and the concluding chapters are entitled 'The Canonisation of the Common People', 'Moral Obligation and Politics in the Commemoration of the Dead' and 'Sacred Union' (King, 1998). In the context of a discussion of civil religion it is the last of these that is, in many respects, the most significant. In reality, and also inevitably, as the chapter acknowledges, the emergence and annual observance of rituals and symbols of remembrance were surrounded by a variety of disagreements and differing perspectives. What should memorials look like? What sentiments should they express? What did such memorials mean? Indeed, what exactly was the meaning of the sacrifice that was commemorated by them? What were the political implications of remembrance? These and many other similar questions were debated at both local and national level as war memorials were erected and the annual rituals associated with them became established.

Yet such disagreements remained secondary to a broad consensus that the dead should be properly honoured, that the silence on Armistice Day should be observed, that wreaths should be laid where the names of the dead were recorded, and that – despite differences in interpretation and meanings attributed to them – there should, indeed, be public expressions of commemoration, remembrance and reverence. Such extensive unity – despite the wide diversity of particular perspectives and interpretations of the meaning of remembrance – was achieved by various strategies and factors. In particular, there was usually general agreement that memorials and rituals of remembrance should be regarded as sacred. Individuals and groups might disagree deeply about the meaning a memorial was supposed to have, or about the appropriateness or otherwise of the particular design or imagery, but there would characteristically be agreement on the sanctity of the memorial itself. That sanctity was derived, moreover, from the respect of the community for those commemorated in the memorial or the act of remembrance, not from the ideas that the memorials might be held to express. The memorial unveiled at Bradford in 1922 illustrated this process. It included two figures, of a soldier and sailor, each advancing holding a rifle with a fixed bayonet. The figures prompted criticism because they were thought by some to suggest a celebration of aggression. Others defended the figures, arguing that they did not celebrate aggression and militarism but rather the spirit of self-sacrifice of Bradford's dead. But despite such differences of opinion, there was consensus on all sides in respecting the memorial itself as sacred, and an overriding concern to share in a genuinely collective process of commemoration (King, 1998, pp.207–8 and 230–1; 1999, p.162).

Another key factor in securing widespread acceptance of both memorials and acts of remembrance was the deliberate reticence and simplicity that were characteristic of most of them. Memorials frequently tended to be of simple design – a characteristic embodied above all in the austere simplicity of the Cenotaph, which has been described as 'a particularly successful embodiment of reserve and iconographical emptiness, allowing it to become a container for the emotions of those with widely different attitudes and beliefs' (King, 1999, p.161). Similarly, ceremonies such as that at the Cenotaph, or at local memorials, were kept simple and sombre, even to the point of austerity, focusing above all on the sober remembrance of the dead and respect for their sacrifice. Characteristically such events avoided explicit or detailed commentary on the meaning of the war and of the deaths being commemorated, but emphasized instead the most general of propositions, such as the appropriateness of remembering the sacrifice of those who died, and the need for the living to commit themselves to upholding the ideals for which those remembered had died. The two minutes' silence was, arguably, the most effective example of this tendency. Like the Cenotaph, it too provided at once a commonly accepted and collectively expressed focus for remembrance, yet also a time and a space for countless personal expressions of memory, reflection, conviction or commitment. Even when political, moral or religious disagreements over the war and its legacy prevented any generally agreed expression of the meaning and significance of remembrance, yet the silence provided 'something to cherish and defend as a transcendent moment' above the divisions within any particular community (King, 1999, pp.161–2).

The present discussion of the ways in which traditions of remembrance may be said to fulfil one of the key roles of civil religion by providing a sense of unity and shared history has already – and inevitably – focused on the importance of the particular rituals, ceremonies and symbols that seek to express such shared experiences and histories. Initially, the importance of many rituals of remembrance in both the USA and the UK was the provision of national and local 'rites of passage', marking the transition from war to peace and the recognition of the cost and loss involved in war. In origin, therefore, such rituals were the national and local communal equivalents of family funerals and services of commemoration – a vital part of the process of mourning. In the longer term, however, such rituals have, necessarily, moved from being exercises in mourning and become annual occasions for national recollection of both the dedication and the loss experienced by past generations. The relationship between national and local versions of such annual rituals of remembrance is also crucial. The fact that innumerable local communities perform their own versions of national commemorative acts, such as those for Remembrance Sunday, Memorial Day or Veterans Day, is a further important demonstration of the way in which rituals of remembrance perform an integrative function within the civil religion of both the UK and the USA. As one scholar has observed of British remembrance and commemoration after the First World War:

> With respect to its dead, each local or institutional community did draw together and form a united movement transcending its charac-teristic internal differences, and enacted the ideal civic vision of itself. At the same time, each community was drawn into a larger whole. The symbols, ceremonies, speeches and writing of commemoration proposed the existence of a greater community amongst all who commemorated the dead ... Through commemoration, a movement was assembled which insisted on remembering the war and the dead, and assigning value to them ... People joined together not because they shared a single attitude to the war, but in the belief that it was necessary to make something valid out of it, whether seeking consolation for personal loss, or out of a sense of political commit-ment, or often from both. Something of value must be saved from the wreck of so many lives, if only a lesson that the disaster of war must not occur again.
>
> (King, 1998, pp.238–9)

If rituals of remembrance amply fulfil the functions of civil religion in providing unifying rituals and emphasizing shared perceptions of national histories, what of the further role of relating the societies concerned to 'a realm of absolute meaning'? As the earlier discussion of attitudes to the American Civil War noted, for some Northern interpreters of the meaning of the war, the association between the sacrificial death of Christ and the deaths of Northern soldiers was explicit and was even enshrined in Julia Ward Howe's 'Battle Hymn of the Republic'. Similarly, both during the First World War and after it, there was no lack of British attempts to draw a parallel between the 'sacrificial' deaths of soldiers and Christian understandings of the death of Christ. It has been noted that the language of remembrance in both the press and in pulpits was often underpinned – implicitly if not explicitly – by ideas such as the potential redemption of the living by the sacrifice of the dead; that death in war could somehow atone for, or expiate, the moral failings of the world; or even that the dead died in a state of grace – and would therefore go to heaven – because of the sacrificial nature of their deaths. Such ideas would not stand up to close or detailed scrutiny and were certainly not consistent with orthodox or traditional Christian theology and belief. Indeed, it has been suggested that they might appropriately be described as 'theologically lazy to the point of heresy' (Bushaway, 1992, pp.158–9; Gregory, 1994, pp.34–5). But they can also be interpreted as the basis of a genuinely popular attempt to find positive meaning in the midst of a scale of loss and suffering that apparently did not find adequate consolation in conventional Christian belief. Moreover, if, as has been suggested, the meaning widely given to the many deaths was 'predicated on the transformative power of self-sacrifice' and the transformation had to be realized by the actions of the living (King, 1999, pp.156–7), then it may also be argued that this amounted to an 'alternative theology' rather than merely a lazy one.

British rituals of remembrance also included – and still include – specifically Christian elements. The official role of the Church of England at the Cenotaph and the use of Christian hymns and prayers, the similar involvement and roles of Christian clergy at local remembrance services, and the burial of the Unknown Soldier in Westminster Abbey, are obvious examples. Many – though by no means all – local war memorials included a cross within their symbolism. And in the cemeteries created by the Imperial War Graves Commission, and still maintained by the Commonwealth War Graves Commission, two of the most prominent symbols were and are the Cross of Sacrifice and the Stone of Remembrance. The former, designed for the Commission by the architect Reginald Blomfield, consists of a large free-standing cross on which is superimposed a sword, pointing downwards. The latter is a large rectangular stone, the size and shape of which could be interpreted as suggestive of a Christian altar, on which appear the words 'Their names liveth for evermore'. The latter text is taken from the biblical Book of Ecclesiasticus. It had been suggested by the poet Rudyard Kipling who was a member of the War Graves Commission, and who had also suggested the simple phrase, 'A Soldier of the Great War known unto God', which was placed on the headstones of unidentified dead in British war cemeteries. Kipling's own – and only – son had been killed in 1915 at the battle of Loos. He had simply disappeared (Longworth, 1985, p.36; Bushaway, 1992, p.145; Laqueur, 1994, p.153).

Figure 1.10 The Cross of Sacrifice in the
Commonwealth War Graves Cemetery, Tyne
Cot, Belgium. Courtesy of the Photograph
Archives of the Commonwealth War Graves
Commission.

Figure 1.11 The Stone of Remembrance in the Commonwealth War Graves
Cemetery, Arnhem, the Netherlands. Courtesy of the Photograph Archives of
the Commonwealth War Graves Commission.

But the very examples of the Cross of Sacrifice and the Stone of Remembrance also point to the tensions between traditional Christian teaching and the rituals and 'liturgies' of British remembrance. For example, the Cross of Sacrifice could be read primarily as an evocation of the crosses that are found in British churchyards, but adorned with a downturned sword symbolizing death in war, rather than as a specifically Christian reference (Stamp, 1977, p.10; Mosse, 1990, p.83). It could also be read as a permanent memorial of the temporary wooden crosses that were used to mark the graves of the dead before the establishment of permanent cemeteries. It is significant, moreover, that a suggestion that each Cross of Sacrifice should be inscribed with a Christian text ('O grave where is thy victory? Thanks be to God which giveth the victory through our Lord Jesus Christ': from the biblical book 1 Corinthians 15) was rejected, despite having the support of the Archbishop of Canterbury (Wilkinson, 1978, p.303; Longworth, 1985, p.51). The Stone of Remembrance is similarly open to an alternative interpretation. It was designed by Edwin Lutyens, and was intended to have no specifically Christian significance at all. He had aimed, rather, to achieve an abstract form that was religiously non-specific and ecumenical in its appeal, and which avoided what he regarded as the narrowness and parochialism of Christian imagery. In so far as it had religious roots or inspiration of any kind, it was the result of Lutyens' own interest in pantheism and his connections with members of the theosophist movement who fostered an inclusive attitude to all spiritual beliefs (Stamp, 1977, p.10; Mosse, 1990, p.84; Borg, 1991, p.73; Winter, 1995, pp.103–7).

Nor are these the only examples of the limits to the specifically Christian content of British rituals and symbols of remembrance. The Cenotaph itself provides another excellent example. Again Lutyens, its architect, determinedly avoided either patriotic or Christian symbolism. It was – and remains – an austere monument, derived from classical Greek commemorative architecture, but without any of the sense of celebration that such classical monuments would have included. Much of the emotional power of the Cenotaph, it has been suggested, derives precisely from its simplicity and lack of overt or explicit religious or spiritual symbolism. By presenting itself simply as a tomb – indeed, an empty tomb – it provided 'a form on which anyone could inscribe his or her own thoughts, reveries, sadnesses' (Winter, 1995,. p.104; Lloyd, 1998, p.91). Significantly, calls for the Cenotaph to include a Christian inscription were rejected, even though they were supported by the Archbishop of Canterbury (Lloyd, 1998, p.88). It has even been suggested that the burial of the Unknown Warrior in Westminster Abbey was a deliberate attempt to create a rival and overtly Christian shrine to the Cenotaph (Inglis, 1993, p.10). Indeed, Lutyens is reported to have said in conversation that:

> There was some horror in Church circles. *What!* a pagan monument in the midst of Whitehall! That is why we have a rival shrine in the Abbey, the Unknown Warrior, but even an unknown soldier might not have been a Christian, the more unknown the less sure you could be.
>
> (Quoted in Lloyd, 1998, p.87)

The possibility that the unknown soldier might not have been a Christian was also raised in relation to the decision that the tomb in Westminster Abbey should include the text, 'In Christ shall all be made alive'. When faced with a Jewish complaint that the religion of the unknown soldier might not have been Christianity, the Dean of Westminster responded by saying that the words expressed the faith of those who had buried the dead man, not of the unknown himself. He also argued that it was justified because the overwhelming majority of those who visited the tomb were Christians, as were the majority – by personal conviction or formal profession – of those who were killed in the war (Wolffe, 1994, p.246; 2000, p.264). In the long run, however, it was the Cenotaph and not the Tomb of the Unknown Warrior in Westminster Abbey that became both the popular and the principal official focus for British rituals of remembrance. When, in 1923, the Archbishop of Canterbury proposed that the service on Armistice Day should be moved from the Cenotaph to Westminster Abbey – because Armistice Day fell on a Sunday – there was widespread opposition. The service remained at the Cenotaph and has done so ever since (Inglis, 1993, p.23; Lloyd, 1998, pp.88–9).

The regulations established for the marking of the permanent graves in British war cemeteries also illustrated the limits to the specifically Christian in British remembrance. In 1918, the Imperial War Graves Commission decided that all the graves would be marked by simple and standard headstones, replacing the wooden crosses that had served this purpose until this time. To these could be added an engraving of a religious symbol – such as a Cross, a Star of David, a Muslim Crescent or a Sikh, Hindu, Buddhist or Confucian symbol – or a regimental insignia, or a short text, but the standard grave marker was to be a non-religious headstone. The policy provoked controversy and resulted in a debate in Parliament. Nevertheless, the wishes of the Commission prevailed, and the simple headstones were established throughout the cemeteries for which the Commission had responsibility. Lutyens once again succinctly expressed the aim behind the policy: besides Christians, he observed, there would be Jews, Muslims and Hindus buried in these cemeteries and their remains deserved equal record and remembrance (Stamp, 1977, p.10; Longworth, 1985, pp.40–55; Moriarty, 1991, pp.65–6; King, 1998, p.187).

Such concern to recognize the diversity of the religious beliefs of those killed fighting for Britain and its empire during the First World War was expressed with particular clarity at the unveiling of a memorial to soldiers of the Indian Army at Patcham, near Brighton, in 1921. During the First World War, many Indian soldiers who had been wounded in France were treated in hospital in Brighton. Inevitably some died and arrangements had to be made for appropriate funeral rites for Muslims, Hindus and Sikhs. The bodies of Muslim soldiers were taken to the mosque that already existed at Woking, and were buried with Muslim rites and military honours. The bodies of Hindu and Sikh soldiers who died were cremated, according to the appropriate religious rites, at a site near the village of Patcham. The memorial subsequently built there was to the memory of all Indian soldiers who had been killed in the war. At its dedication the chairman of the Memorial Committee asserted that:

> There is a religion underlying all religions. It is the consecration of the principles of justice, righteousness, mercy, goodwill, towards men. It is the orientation towards the unseen Giver of life, of our thoughts on those principles of conduct divinely implanted in mankind.
>
> (Quoted in Robinson, 1996, p.45)

Analysis of some of the hymns most closely associated with British rituals of remembrance similarly suggests a preference for a more generalized religious sentiment rather than the specificity of Christian orthodoxy. 'O God our help in ages past' – as suggested earlier in this chapter – appeals to concepts such as the brevity and transience of human life in the face of the eternity and timelessness of God and to trust in God as 'our eternal home'. Such sentiments are, of course, entirely compatible with the most impeccably orthodox Christian belief – but they are also compatible with a variety of much less explicit theologies and beliefs. 'O valiant hearts', meanwhile, a hymn specifically written for the purpose of remembrance, was striking for its celebration of the sacrifice of fallen soldiers and its explicit association of their sacrifice with that of Christ. According to this hymn, the dead had given all to save mankind, but had scorned to save themselves. Christ had passed 'the self-same way' and now blessed 'our lesser Calvaries'. As he rose, so would the dead, who had shared 'his cup of sacrifice'. Certainly, these were overtly Christian associations, yet once again the sentiments were hardly orthodox Christian theology – even though the hymn was included in official hymnbooks – but tended, rather, to focus attention on the dead and their sacrifice and its redemptive power and significance. Indeed, it might reasonably be argued that 'O valiant hearts' is not essentially a hymn of Christian worship, but rather primarily a celebration of those who died in war whose sacrifice is, as it were, 'blessed' or 'baptized' by Christian concepts and associations.

Such considerations have prompted the observation that, despite being associated with Christian hymns, language and concepts, remembrance was 'also strangely *a*-religious' – largely because deliberate efforts were made to avoid precise reference to specific Christian doctrines in order to avoid offending the relatives of those of other faiths who had died. Rituals of remembrance, the same commentator suggests, were 'bathed in religious and specifically Anglican' sentiment, liturgy and hymnody, yet 'were religious occasions in form only' (Bushaway, 1992, p.158). But it has been the argument of this essay that the rituals of remembrance were, in fact, highly religious – albeit in the service of a deliberately imprecise and unspecific civil religion. This argument is supported by the language used by historians to describe the rituals involved, as for example in the concepts of the 'transcendent sacred time of the two minutes' silence'; the 'sacred symbol of the Cenotaph'; or the 'canonization of the common people'. So did – and do – such expressions of civil religion connect people with a realm of absolute meaning?

They certainly connected, and can still connect, people with profound reflection on enduring questions about human existence and experience. What was the meaning of so much human suffering and loss? Was there, indeed, any meaning in it at all? What are the appropriate ethical and moral conclusions to be drawn from such episodes in history? What hope, if any, might be derived from contemplation of such loss and sacrifice? And, as we have seen, at least one of the consistent explanations offered by rituals of remembrance is that the sacrifice of past generations should be remembered and honoured, and that the living should seek to lead better lives as a result of such remembrance. Whether such questions and responses as these constitute contact with 'a realm of absolute meaning' is an open question – as indeed is the very concept and nature of 'a realm of absolute meaning' itself. But it is surely clear that rituals of remembrance which raise such issues and focus such thoughts are engaged in an activity that decisively transcends the ordinary, the everyday and the mundane, and which insistently demands that both individuals and societies reflect on their deepest beliefs and values.

Causes of division

If British and American rituals of remembrance thus fulfil many of the roles and functions of civil religion, it is nevertheless also important to note the limits to such fulfilment as well. Indeed, the rituals of remembrance themselves can become the focus for dispute and disunity as well as unity. For those who tend to favour pacifism or have a strongly internationalist disposition, the rituals of remembrance – with their inevitable associations with the military and with the recollection of war – may appear to glorify an undesirable nationalism or promote an uncritical patriotism and therefore constitute a cause of offence. Many clergy, for example, will be familiar with the tensions that can arise on Remembrance Sunday, when the attendance of members of the British Legion at a Remembrance Service and the orientation of worship towards the theme of remembrance may offend some regular churchgoers whose own beliefs lead them to reject the continuing rituals of remembrance (Wilkinson, 1978, pp.300–1). Conversely, clergy may themselves resist what they see as inappropriate emphases within the traditional rituals of Remembrance Sunday (Pawley, 1950; Coppin, 1965). A different kind of conflict or controversy may also arise if local attempts are made to include representatives of religious traditions other than Christianity within the rituals of Remembrance Day. Such an example occurred at Southampton in 1994, when representatives of the local Jewish, Hindu, Muslim and Sikh communities were invited to participate in the service held at the local war memorial on Remembrance Sunday. In fact, the majority response was positive, and an editorial in the local paper quoted approvingly from the comments of the local Member of Parliament who echoed – consciously or unconsciously – the attitudes and intentions of the Imperial War Graves Commission and figures such as Lutyens some three-quarters of a century earlier: the inclusion of Jews, Hindus, Muslims and Sikhs alongside Christians was an overdue recognition that members of their faiths had died in the wars commemorated by the memorial and the ceremony. There was, however, also a fierce attack on this initiative from a vocal minority opposed to the modification of the traditional rituals. For this minority, the inclusion of prayers for peace in Arabic, Punjabi, Hebrew and Sanskrit was a 'non-Christian betrayal' of the values and way of life that the dead had died to preserve (Gilliat-Ray, 1999, pp.238–40).

Similarly, at the national level tensions may become apparent at particular moments. In the UK, for example, in 1982, the Memorial Service at St Paul's Cathedral after the Falklands War prompted protests from some Conservative MPs who objected to the fact that in

his sermon, the Archbishop of Canterbury had condemned nationalism and spoken of the need for peace and reconciliation – although
he also accepted the need for the Falklands War and praised the
courage of the British forces (Wolffe, 1993, p.325; 1994, pp.263–4). In
the USA, meanwhile, in the late 1960s and the early and mid-1970s, as
the Vietnam War was being fought and was also deeply dividing the
nation, the celebration of both Memorial Day and Veterans Day was
downplayed (Albanese, 1974, pp.391–2; Hass, 1998, p.91). Veterans
Day was even moved from its traditional date of 11 November to the
fourth Monday in October. It was subsequently restored to 11
November in the late 1970s, although the issue of the commemoration of those killed in the Vietnam War was to prompt further
controversy in the 1980s – as Chapter 3 will explore in some detail.

There are also other more profound ways in which, historically,
both American and British rituals of remembrance fail to secure the
overarching collective unity that is one of the main aims and
purposes of civil religion. By constructing particular histories and
interpretations of the conflicts that led to the emergence of rituals of
remembrance, it is possible to avoid confronting other issues that
might intrude on or undermine the officially preferred understanding
of the significance of the rituals in question. Two brief examples may
be cited from both the American and British rituals of remembrance
discussed in this chapter.

As we have seen, the origin of many of America's continuing
traditions and rituals of remembrance lay in the Civil War and its
recollection and commemoration. That process of commemoration,
however, had at its centre the 'ideology of reconciliation', which
enabled both North and South to develop a shared understanding of
the Civil War in which the sacrifice of the soldiers of both sides was
remembered and honoured. But this ideology also excluded from
view the contribution of black Americans to the war, and carefully
avoided the issues of slavery and race – either as causes of the war or
as ongoing issues after it. Late-nineteenth-century black American
intellectuals such as Frederick Douglass made strenuous efforts to
establish an alternative memory of the Civil War, one that emphasized
the themes of black emancipation, freedom, citizenship, suffrage and
dignity, and that continued to recognize slavery as a fundamental
cause of the war (Blight, 1989).

Douglass had been born into slavery in 1818, but had escaped in
1836 and arrived in New York in 1838. There he worked for the anti-
slavery movement and become an influential orator, journalist and
social reformer, and in his later years, he was appointed to several
government posts. From the early 1870s until his death in 1895,
Douglass wrote and spoke against the growing acceptance of the

ideology of reconciliation between North and South and the nostalgic romanticism of the myth of the 'Lost Cause' (see pp.16–17). At the same time he stalwartly resisted the resurgence of racism and the marginalization of the black contribution to the Civil War, and he advocated the continued memorial and celebration of Northern victory as a moral triumph over the evil of slavery. Significantly, many of Douglass' most passionate expressions of this alternative memory of the Civil War and its meaning occurred in the Memorial Day addresses which he was regularly invited to deliver. For example, as early as 1871, in his Memorial Day address at the grave of the unknown Union dead in Arlington National Cemetery, Douglass proclaimed that:

> We are sometimes asked in the name of patriotism to forget the merits of this fearful struggle, and to remember with equal admiration those who struck at the nation's life, and those who struck to save it – those who fought for slavery and those who fought for liberty and justice. I am no minister of malice ... I would not repel the repentant, but ... may my tongue cleave to the roof of my mouth if I forget the difference between the parties to that ... bloody conflict.
>
> (Quoted in Blight, 1989, p.1160)

Again, in 1878, Douglass argued that what drew Northerners to celebrate Memorial Day was 'the moral character of the war ... the far-reaching ... eternal principles in dispute, and for which our sons and brothers encountered ... danger and death'. It had been, he insisted, 'a war of ideas, a battle of principles ... a war between the old and new, slavery and freedom, barbarism and civilisation' (quoted in Blight, 1989, pp.1162–3). And at the end of his life, in one of his last public speeches, Douglass addressed the Memorial Day gathering in May 1894 in Rochester Cemetery, where he would be buried only nine months later. He again opposed the ideology of reconciliation that so deliberately avoided the moral issues and causes of the Civil War. 'Death has no power to change moral qualities', he declared.

> What was bad before the war, and during the war, has not been made good since the war ... Whatever else I may forget, I shall never forget the difference between those who fought for liberty and those who fought for slavery; between those who fought to save the Republic and those who fought to destroy it.
>
> (Quoted in Blight, 1989, p.1178)

Despite such efforts, however, the interpretation of the war that steadily came to predominate in American rituals of remembrance was, indeed, that of the ideology of reconciliation between North and South. And it was central to the ideology of reconciliation that the focus should be on the shared respect of the two sides for those who fought, and that the vexed issues of slavery and the origins of the war and of black emancipation and its post-war implications should not be addressed (Foster, 1987, pp.69–70, 140 and 194–6; O'Leary, 1994, pp.21–7; Savage, 1994, pp.131–4; Grant, 1998, pp.177–8).

As black Americans continued to be excluded from full participation in American society and culture – in both the North and South – so also they were largely excluded from the memorials to the Civil War dead. Thus, in a survey of American monuments completed in 1916, only three Civil War monuments that included representations of black soldiers were identified. Of these, two portrayed a single black soldier in the midst of larger groups of white soldiers. The third was the Shaw Monument in Boston which commemorates both Robert Gould Shaw – the white commanding officer of the first black regiment to be raised in the North – and also the black soldiers of the regiment, among whom were the two sons of Frederick Douglass (Savage, 1994, pp.136–7; Blight, 1989, p.1174). Indeed, so comprehensive was the exclusion of black participation in the war from physical memorials, and so prevalent was the ideology of reconciliation between North and South, that it has been argued that the commemoration of the Civil War in physical memorials 'is ultimately a story of systematic cultural repression, carried out in the guise of reconciliation and harmony' (Savage, 1994, p.143). The continuing relevance of the issue – and also the continuing relevance of rituals of remembrance in relation to the Civil War – was further demonstrated by the unveiling of a new memorial in 1998 to black soldiers who fought in the Civil War. Called the African-American Civil War Memorial, it is located in the Shaw neighbourhood of Washington and is inscribed with 208,943 names – thus recalling each of the black soldiers who fought for the Union, together with the white officers with whom they served. Both the location of the memorial and the date of the unveiling are replete with symbolism. The Shaw neighbourhood in Washington is named after Robert Gould Shaw and the monument was unveiled on the 135th anniversary of the battle in South Carolina in which Gould and most of his regiment were killed (*New York Times*, 12 July 1998).

Black Americans are not, however, by any means the only group within American society to have been excluded from, or marginalized within, the civil religious traditions associated with American rituals of remembrance. The Civil War was only one of two wars fought by Americans in the second half of the nineteenth century to establish national unity across the continent from the Atlantic to the Pacific and from Mexico to Canada. The second war to achieve this aim was with the Plains Indians, and resulted in the military defeat and subjugation

Figure 1.12 The Shaw Monument in Boston, Massachusetts. Courtesy of The Bostonian Society/Old State House.

Figure 1.13 A descendant of a black American Civil War soldier touching the African-American Civil War Memorial in Washington, DC. Associated Press/Wide World Photos/William Philpott.

of the last of the independent Native American peoples. Significantly, it provided the first opportunity after the Civil War for Southerners and Northerners to fight together against a common enemy (O'Leary, 1994, p.22). It also provided another battlefield that became a sacred site for many Americans.

In late June 1876, General George Armstrong Custer led over 250 of his soldiers of the Seventh Cavalry to their deaths at the battle of the Little Bighorn in Montana. For white Americans it was a moment of shock – a shock made symbolically greater by the fact that the defeat of Custer coincided with the first centenary of the American Declaration of Independence. For the Plains Indians it was a short-lived but proud moment of victory in their unequal and ultimately doomed struggle to maintain their independence in the face of the overwhelmingly superior resources and technology of the whites. The site of the battle was marked in 1881 by a granite obelisk bearing the names of Custer's soldiers. The site was also set aside by the government as a national cemetery. Custer and his men rapidly became venerated as martyrs to the final fulfilment of (white) America's perceived destiny to expand across the entire continent.

Over the decades the battlefield became the location for commemorative events which, characteristically, celebrated Custer and his soldiers as heroes but cast the Plains Indians as a savage enemy. By the 1970s, however, alternative versions of the Custer myth were increasingly aired, and the descendants of the Plains Indians who had defeated Custer increasingly made their voices heard at the site of the battle – and especially at public events held there. The Custer battlefield thus became a highly contested 'sacred site'. Traditional 'patriotic' enthusiasts of the Custer myth clashed, often highly controversially, with groups such as the American Indian Movement, who sought to secure equal commemoration of – and thus equal honour towards – the Native Americans who had fought and died there over 100 years earlier. By the early 1990s it had been agreed that the official title of the site would be changed from the Custer Battlefield National Monument to the Little Bighorn National Monument, and that a monument to the Plains Indians who fought there would also be erected (Mayo, 1988, pp.150–4; Linenthal, 1991, chapter 4; Sellars and Walter, 1993, pp.180–4; Foote, 1997, pp.325–7). This, however, did nothing to stop the controversies over the site. On the contrary, by the mid-1990s, the proposal to build a monument to the Sioux and Cheyenne who died in the battle had led Custer enthusiasts to accuse the National Park Service of seeking to achieve the 'Indianization' of the battlefield (*New York Times*, 23 June 1996; 24 August 1997; 28 August 1997). The intense controversy that this site continues to generate provides another striking example of the limits to the effectiveness and inclusiveness of the civil religion that is sustained by American rituals of memorial and remembrance.[11]

Critical consideration of British rituals of remembrance similarly reveals the limits to their role as expressions of a unifying civil religion. The very fact that, between the two world wars, the annual cycle of rituals of remembrance was such a powerful and effective means of reaffirming social and political unity meant that other, alternative, views of the war, and of the social and economic inequalities and political divisions of the inter-war years, were correspondingly more or less severely marginalized. The very fact that, as we have seen, disagreements over the imagery or meaning of a memorial were commonly set aside in order to preserve and emphasize the sacred status of the memorial itself illustrates this point. Moreover, the annual rituals of remembrance not only provided occasions on which differing political opinions were united and in which the royal family led the nation's honouring of the dead: they also affirmed an existing social order and enshrined a particular view of the nation's participation in the war. Indeed, it has been argued that, in the annual act of remembrance, 'the demons of discontent and disorder were purged', and that in the universal motto, 'Lest we Forget', British society was 'denied access to a political critique of the war' (Bushaway, 1992, p.161). Similarly, it is notable that, between the two world wars, the transmission of the Armistice Day rituals and the British Legion Festival of Remembrance on BBC radio was a key element – along with broadcasts on Empire Day and Christmas Day – in the development of the BBC's broadcasting to the empire. Indeed, the annual British Legion Festival of Remembrance was originally called 'the Empire Festival of Remembrance'. But the vision of empire to which such broadcasting contributed was a carefully and conservatively defined one. It strenuously avoided political critiques of empire and imperialism and carefully cultivated a nostalgic, heroic and patriotic mood (Mackenzie, 1986, pp.167, 179 and 186–7; Gregory, 1994, p.79).

Nor could the unifying role and function of British rituals of remembrance encompass all communities within Britain. The example of Northern Ireland provides a particularly compelling and still relevant case in point. Remembrance and commemoration of

---

[11] The whole concept of civil religion in the USA has also been subjected to searching criticism from a Native American perspective by Vine Deloria, a professional historian and a member of the Standing Rock Sioux Tribe of North Dakota. Deloria argues that American civil religion, as defined by Bellah, is in fact essentially a product of a Christian world-view, and that Native American religious values and concepts do not fit within it but present a radically different understanding of the universe (Deloria, 1999, chapter 17).

the legacy of the First World War in Northern Ireland may unite particular communities *within* Northern Ireland, but it emphatically does not provide the overarching unity between diverse and otherwise opposed groups that a civil religion is supposed to provide. In Northern Ireland the rituals of remembrance associated with British commemoration of those killed in war provide a striking focus for the sense of historical identity of the Protestant and Unionist section of the community. Indeed, the commemoration of the anniversary of the battle of the Somme in 1916 – when 5,500 members of the Protestant Ulster division were killed or wounded on the first day of the battle alone – has become the focus for marches in which Protestant Orange Lodges in Belfast remember the losses of the Ulster division on that occasion, and interpret the event as an example of the sacrifice of the Protestant community on behalf of the UK and thus a reaffirmation of Ulster's British identity. Banners and wall paintings similarly celebrate the actions of the Ulster division at the Somme – in the latter case often explicitly associating the deaths of Ulster soldiers on the Somme with the deaths of members of Protestant paramilitary groups in the conflict in Northern Ireland since the 1970s. In so doing, recent and contemporary banners and murals recall earlier examples of such images that appeared in the 1920s and 1930s (Jarman, 1997, pp.71–2, 97, 120–1, 224–6; 1999, pp.176–84). By contrast, for strongly republican and nationalist members of the Catholic community in Northern Ireland, it is a quite different event in 1916 that is the focus of acts of remembrance and commemoration. For many members of the Catholic community it is the commemoration of the Irishmen who died in the Easter Rising against the British in Dublin in 1916 – or who were executed by the British after the failure of the rising – that is the focus for murals and annual parades. Again, in both images and events, explicit associations and connections are made between those who died for the ideal of an independent Ireland in 1916, and those who have died on the republican and nationalist side since 1969 (Jarman, 1997, pp.144–7, 236–8; 1999, pp.184–8).

In both cases, the theme of sacrifice is again central to the process of commemoration and remembrance. And in both cases, also, the process of remembering – precisely in order to commemorate highly specific and contrasting memories and communal identities – has also involved a process of forgetting. Just as critics of British rituals of remembrance between the two world wars may argue that the liturgy of remembrance prevented critical discussion of the war and recognition of ongoing social and economic divisions in British society, so critics of both Protestant/Unionist and Catholic/Republican commemorations of 1916 in Northern Ireland may point to the complexities that are overlooked in these processes. Both Unionist Protestants and Republican Catholics largely choose to ignore and forget that many Catholic Irishmen fought in the British army in the First World War, while in 1914 it had been Ulster Protestants who had been ready to undertake an armed uprising against Britain (Jarman, 1997, pp.155–8; 1999, pp.191–3; Aldridge, 2000, pp.151–2). Northern Ireland, it has thus been suggested, 'is the stage for a conflict of civil religions' (Aldridge, 2000, p.149). Two communities assert and define their respective unities through a variety of rites, rituals, images and symbols, deliberately excluding the 'other' community in the process. The symbols and rituals of remembrance, moreover, are central elements in such self-definition and exclusion.[12]

Conclusion

The evidence and argument of this chapter suggest that, in both the American and British cases, the origins and history of rituals of remembrance of those killed in war do, indeed, fulfil many of the classic roles and functions of a 'civil religion'. They are designed to create and foster a sense of unity that transcends internal differences and disagreements. They do seek to cultivate a shared sense of history and destiny. They do provide symbols, rites and ceremonies that seek to give sacred meaning to the life of the community. And they do attempt to connect the community and individuals within the community, if not to 'a realm of absolute meaning', then at least to profound questions of meaning in the face of suffering, loss, sacrifice, and the threat of the utter absence of meaning that the losses inflicted by modern war can cause. At the same time, however, neither American nor British rituals of remembrance fulfil these roles fully or without ambiguity. In both cases, aspects of the history and

[12] An event at Messines, in Belgium, on the afternoon of 11 November 1998, however, provided a striking example of the way in which rituals of remembrance may also serve to address long-standing and continuing divisions. On that occasion a monument, in the form of a traditional Irish stone tower, was unveiled in the presence of the Belgian king, the Irish president and the British queen. The tower was the work of both Protestants and Catholics from both Northern Ireland and the Republic of Ireland and was dedicated to the memory of all the Irish killed in the First World War. It was located at Messines because, at the battle for the Messines Ridge in 1917, both Protestant and Catholic Irish divisions fought side by side. The dedication of the monument, read simultaneously by a Protestant and a Catholic, was to the hope of present and future reconciliation as well as to the memory of the dead. For discussions of some of the many ambiguities involved in the remembrance of the First World War in Ireland as a whole – and not only in Northern Ireland – see Leonard (1988) and Jeffrey (1993).

development of rituals of remembrance serve not to unite but to alienate or divide particular sections of the American or British population.

There also remains the question of the current status and future prospects of American and British rituals and traditions of remembrance. Discussion here has focused predominantly on the origins and earlier development of these rituals and traditions. But what of the question of their future? Are they likely to sustain their place within American and British national life in the twenty-first century? Or are they inevitably destined to decline and become increasingly marginal as the generations pass and the connection with the wars that first gave rise to them becomes ever more distant and remote? In respect of the way in which Remembrance Sunday in Britain never assumed the same status or significance after the Second World War that Armistice Day had achieved in the years between the two world wars, it has been argued that:

> The day no longer carries the mystical conviction that it should be a transforming experience, one that makes sense of all the suffering and which rededicates the nation to high aspirations. It is increasingly the memory of a memory. It can survive as long as those who remember what Armistice Day once was survive, or in other words, while those who fought a war remembering another war are still alive. But the language which surrounds the ritual is dead. Without the conviction of a transformative redemption we cannot understand sacrifice; the word becomes part of an empty rhetoric. We can respect the suffering but we cannot understand it.
>
> (Gregory, 1994, pp.226–7)

Perhaps this is correct. But there are at least modest grounds for suggesting that the eclipse and decline of traditional British and American rituals of remembrance may be less absolute than this assessment allows.

For example, in both countries, the continuing relevance of 11 November as an occasion and symbol of national commemoration and remembrance of those killed in war was clearly demonstrated by events in the last quarter of the twentieth century. In the USA in the late 1960s, in the midst of the Vietnam War, it was decided that the national celebration of Veterans Day should be changed from 11 November to the fourth Monday in October, and from 1971 to 1977 this was the practice. It rapidly became clear, however, that this was not a popular innovation and that many Americans continued to regard 11 November as the appropriate date for Veterans Day. In 1978, therefore, the government returned the observance of Veterans Day to 11 November. Similarly, in the UK in 1995, the custom of observing two-minutes of silence across the nation at 11 a.m. on 11 November – whatever day of the week it might be, as had been the custom between the two world wars – was reintroduced as an experiment. The attempt to reintroduce the observance of two minutes' silence on 11 November itself – some 50 years after it had last been observed in this way – might well have proved an embarrassing failure. In fact, it proved sufficiently successful to be continued in subsequent years. According to the Royal British Legion, in 1998 the silence on 11 November was observed by 72 per cent of the population in the UK, and may even be regarded as being re-established within the annual British calendar. In particular, the British Legion has emphasized the extent to which younger people have been aware of and participated in the reintroduced silence.[13]

In both the UK and the USA there were also other examples of the desire to continue and sustain rituals of remembrance as the twentieth century turned into the twenty-first. In the UK the Royal British Legion Festival of Remembrance and the Remembrance Sunday ceremony at the Cenotaph in 2000 involved self-conscious innovation. The Festival of Remembrance was deliberately oriented towards the young and to the handing on of traditions of remembrance to another generation in a new century and a new millennium. At the Cenotaph, meanwhile, in addition to representatives of a variety of Christian denominations and of the Jewish community, for the first time there were also official representatives of the Buddhist, Muslim, Sikh and Hindu communities at the Remembrance Sunday service. The British government also announced that an official memorial to British service personnel killed in all wars since the Second World War was to be built. In the USA, meanwhile, on Veterans Day 2000, an official ceremony was held in Washington DC to begin the construction of a National Memorial to the American experience in the Second World War, an initiative that will be discussed briefly at the end of Chapter 3. Earlier the same year, on 3 May, the government had called on Americans 'to pause for one minute at 3.00 p.m. (local time) on Memorial Day, to remember and reflect on the sacrifices made by so many to provide freedom for all'. Subsequently, in December 2000, it was formally resolved that Memorial Day would include such a 'National Moment of Remem-

---

[13] These claims were made, in 2000, on the official web site of the Royal British Legion, details of which are included in the bibliographical references for this chapter.

brance', in which all Americans would observe a brief act of remembrance and respect.[14]

Thus, as the discussion of visits to war cemeteries and memorials in the next chapter will also suggest, even if the passing of the generations necessarily changes many of the meanings associated with British and American rituals of remembrance, it is far from clear that the future of these rituals is bound to be one of simple or inexorable decline. It would still be a brave and bold politician, indeed, who proposed the abolition or substantial reduction of the traditional British and American rituals of remembrance. Arguably, therefore, the more interesting question is not whether they are likely to survive at all, but whether recent experience suggests there are any grounds for supposing that such rituals, traditions and sites of remembrance are still capable of exciting interest and therefore of developing new and continuing significance as symbols of civil religion.

References

Ahlstrom, S. (1972) *A Religious History of the American People*, New Haven: Yale.

Albanese, C. (1974) 'Requiem for Memorial Day: dissent in the redeemer nation', *American Quarterly*, 26, pp.386–98.

Aldridge, A. (2000) *Religion in the Contemporary World: A Sociological Introduction*, Cambridge: Polity Press.

Bell, G. (1952) *Randall Davidson: Archbishop of Canterbury*, Oxford: Oxford University Press.

Bellah, R. (1967) 'Civil religion in America', *Daedalus*, 96, pp.1–21.

Bellah, R. (1974) 'American civil religion in the 1970s', in R. Richey and D. Jones, *American Civil Religion*, New York: Harper & Row, pp.255–72.

Bellah, R. (1975) *The Broken Covenant: American Civil Religion in Time of Trial*, New York: The Seabury Press.

Blight, D. (1989) '"For something beyond the battlefield": Frederick Douglass and the struggle for the memory of the Civil War', *The Journal of American History*, 75, pp.1156–78.

Bocock, R. (1985) 'Religion in modern Britain', in R. Bocock and K. Thompson (eds) *Religion and Ideology*, Manchester: Manchester University Press, pp.207–33.

---

[14] For the origins of the National Moment of Remembrance, see the web site dedicated to Memorial Day listed at the end of the bibliography.

Borg, A. (1991) *War Memorials: From Antiquity to the Present*, London: Leo Cooper.

Briggs, A. (1965) *The History of Broadcasting in the United Kingdom, Volume II: The Golden Age of Wireless*, London: Oxford University Press.

Brown, S. (1994) '"A Solemn Purification by Fire": responses to the Great War in the Scottish Presbyterian Churches, 1914–19', *Journal of Ecclesiastical History*, 45, pp.82–104.

Bushaway, B. (1992) 'Name on name: the Great War and remembrance', in R. Porter (ed.) *Myths of the English*, Cambridge: Polity Press, pp.136–67.

Cannadine, D. (1981) 'War and death, grief and mourning in modern Britain', in J. Whaley (ed.) *Mirrors of Mortality: Studies in the Social History of Death*, London: Europa, pp.187–242.

Clements, K. (1975) 'Baptists and the outbreak of the First World War', *Baptist Quarterly*, 26, pp.74–92.

Coppin, R. (1965) 'Remembrance Sunday', *Theology*, 68, pp.525–30.

Deloria, V. (1999) *For This Land: Writings on Religion in America*, New York: Routledge.

Foote, K. (1997) *Shadowed Ground: America's Landscapes of Violence and Tragedy*, Austin: University of Texas Press.

Forty, A. and Kuchler, S. (eds) (1999) *The Art of Forgetting*, Oxford: Berg.

Foster, G. (1987) *Ghosts of the Confederacy: Defeat, The Lost Cause, and the Emergence of the New South 1865 to 1913*, New York: Oxford University Press.

Gilliat-Ray, S. (1999) 'Civic religion in England: traditions and transformations', *Journal of Contemporary Religion*, 14, pp.233–44.

Gillis, J. (ed.) *Commemorations: The Politics of National Identity*, Princeton: Princeton University Press.

Grant, S-M. (1998) '"The charter of its birthright': the Civil War and American nationalism', *Nations and Nationalism*, 4, pp.163–85.

Gregory, A. (1994) *The Silence of Memory: Armistice Day 1919–1946*, Oxford: Berg.

Hass, K. (1998) *Carried to the Wall: American Memory and the Vietnam Veterans Memorial*, Berkeley: University of California Press.

Hoover, A. (1989) *God, Germany, and Britain in the Great War*, New York: Praeger.

Hüppauf, B (1985) 'War and death: the experience of the First World War', in M. Crouch and B. Hüppauf, *Essays on Mortality*, Kensington NSW: University of New South Wales, pp.65–87.

Inglis, K. (1992a) 'War memorials: ten questions for historians', *Guerres Mondiale et Conflits Contemporains*, 167, pp.5–21.

Inglis, K. (1992b) 'The homecoming: the War Memorial Movement in Cambridge, England', *Journal of Contemporary History*, 27, pp.583–605.

Inglis, K. (1993) 'Entombing unknown soldiers: from London and Paris to Baghdad', *History and Memory*, 5, pp.7–31.

Jarman, N. (1997) *Material Conflicts: Parades and Visual Displays in Northern Ireland*, Oxford: Berg.

Jarman, N. (1999) 'Commemorating 1916, celebrating difference: parading and painting in Belfast', in A. Forty and S. Kuchler (eds) pp.171–95.

Jeffery, K. (1993) 'The Great War in modern Irish memory', in T. Fraser and K. Jeffery (eds) *Men, Women and War*, Historical Studies XVIII, Dublin: The Lilliput Press, pp.136–57.

King, A. (1998) *Memorials of the Great War in Britain: The Symbolism and Politics of Remembrance*, Oxford: Berg.

King, A. (1999) 'Remembering and forgetting in the public memorials of the Great War', in A. Forty and S. Kuchler (eds) pp.147–69.

Laqueur, T. (1994) 'Memory and naming in the Great War', in J. Gillis (ed.) pp.150–67.

Leonard, J. (1988) '"Lest We Forget": Irish War Memorials', in D. Fitzpatrick (ed.) *Ireland and the First World War*, Dublin: The Lilliput Press, pp.59–67.

Linder, R. (1996) 'Universal pastor: President Bill Clinton's civil religion', *Journal of Church and State*, 38, pp.733–49.

Linenthal, E. (1991) *Sacred Ground: Americans and Their Battlefields*, Urbana Illinois: University of Illinois Press.

Lloyd, D. (1998) *Battlefield Tourism: Pilgrimage and Commemoration of the Great War in Britain*, Oxford: Berg.

Longworth, P. (1985) *The Unending Vigil: A History of the Commonwealth War Graves Commission*, London: Leo Cooper/Secker & Warburg.

Lowell, R. (1964) 'On the Gettysburg Address', in A. Nevins (ed.) *Lincoln and the Gettysburg Address*, Urbana, Illinois: University of Illinois Press.

Mackenzie, J. (1986) '"In touch with the infinite: the BBC and the Empire 1923–53', in J. Mackenzie (ed.) *Imperialism and Popular Culture*, Manchester: Manchester University Press, pp.165–91.

Marrin, A. (1974) *The Last Crusade: The Church of England and the First World War*, Durham NC: Duke University Press.

Matheson, P. (1972) 'Scottish war sermons', *Records of the Scottish Church History Society*, 17, pp.203–13.

Mayo, J. (1988) *War Memorials as Political Landscape: The American Experience and Beyond*, New York: Praeger.

Mestrovic, S. (1993) *The Road from Paradise: Prospects for Democracy in Eastern Europe*, Lexington, Kentucky: University Press of Kentucky.

Morgan, D. (1997) '"Christ and the War": some aspects of the Welsh experience, 1914–1918', *The Journal of Welsh Religious History*, 5, pp.73–91.

Moriarty, C. (1991) 'Christian iconography and First World War memorials', *Imperial War Museum Review*, 6, pp.63–75.

Moriarty, C. (1995) 'The absent dead and figurative First World War memorials', *Transactions of the Ancient Monument Society*, 39, pp.7–40.

Moriarty, C. (1997) 'Private grief and public remembrance: British First World War Memorials', in M. Evans and K. Lunn (eds) *War and Memory in the Twentieth Century*, Oxford: Berg, pp.125–42.

Mosse, G. (1990) *Fallen Soldiers: Reshaping the Memory of the World Wars*, Oxford: Oxford University Press.

O'Leary, C. (1994) '"American All": reforging a national brotherhood, 1876–1917', *History Today*, 44, pp.20–7.

Patterson, J. (1982) 'A patriotic landscape: Gettysburg, 1863–1913', *Prospects*, 7, pp.315–33.

Pawley, B. (1950) 'The theology of Remembrance Sunday', *Theology*, 53, pp.178–84.

Pierard, R. and Linder, R. (1988) *Civil Religion and the American Presidency*, Grand Rapids, Michigan: Zondervan.

Robinson, C. (1996) 'Neither East nor West: some aspects of religion and ritual in the Indian army of the Raj', *Religion*, 26, pp.37–47.

Savage, K. (1994) 'The politics of memory: black emancipation and the Civil War Monument', in J. Gillis (ed.) pp.127–49.

Sellars, R. (1986) 'Vigil of silence: the Civil War memorials', *History News*, 41, pp.19–23.

Sellars, R. and Walter, T. (1993) 'From Custer to Kent State: heroes, martyrs and the evolution of popular shrines in the USA', in I. Reader and T. Walter (eds) *Pilgrimage in Popular Culture*, London: Macmillan, pp.179–200.

Stamp, G. (1977) *Silent Cities: An Exhibition of the Memorial and Cemetery Architecture of the Great War*, London: RIBA.

Walter, T. (1990) *Funerals and How to Improve Them*, London: Hodder & Stoughton.

Wilkinson, J. (1978) *The Church of England and the First World War*, London: SPCK.

Wilson, C. (1980) *Baptised in Blood: The Religion of the Lost Cause, 1865–1920*, Athens: University of Georgia Press.

Winter, J. (1992) 'Spiritualism and the First World War', in R. Davis. and R. Helmstadter (eds) *Religion and Irreligion in Victorian Britain: Essays in Honor of R.K.Webb*, London: Routledge, pp.185–200.

Winter, J. (1995) *Sites of Memory, Sites of Mourning: The Great War in European Cultural History*, Cambridge: Cambridge University Press.

Wolffe, J. (1993) 'The religions of the silent majority', in G. Parsons (ed.) *The Growth of Religious Diversity: Britain from 1945, Volume 1: Traditions*, London and New York: Routledge, pp.305–46.

Wolffe, J. (1994) *God and Greater Britain: Religion and National Life in Britain and Ireland 1843–1945*, London and New York: Routledge.

Wolffe, J. (2000) *Great Deaths: Grieving, Religion and Nationhood in Victorian and Edwardian Britain*, Oxford: Oxford University Press and The British Academy.

Internet sources consulted

http://www.britishlegion.org.uk/ – the official web site of the Royal British Legion.

http://www.cwgc.org – the official web site of the Commonwealth War Graves Commission.

http://www.mdw.army.mil/ – the official web site of the US Army Military District of Washington, including pages on various aspects of the history of Arlington Military Cemetery, the Tombs of the American Unknown Soldiers, the Confederate Memorial at Arlington, and both Memorial Day and Veterans Day.

http://www.nps.gov/gett/ – the official web site of the Gettysburg National Military Park, run by the US National Park Service.

http://www.afroamcivilwar.org. – the official web site of the African-American Civil War Memorial and its history.

http://www.usmemorialday.org/ – a web site on the history of Memorial Day in the USA, with links to other related sites.

http://www.veteransview.com. – a web site run for American military veterans, including information on the history of Veterans Day.

CHAPTER 2

Public monuments and private grief: war graves, war memorials and personal pilgrimage

One of the items in an edition of the BBC Saturday morning radio programme *Home Truths*, broadcast in May 2000, was a tape-recorded diary by a listener who had recently visited the graves of friends with whom he had joined the army in 1943. The graves are situated in a Commonwealth War Graves Cemetery in Germany. At the time of the visit, the listener, John Schwartz, was 73 years old. He had joined the army some 57 years earlier in 1943 – though under age to do so – along with three of his closest friends from school and youth club. His friends were killed and Schwartz now goes back to Germany each year with a pilgrimage organized by the Royal British Legion.

The diary recorded the journey to Germany and the sense of community among many of those on the pilgrimage who knew each other from previous years. The climax of the trip was the visit to the cemetery. After describing the cemetery with its 'row, upon row, upon row of identical white headstones' and the Cross of Sacrifice where they would later hold a short service, Schwartz recorded his reaction to visiting the graves of his friends. He remembered them with a combination of affection and sadness. He recalled that they had been killed on different days, miles apart; but now their graves were only 30 yards from each other. He placed a plant on one of the graves on behalf of the sister of the dead soldier who could not visit the grave herself. He took a photograph of the gravestone, with the plant in front of it, to send to the soldier's sister, observing that, 'Really, I suppose, it's as near as she'll get.'

He went to the next grave, to place a wreath of poppies and a cross, knowing, he said, that this would be the moment when he would 'choke up', because the man buried there had been his best mate. He read the headstone: '14491053 Lance Corporal John Timpson. Aged 18 years', and added, 'That's no age to die is it? I was only 17 myself at the time. It all seems so bloody futile.' The recording included a brief extract from the religious service held at the Cross of Sacrifice, with the notes of the 'Last Post' being sounded on a bugle and the ritual promise that those buried in the cemetery would be remembered. It ended with Schwartz' concluding thoughts on his visit:

> Well, that's it. The service is over, all the pomp and ceremony is finished. God, I've got a love and a hate feeling for this place. I love coming here, but I hate what it stands for. All that killing; them and us. Why? What was it all for? The world's still in a hell of a state. There's trouble everywhere. I wonder why we bothered, what was it all for?

> Well, I'm back at the hotel now. It's been one of those days. You get a bit choked up at times, but then it's all worthwhile. After all, I've waited all year for this day. Please God, I'll live long enough, I'll do it all again next year.

(Home Truths, BBC Radio 4, 20 May 2000)

The whole item was a moving testimony to the potential emotional and psychological power of war graves and war memorials, and of visits to such sites. It also, implicitly if not explicitly, raised profound questions about the religious meaning and significance of such phenomena and such visits. Thus, it was notable that Schwartz and the British Legion chose to call the visit a 'pilgrimage'. The visit was centred on personal and collective ritual acts of remembrance. God was invoked at some of the most emotional moments of the account – in an informal, unorthodox, instinctive way, perhaps, but precisely at the points of greatest personal feeling and perplexity. And above all, the account of the visit was permeated by a desperate desire to find meaning and a sense of worth in spite of the manifest evidence of loss and futility to which the cemetery bore witness.

The item is also another example, at a popular level, of the marked interest in the phenomenon of war graves, war memorials and visits to such sites that has been increasingly evident in recent years. This chapter will explore this recent and contemporary interest in pilgrimage to war graves and war memorials by examining two case studies. The first will consider the resurgence of interest in such pilgrimage in the British context since the mid-1980s, placing it within the historical context of earlier pilgrimages to the cemeteries and memorials of the First World War in the 1920s and 1930s. The second case study, using an American context, will examine the particular example of the traditions of pilgrimage and personal rituals that have developed in relation to the Vietnam Veterans Memorial in Washington DC. Finally, a brief conclusion will explore some of the possible relationships between personal pilgrimages to war graves and memorials, and the concept of 'civil religion'.

The resilience of remembrance: war grave pilgrimage at the end of the twentieth century

'If you've never seen a war cemetery, I defy you not to be moved.'
(A guide on a visit to the cemeteries of the First World War in Belgium and Northern France, quoted in the *Sunday Times*, 8 November 1998)

In the two decades after the First World War and before the Second, many thousands of people visited the battlefields, cemeteries and war memorials that were erected to commemorate the British dead of the war of 1914–18. Although the majority of such travellers visited northern France and Belgium, others visited similar sites in Italy, Greece, Turkey and Palestine. The visits were often organized by veterans' associations or by the British Legion. Benevolent organizations were founded – such as the St Barnabas Society and the War Graves Association – to assist bereaved relatives who could not afford the prices charged by commercial tour operators. From Australia, New Zealand, Canada and South Africa, similar pilgrimages were organized to the battlefields and memorials associated with the soldiers of those countries who had fought and died in the war (Walter, 1993; Lloyd, 1998).

The tradition of pilgrimage to battlefields, cemeteries and memorials thus has a well-established history. After the Second World War, however, the scale of such visits was much smaller. Until 1951 the British government gave financial assistance to next of kin to visit a war grave and the British Legion continued to provide tours to war cemeteries (Walter, 1993, p.65). But the scale of these initiatives never rivalled those of the 1920s and 1930s, and reached an all-time low in the 1960s. Similarly, in the mid-1960s, the Commonwealth War Graves Commission received fewer than 1,500 enquiries a year about the location of graves (Longworth, 1985, p.237; Walter, 1993, p.63).

By contrast, since the mid-1980s there has been a remarkable resurgence of interest in the cemeteries, battlefields and memorials of the two world wars and in the frequency of visits to these sites. Enquiries to the Commonwealth War Graves Commission began to rise again. After increasing slowly during the 1970s and 1980s, in 1990 the Commission received 28,000 enquiries and by 1998 the figure had risen to 40,000 (Walter, 1993, p.63; *Independent*, 6 November 1998). By 2000, and with the advent of the Internet, the web site of the Commission claimed to be registering 250,000 hits per week. Clearly, by no means all of these will have resulted in a specific enquiry – but the level of general interest in the Commission and its work implied by this number of weekly contacts is striking, and the web site provides the means to search electronically for the location of a particular grave and to secure detailed information about travel to the location concerned.

The number of tour operators offering organized visits to battlefields, memorials and cemeteries has also increased markedly. In the early 1990s, in a pioneering article on this theme, Tony Walter pointed out that, whereas in the mid-1970s there were no firms offering tours and pilgrimages to battlefields and memorials, by 1991 there were six large companies and several smaller ones, providing over 200 visits to places as varied as France and the Far East. Walter estimated that, together with the visits organized by the British Legion Pilgrimage Department, these tours might cater for between eight and ten thousand people, in addition to which there would be many other pilgrimages organized by veterans and regimental associations, private groups and schools (Walter, 1993, pp.67–9). More recently it has been observed that the 'memorial sites of the First World War now receive more visitors than ever before' (Rowlands, 1999, p.129). The habit of school history classes making visits to battlefields and cemeteries is particularly significant because of the way in which it transmits the practice of pilgrimage to such sites to new generations. An initiative that began in the mid-1980s, such educational visits have not only continued to flourish but also demonstrate a capacity to exercise potentially profound effects on the students who experience them.[1] Similarly, despite the increasing age of veterans of even the Second World War, veterans' associations continue to organize pilgrimages, travelling not only to the geographically relatively close battlefields and cemeteries of Europe, but also to the cemeteries and memorials of North Africa and the Far East.

It is not merely the statistics of such visits, however, that provide evidence of the renewed interest in such phenomena. Since the early 1990s, articles in the press have frequently drawn attention to the growth of interest in these sites. Characteristically, these articles emphasize themes such as the element of personal or family pilgrimage involved, and the extent to which interest in the sites

---

[1] See, for example, reports in *Daily Telegraph* (12 November 1998) and *Observer* (7 November 1999).

Figure 2.1 The Commonwealth War Graves Cemetery, Tyne Cot, Belgium. Courtesy of the Photograph Archives of the Commonwealth War Graves Commission.

crosses generational boundaries and is most definitely not confined to veterans or widows. Indeed, in the case of the surge of interest in the battlefields, cemeteries and memorials of the First World War it is now, by definition, later generations that are moved to enquire, to learn and to visit. Such newspaper articles also characteristically seek to explore the reasons for the renewed interest in these places and their meaning.[2]

The popular culture of both films and novels has also reflected and contributed to this renewed interest. Thus, for example, in Steven Spielberg's much discussed film *Saving Private Ryan* (1998), the theme of a veteran's return to a cemetery in Normandy was the essential context for the main narrative of the film. The film was controversial principally because of the brutal realism of the portrayal of the fighting on one of the beaches in Normandy where American soldiers landed in June 1944. In fact, the entire narrative of events located in June 1944 took the form of an extended flashback, framed by the opening and closing sequences in which a veteran visited an

[2] For a sample of such newspaper articles see *Guardian* 'Weekend' (3–4 November 1990); *Daily Telegraph* (11 November 1994); *Independent* (6 November 1998); *Sunday Times* 'Travel' (8 November 1998); *Daily Telegraph* (9 November 1998); *Observer* (7 November 1999); *Observer* 'Review' (7 November 1999).

American military cemetery and found the grave of a man who had died rescuing him some 50 years earlier. In this particular fictional narrative, it was the moment of finding the grave that provided the occasion for the recollection of the events of half a century earlier.

Similar themes were also an important feature of widely acclaimed novels published during the 1990s. Thus, in *Birdsong*, a novel by Sebastian Faulks about the horrific experiences of British soldiers in the trench warfare of the First World War, one of the important subplots concerns the need experienced by the principal character's granddaughter to find out about her grandfather's wartime experience. A key moment in her process of discovery occurs when she visits the memorial at Thiepval to the missing of the battle of the Somme (Faulks, 1994, pp.210–11). Similarly, in Pat Barker's novel *Another World*, the continuing legacy of his traumatic experiences in the First World War haunts the last days of one of the characters, now an old man of 101, dying of cancer. The relationship between the old man, Geordie, and his grandson, Nick, is central to the novel – and a crucial moment in their relationship occurs when Nick takes Geordie to visit the cemeteries of the Somme and the Thiepval monument (Barker, 1998, pp.72–5).

At the level of academic study, meanwhile, the 1990s witnessed a growing recognition that the whole area of war memorials, remembrance, and the cultural significance of such phenomena and activities, had been curiously neglected by historians hitherto. Articles and books duly began to appear with increasing frequency. Seminal articles of the earlier 1990s included studies of war memorials (Inglis, 1992a; 1992b; 1993; Moriarty, 1991; 1995) and of war grave pilgrimage (Walter, 1993). From the mid-1990s onwards, important book-length studies began to appear examining, for example, the emergence of the rituals of Armistice Day in the UK between 1919 and 1946 (Gregory, 1994); the significance of places and practices of mourning in Europe after the First World War (Winter, 1995); the design, symbolism and function of war memorials in the UK after the First World War (King, 1998); and the history of pilgrimages to battlefields and cemeteries between 1919 and 1939 (Lloyd, 1998).

Major anniversaries also played an important role in focusing public interest on the two world wars of the twentieth century, and in raising public and popular consciousness of the memory of them. From 1989 until 1995, an entire sequence of fiftieth anniversaries of key moments, battles, crises and turning points of the Second World War provided the occasion for fiftieth anniversary reunions of veterans, for official ceremonies commemorating particular events, and for documentary film-makers to retrieve old film and interview now ageing survivors (Evans and Lunn, 1997, p.xv). It is difficult to assess the precise impact of such events, but it is likely that the media coverage of successive anniversaries was a significant factor in the steady resurgence of interest in remembrance and in the increased numbers of enquiries to organizations such as the Commonwealth War Graves Commission. The palpable sense of the imminent passing of the majority of the generation that had lived through the events being remembered added to the impact of news reporting and documentaries. The dignity of many now elderly interviewees as they remembered often traumatic events from their own youth was apt to prompt reflection in those too young to remember – and then, in many cases, to lead to questions about family history, about parents, grandparents, uncles and aunts, perhaps not even known personally, but recalled in family photograph albums and anecdotes.[3]

The sequence of Second World War fiftieth anniversaries was followed in November 1998 by the eightieth anniversary of the end of the First World War. Documentaries again focused on this event, and on the war itself, and included interviews with the now very few surviving veterans, all of whom were in their late nineties or over 100 years old. Finally, from 1999 onwards, a sequence of sixtieth anniversaries of the various stages of the Second World War began and, at the time of writing, these continue. Again, there are documentaries and coverage of official ceremonies, while the sense of the ageing and passing of a generation is yet more striking ten years on from the fiftieth anniversary events and documentaries. The same questions about family histories have been prompted, but with even greater poignancy and effect.

The significance of anniversaries and the link between them and television documentaries had already been noted by Tony Walter in the early 1990s in relation to the seventieth and fortieth anniversaries of, respectively, events in the First and Second World Wars. He also associated this resurgence of interest in visits to cemeteries, memorials and battlefields with broader social and cultural trends. Modern travel made visits to cemeteries and memorials easier, and increasing prosperity similarly made it possible for more people to consider such trips. At the same time attitudes to death, grief and bereavement were also changing. The tradition of reserve and

---

[3] Even before the sequence of fiftieth anniversaries, the Commonwealth War Graves Commission had noted that, whereas the numbers of veterans attending ceremonies of remembrance inevitably declined, the number of younger people 'seeking the graves of their ancestors and the circumstances and the reasons for their deaths' was increasing (Longworth, 1985, p.252). Moreover, as Walter has observed, as the years pass, more, not fewer, people have an ancestor who died in the First World War (Walter, 1993, p.72).

suppressed or unexpressed emotion that was so characteristic of British attitudes to death even until the 1960s was replaced by a more open expression of feelings. The age structure of the population was also relevant. It was only in the 1970s and 1980s that most of those who fought in or were bereaved as a result of the Second World War reached retirement. Having perhaps shelved grief for many years in the course of busy lives, retirement allowed time and opportunity to reflect, to revisit the past, and to address unfinished business. The opportunity to visit the graves of husbands, uncles, friends or old comrades became both a practical possibility and a desirable one. The increase in visits to cemeteries and memorials was not, however, restricted to the elderly and the retired: younger people were also represented. People in their forties and fifties visited the graves of fathers or uncles they hardly or never knew – either to accompany older relatives, or because they themselves wished to honour family memories or give greater meaning to old photographs (Walter, 1993, pp.69–72).

But why call such visits 'pilgrimages'? Walter addressed this issue in his article and suggested that visits to battlefields, memorials and cemeteries had several characteristics that were closer to traditional religious pilgrimage than to modern tourism. Thus, many people undertake their visits with a specific personal goal – to see a particular grave, memorial or name. They do not go simply to see new places and find new experiences. There is also an intimate relationship between the rest of their lives and the focus of this visit. Pilgrims to war cemeteries and memorials characteristically speak of the experience as one of completion: perhaps of completing a promise made many years ago; perhaps of paying a personal debt of honour and keeping faith with those killed; perhaps of being able to complete unfinished aspects of their own lives. The places visited are also sacred places, not merely interesting sites to see, for they are the location of the remains – even if all that remains is a name – of a loved individual, and to be in the presence of the remains is to experience some form of healing. In another age or more traditional religious way of speaking, the remains might have been called 'relics', and the hoped for healing might have been physical. In the case of war grave and war memorial pilgrimage, however, the healing is emotional and psychological (Walter, 1993, pp.85–6). Depending on one's definition of 'religion' or 'spirituality', however, such healing might also reasonably be described as religious or spiritual. Certainly, it would seem perverse to deny as a matter of principle that experiences that enable individuals to resolve unresolved tensions, confront long-suppressed emotions and regrets, or achieve a sense of personal fulfilment, could reasonably be described in this way: and the evidence is clear that war grave and war memorial pilgrimage does indeed facilitate such ends.

Walter's article cited many examples of such evidence, much of it, strikingly, from women: a woman in her eighties who visited her fiancé's grave for the first time, only just having learnt how to organize such a visit; a woman in her nineties who visited her husband's grave for the first time – having last seen him at a station in 1915, shortly before he was killed; a woman of forty who visited her father's grave in Italy and felt a sense of completeness on seeing his gravestone; a middle-aged woman who visited her father's grave in Singapore and felt that tending flowers there had somehow enabled her to care for him – which she had never been able to do in fact; a woman who was overwhelmed by the unexpected beauty of the cemetery in North Africa where her first husband was buried.

The capacity of visits to war cemeteries and memorials to take on a quality of pilgrimage and culminate in an experience of completion can even extend to a further generation. In 1990, Timothy Pain described in a newspaper article why and how he had come to travel to Belgium to find his grandfather's name on the Menin Gate, the memorial to the 56,000 British soldiers who had simply vanished in the battles around Ypres during the First World War (Pain, 1990). He described how his maternal grandmother's sadness on Remembrance

Figure 2.2 Commonwealth war graves in a cemetery in Tangiers, Morocco. Courtesy of the Photograph Archives of the Commonwealth War Graves Commission.

Figure 2.3 The Menin Gate, Ypres. Courtesy of the Photograph Archives of the Commonwealth War Graves Commission.

Figure 2.4 Detail of the Menin Gate. Photo: © Jeremy Cooper/Oliomedia.

Sunday in the 1950s and 1960s was one of the most powerful memories of his childhood. As he grew up, his grandmother and other relatives of her generation said that he looked like his grandfather, Alfred. He explained that he found this embarrassing, but that he also developed a sense of responsibility, though he did not know to whom or to what. As he reached his twenties he also came to see his resemblance to his grandfather, and he became fascinated by his grandfather's eyes in the last photograph of him before he died. 'I was gripped by his eyes, and something happened which I can neither understand nor rationalise. I knew that there was something for me to do.' After his grandmother died, aged 94, Pain asked his mother whether her mother had ever visited her husband's grave. His mother explained that her mother had always said there was no grave, because there was no body. 'Instantly I knew what I had to do. I knew what I had seen in the eyes of my grandfather. I knew what the burden of my resemblance meant.' He took his mother to the Menin Gate and found his grandfather Alfred's name. They looked at it. He took some photographs. His mother cried. He prayed that Alfred would know that they had come. And he left behind, leaning against the wall of the Menin Gate, his grandfather's sergeant's drill stick that he and his mother had found at the back of his grandmother's wardrobe after she had died. Pain had begun the brief article with the words: 'I have never believed that the dead can speak to the living, and I'm not quite sure what the visit achieved, but something deep within me is convinced that my grandfather is pleased.' He concluded it:

> Of course I realise that the visit was really about meeting emotional needs in my mother and myself; and of course I know that Alf is probably unaware of our visit. But an irrational, incomprehensible part of my inner being needs to believe that he knows and is pleased by our overdue visit. I won't be going back to the Menin Gate. I don't need to; for now I can look into those eyes without any sense of discomfort. I have done my duty. Someone has at last said 'Goodbye.'
>
> (Pain, 1990, p.28)

Pain – like many others who travel to war graves or memorials – visited the Menin Gate with a sense of purpose and expectation. He did not know exactly what to expect or fully understand the meaning his visit would prove to have, but he travelled in the manner of a pilgrim, to a special place, in search of some kind of resolution, some kind of answer. Others travel to such places without comparable intentions. Many people set out to visit war graves, memorials and battlefields as tourists rather than pilgrims, interested in the phenomenon, but without a personal aim or expectation of encountering a moment of profundity. Others again may stumble across a cemetery or memorial by chance. It has been noted, however, that it is not unusual for tourists or chance visitors to war cemeteries and memorials to find themselves unexpectedly confronted by moments of great emotional intensity. Walter has described the process as one in which 'unintentional pilgrims' find that 'for a few moments they have ceased to be tourists and have connected with something very deep' – a process that he has experienced himself (Walter, 1990, pp.212–13; 1993, pp.72–3).

The kind of experience that Walter describes in this way was also described in another more recent account of a couple who went to find the grave of a great uncle, Edmund Ashworth, who had been killed in 1915, long before either of them had been born. Prompted to visit the grave by a photograph, they went for a half-term break, not just to visit the grave, but also to see an art exhibition and to see the monument at Thiepval – it was therefore emphatically not a pilgrimage that they set out to undertake. Yet, when they found the grave in a small cemetery with 528 other graves, their reaction was thus:

> Both Sally and I find it strange to be here. After all, Edmund Ashworth is someone we have never met, only heard about and seen in a photograph. We know almost nothing about his life or his death. I feel an odd mixture of abstraction and overwhelming sadness. I don't think it relates directly to Edmund Ashworth. It is the emotion produced by the cemetery on this cold, inappropriately beautiful day.
>
> We take snapshots, feeling like out-of-place tourists (we get edgy about which shots to take and how many). We make sure that the snapshots show only his grave and the cemetery. We don't want pictures of ourselves. It would be wrong. This isn't a seaside outing.
>
> (Barker, 1999, p.2)

The experience of being surprised by the sheer impact of war memorials and cemeteries is also central to the incidents involving such visits in the novels *Birdsong* and *Another Country*. In *Birdsong*, when the granddaughter of the central character visits the Thiepval monument she is overcome by the sheer scale of the loss that it represents:

> As she came up to the arch Elizabeth saw with a start that it was written on. She went closer. She peered at the stone. There were names on it. Every grain of the surface had been carved with British names; their chiselled capitals rose from the level of her ankles to the height of the great arch itself; on every surface of every column as far as her eyes could see there were names teeming, reeling, over surfaces of yards, of hundreds of yards, over furlongs of stone [...]

'Who are these, these ...?' She gestured with her hand.

'These?' The man with the brush sounded surprised. 'The lost.'

'Men who died in this battle?'

'No. The lost, the ones they did not find. The others are in the cemeteries.'

[...]

When she could speak again, she said, 'From the whole war?'

'The man shook his head. 'Just these fields.' He gestured with his arm.

Elizabeth went and sat on the steps on the other side of the monument. Beneath her was a formal garden with some rows of white headstones, each with a tended plant or flower at its base, each cleaned and beautiful in the weak winter sunlight.

'Nobody told me.' She ran her fingers with their red-painted nails back through her thick dark hair. 'My God, nobody told me.'

(Faulks, 1994, pp.210–11)

The equivalent moment in *Another World* is no less striking. Nick takes his grandfather Geordie on what they both know will be his last visit to the cemeteries of the Somme and the Thiepval monument – though for Nick it is his first visit there.

Nothing Nick had heard, nothing he had read, prepared him for the cemeteries ... One of Nick's clearest memories is of Geordie standing in a German cemetery, the thin dark crosses casting blue shadows on the snow, like the footprints of birds.

Just as nothing had prepared him for the cemeteries, so the cemeteries, with their neatly tended plots and individual inscriptions, failed to prepare him for the annihilating abstractions of Thiepval ...

If, as Nick believed, you should go to the past, looking not for messages or warnings, but simply to be humbled by the weight of human experience that has preceded the brief flicker of your own few days, then Thiepval succeeded brilliantly.

(Barker, 1998, pp.72–3)

Both of the latter two examples are fictional. Neither explicitly uses the language of 'pilgrimage' or of 'religion'. But both bear testimony to the recognition that the impact of war cemeteries and memorials can prove not merely surprising, but potentially transforming or revelatory in its intensity. The implication, in both novels, is that the character has been changed by the experience at a profound level. Arguably, these too are portrayals of moments when visits take on the character of pilgrimages.

Figure 2.5 The Thiepval Monument to the missing of the Somme. Courtesy of the Photograph Archives of the Commonwealth War Graves Commission.

Visits to cemeteries and memorials by school groups, though self-evidently educational rather than religious in aim and intention, also possess the capacity to prompt profound reactions. One journalist described the impact of Sanctuary Wood museum and the Tyne Cot cemetery in Flanders on one group of British schoolchildren in 1999. At the museum they viewed a particularly graphic photograph of a dead soldier with no face: they 'stared at the photograph, and walked away in silence'. Later they visited the cemetery.

> They file out [of their coach] – some spotty, some out for a bit of flirting – and then walk through the gravestones. You could watch their body language change. By the time they had passed the first ten rows they were no longer moving like jittery adolescents. They were grown-ups, coming to terms with the smudging out of a generation.
>
> (Sweeney, 1999, p.14)

Afterwards, some of them offered their reactions. One girl commented, 'What really gets to me is the ones with no names.' Another girl said, 'You read all about so many dead but it doesn't affect you. To see with your own eyes all these graves, it's different.' One of the boys looked up his own name in the books containing the names of the dead commemorated there – and was shocked to find an exact namesake there. Later, the journalist repeated the experiment with his own name and also found a namesake among the panels recording the 34,000 missing commemorated at Tyne Cot (Sweeney, 1999).[4]

It would seem, then, that at the beginning of the twenty-first century, the war graves and war memorials to the British dead of the twentieth century's two world wars still retain a power to move and to provoke those who visit them into unexpected reflection. It is a power that apparently extends beyond those who deliberately set out to visit these places as pilgrims; and it is a power that crosses generations. It is a power that apparently prompts, perhaps above all, humility in the face of the silent record of so much human suffering and loss. The next section will examine another, more recent, war memorial that has come to exercise a similar influence and power.

An American sacred space: the Vietnam Veterans Memorial

'I think it's one of the most reverential places I've ever been. It never lets you out.'

(Quoted in Katakis, 1988, p.69)

Popularly, it has come to be known, simply, as 'The Wall'. It is one of the most visited sites in the American capital city, Washington DC, attracting more than two million visitors a year. Since its dedication in 1982, over twenty million people have visited it (Hass, 1998, p.8), and sometimes as many as 20,000 people visit it in a single day (Scruggs and Swerdlow, 1985, p.159). In 1994, the *New York Times* (11 November 1994, section A, p.12) described it as a 'hallowed national shrine', a 'sacred place' where Americans make pilgrimages to see a wall of names and grieve. It has also been called 'America's Wailing Wall', a 'Mecca for the Vietnam generation' (Powell, 1995, p.xi.), and 'one of the most evocative shrines ever erected by Americans' (Foote,

---

[4] Although of no more than anecdotal significance, two incidents from my own experience suggest that such examples of being surprised into profound or unexpected reactions by war cemeteries and memorials may not be that unusual. In one case I listened to a friend in her forties describe her own amazement and shock at visiting the First World War cemeteries at Arras while seeking the name of her husband's grandfather. The visit was notable too for being connected with the resolution of aspects of family history. In the other case I watched a fourteen-year-old girl react to a rural French First World War cemetery. Having been disinclined to walk to the cemetery after a long day of travelling, once there she became almost instantly reflective and absorbed by the place. Her observation after half an hour wandering among the gravestones was simply, 'It's amazing. It's as if they are all still here.' She is not a person given to over-sentimental or emotive pronouncements. Her comment was, accordingly, all the more striking.

1997, p.314). It has been the focus for literally tens of thousands of gifts, letters and mementoes, which now form a huge memorial collection (Allen, 1995; Hass, 1998, pp.22–4). It has sparked an extensive literature – both academic and popular – and has entire web sites devoted to it. It has been called the 'only really alive war memorial in any western nation' (Mosse, 1990, p.224). It consists of a 'V'-shaped wall of polished and reflective black marble, cut into the ground at an angle, so that the visitor descends progressively further below ground level as he or she walks to the point of the 'V'. Engraved on the wall, in the chronological order of their deaths, are the names of 58,209 American service personnel who were killed in the Vietnam War.

The story of the origins of the Vietnam Veterans Memorial, of the fierce controversies over its design and meaning, of its subsequent development into a 'hallowed national shrine', and of its potentially intriguing relationship to the concept of an 'American civil religion', will be the subject of the next chapter. This chapter is concerned with the more specific question of the way in which this particular memorial has become the focus for a remarkable outpouring of personal pilgrimages and rituals of mourning and remembrance.

The process began even as the memorial was being built. When the first panel of names had been completed it was brought to the site provided for the Memorial in Washington. It was arranged that the

Figure 2.6 The Vietnam Veterans Memorial. Photo: © Jeremy Cooper/ Oliomedia.

Figure 2.7 The Vietnam Veterans Memorial. Photo: © Jeremy Cooper/ Oliomedia.

Figure 2.8 The centre point of the Vietnam Veterans Memorial. Photo by the National Parks Service. Courtesy of the National Park Service, National Capital Region and Parks and History Association.

families of several of the dead named on that particular panel would attend a brief unveiling ceremony. The panel was unveiled and each family walked up to it and left one long-stemmed red rose. Then:

> The families also did something unexpected. They touched the stone. Even a six-year-old girl walked calmly through the adults and reached up to an uncle she had never met. The touches were more than soft. They were gentle, filled with feeling – as if the stone were alive.
>
> (Scruggs and Swerdlow, 1985, p.123)

Subsequently, as the builders installed successive panels, people came to watch and to catch a glimpse of the panels of names, often trying to get inside the fenced-off construction area. An ex-navy pilot in uniform brought his dead brother's Purple Heart medal and asked that he be allowed to put it into the concrete that was about to be poured for the foundation of another panel. He was allowed to do so, and saluted as the medal disappeared into the wall (Scruggs and Swerdlow, 1985, p.124). When the memorial was officially dedicated in November 1982, it immediately became obvious that this process was continuing. People came to the Wall day and night, searching for particular names, if necessary by torchlight or using matches or cigarette lighters. Almost always they wanted to touch the names. Veterans devised their own rituals: drinking beers or smoking cigarettes in silence before a sequence of names; pouring a series of whiskies, saluting, drinking them, saluting again and leaving; scattering the ashes of a veteran who had survived the war but subsequently committed suicide; leaving an American flag (Scruggs and Swerdlow, 1985, pp.147–8).

From the beginning, visitors to the memorial left things there – a practice that has continued in subsequent years. Some of them were what might have been expected: letters to the dead, poems, medals, photographs, birthday cards, teddy bears, high school yearbooks, wedding rings, obituaries, old service dog-tags, uniforms, combat jackets, flags and candles. Other items were less obvious, less predictable, and less easily interpreted: bubble-gum wrappers, cans of beer, unopened sardine cans, cigarettes, a pair of cowboy boots, a champagne glass, a car stereo speaker, a television set, records, key chains, a handful of sea shells, a green elephant, an eagle feather, a paper fan, eight pairs of Nike running shoes at eight different panels (Allen, 1995, p.94; Hass, 1998, especially pp.22–9 and 92–5). The items were initially carefully gathered and stored nearby by the staff of the National Park Service who work at the memorial. In 1984, they were then officially organized into the Vietnam Veterans Memorial Collection, since when all items left at the Wall have been catalogued and archived at an official storage centre in Maryland.

Figure 2.9 Personal behaviour at the Vietnam Veterans Memorial. Erich Hartmann/Magnum.

Figure 2.10 Personal behaviour at the Vietnam Veterans Memorial. Photo: © Larry Powell.

Figure 2.11 Items left at the Vietnam Veterans Memorial. Photo: Bill Clark. Courtesy of the National Park Service, National Capital Region and Parks and History Association.

Figure 2.12 Items left at the Vietnam Veterans Memorial. Photo: © Larry Powell.

Most of the things left at the Wall are highly personal and are left by individuals in memory of other individuals. Veterans remember and honour old comrades. They say goodbye to them 'properly' at last. They may visit once or return frequently – but in either case do so to bring some resolution to their own relationship with both their dead comrades and their own past. They leave the beer or the cigarettes they owed but never had the chance to return. They apologize because they could not save their comrades who died. Sometimes they apologize because they survived when their comrades did not – and wonder why this was so. It is in the messages that they sometimes leave that such motives and intentions become explicit. A selection of examples demonstrates both the variety and the intensity of these motives and intentions:

> How angry I was to find you here – though I knew that you would be. I've wished so hard that I could have saved you. I would give my life if somehow it would bring you back. It is only now on my second trip to the monument that I can admit that you, my friends, are gone forever – that I can say your names, call you my friends and speak of your deaths.
>
> (Quoted in Palmer, 1987, p.33)

> This world has changed. I am sorry that you don't share it with me. I am sorry your name is here. I ask why mine is not.
>
> [...]

We grew up together. We served together. You died and I lived. I never could understand that. You were a much better person than me. I'll always remember you. Life has never been the same without you.

[...]

It has been a long time. But I will never forget you – or Nam – but I have finally come home today.

[...]

Well, old friend, this is the first time I've had the guts to come and pay my respects. It's been more than twenty years. But not a day has gone by that I haven't thought about you and some of the talks we had. I wonder why you're there and I'm here and if somehow you wouldn't have done more with your life than I've done with mine. I never did call your family when I came home. Went to Canada for about 15 years. Then it all seemed like so long in the past. I just didn't want to open any of their wounds. I wish I could have traded places with you ... I can even hear your voice sometimes. When I do, I try to jot what I hear. Please keep it up.

[...]

Our skin was not the same but our hearts were. I've missed you soul brother. Travel in peace ... This ten pack is on me. I've come to have one last smooth with you.

[...]

I've been here at this special place three times now, and I always feel like I've somehow gotten closer to many answers to all of it, but mostly what I feel is just an outpouring of love and gratitude that I was your friend and that there's not a day goes by that I don't think of you. Not in a sad dark way, like it used to be before they built this, but the crazy times too, and the laughter – there was a lot of that.

(Quoted in Powell, 1995, pp.12, 13, 14 and 22)

Perhaps, I can bury you now; at least in my soul. Perhaps, now, I won't again see you night after night when the war reappears ... You got a bronze star, a silver star, survived 18 months ... only to walk into a booby trapped bunker and all of a sudden you had no face or chest. I never cried. My chest becomes unbearably painful and my throat tightens so I can't even croak, but I haven't cried. I wanted to, just couldn't. I think I can, today. Damn, I'm crying now.

(Quoted in Palmer, 1987, p.27)

A woman who had served as a nurse in Vietnam and had tried to suppress the pain of the experience visited the Wall and found the name of a man she had nursed. She touched the name and finally cried after years of silence:

> I thought the Memorial was perfect, sad, beautiful – it made me cry and that's what I needed ... It felt so good to cry near the names of those I had touched ... I was with them again. The Wall made me face reality ... It allowed me to grieve.
>
> (Quoted in Marling and Wetenhall, 1989, p.347)

Other veterans leave messages at the Wall that seek to resolve their own continuing moral disquiet and guilt. Thus, one veteran attached a letter to a small picture of a Vietnamese man and young girl. The letter read:

> Dear Sir,
> For twenty two years I have carried your picture in my wallet. I was only eighteen years old that day we faced one another on that trail in Chu Lai, Vietnam ... So many times over the years I have stared at your picture and your daughter, I suspect. Each time my heart and gutts (sic) would burn with the pain of guilt. I have two daughters myself now. One is twenty. The other one is twenty-two, and has blessed me with two granddaughters ... Forgive me Sir, I shall try to live my life to the fullest, an opportunity that you and many others were denied.
>
> (Quoted in Allen, 1995, p.103)

Another message read:

> This wedding ring belonged to a young Viet Cong fighter. He was killed by a Marine unit in Phu Loc province of South Vietnam in 1968. I wish I knew more about this young man. I have carried this ring for 18 years and it's time for me to lay it down. This boy is not my enemy any more.
>
> (Quoted in Palmer, 1987, p.184, and in Powell, 1995, p.23)

If many seek some form of 'resolution' in the messages and gifts that they leave at the Wall, it is difficult not to see in messages such as these a search for 'absolution' and forgiveness. Thus, it is hardly surprising that the rituals and patterns of behaviour observed at the Wall have been described as 'strategies for redemption' (Carlson and Hocking, 1988).

As well as veterans, other 'survivors' – parents, brothers, sisters, lovers, widows, children and grandchildren – also leave messages and gifts. Birthdays and anniversaries provide obvious occasions for those who visit the memorial regularly, as do Christmas, Easter, Father's Day, Memorial Day and Veterans Day. News is sometimes brought to the dead. In the words of one commentator, 'As the years go by, the Wall is where generations meet ... Children talk to their fathers saying, "They tell me I look a lot like you." Brothers and sisters relay family news. Parents introduce their children to grandparents they'll never know' (Powell, 1995, p.33). Again, it is in particular messages left at the Wall that the intensity and depth of feeling that are involved are best revealed:

> Here are the first two images of your first grandchild ... Dad – this child will know you – just how I have grown to know and love you – even though the last time I saw you I was only four months old ...
>
> (Quoted in Allen, 1995, p.103)

> I came to visit you today. I haven't ever felt so close to you before. I never got a chance to know you but I love you very much. There isn't a day goes by that Mom doesn't think of you ...
>
> [...]
>
> Hi Dad. The last time you saw me I was just starting to walk. I really didn't get to know you or you to know me. Well, here it is 22 years later and I am married ... We have been married three years and next year when we come back to the Wall like we do every year, I will be showing your name to your grandchild and will say that this is your grandfather's name.
>
> (Quoted in Powell, 1995, pp.35 and 37)

In addition to the offerings left by individuals, there are also collective acts of remembrance. These too are sometimes marked by items left at the Wall. Thus, Hawaiian veterans left a chain of orchids that stretched the length of the Wall, while Native American veterans have brought beaded eagle feathers, ceremonial war shields and medicine bundles, and have held traditional tribal rituals at the Wall (Allen, 1995, pp.95–6). Other groups leave wreaths, floral tributes and flags on behalf of particular communities or associations (Powell, 1995, p.57).[5] In the early 1990s it was estimated that as many as 1,100 to 1,500 reunions took place each year at the Wall (Wagner-Pacifici and Schwartz, 1991, p.402).

It has been pointed out that leaving something at the Wall – whether an item or a message – has itself become a ritual act. Whereas initially many, probably most, of the things and messages left were the result of spontaneous acts – many of the early messages, for example, were hastily scrawled on scraps of paper or notepaper from local hotels – many subsequent offerings have taken on a more prepared, premeditated quality (Allen, 1995, p.100). This, however, need not lead to the conclusion that more premeditated or prepared

---

[5] The Wall has also been used as a place to register protests over particular issues, again often by leaving items. Thus, veterans protesting over the effect on them of the Agent Orange defoliant, which was widely used in Vietnam, have registered their protest at the Wall, as have campaigners for American prisoners-of-war still believed to held in South-East Asia. The Gulf War also prompted symbolic protests at the Wall.

acts are any less genuine or significant. Indeed, the element of 'pilgrimage' – of intentional travel to a place in the anticipation and expectation of the completion of some ritual act – might even be regarded as greater in such cases. Nor is the leaving of items or messages the only ritual that has grown up around the Wall.

Other characteristic activities include the desire of those who visit a particular name to touch the name itself on the Wall – indeed, even many of those who do not go to the Wall to find a particular name are frequently moved to reach out and touch the surface and the engraved names. Often they also wish to take a rubbing of the name – an act for which the National Park Service staff are prepared by having paper, crayons and envelopes available for those who have not brought them or anticipated requiring them. Step ladders are available to reach names high on the Wall. People not only place their hands on the Wall, but see themselves reflected in it. The polished surface reflects the sky, the trees, and the people who stand in front of it. The experience of seeing oneself reflected back from the wall of names has become a recurrent theme of accounts of visits. This aspect is often interpreted in terms of the memorial being about the present as well as the past, and a symbol of the interaction between the two. It is also a place of quiet. It is not simply silent: some people are silent, but others talk, and many cry. But it is a place characterized by 'hushed whispers, reverential comments, or just silence. Being there is a holy experience' (Sutherland, 1995, p.xi).

The theme of the holiness of the memorial was taken up by another visitor, a veteran of the war, who described the behaviour of veterans who, like himself, came to the Wall: 'They walk as if on hallowed ground. They touch the stone. They speak with the dead.' The memorial, he continued is 'a collection point, an altar on which the living leave tokens of the dead and trappings for an afterlife' (Norman, 1987, pp.15 and 18). The desire to speak with the dead and the sense – real or metaphorical – of actually communicating with them is manifest in the letters and messages addressed to them. One woman reflected on her first visit to the Wall, in 1985, to find the name of her father, who had been shot down over Laos seventeen years earlier in 1968. Officially missing, she knew that, realistically, there was little chance of him being alive.[6] After various delays, she eventually arrived at the memorial at 2.30 in the morning. Even then people were there, and she described herself as feeling safe and protected.

[6] The names on the Wall include all of the American servicemen and women killed in Vietnam, plus those still officially listed as 'missing in action'.

Figure 2.13 Personal behaviour at the Vietnam Veterans Memorial. Photo: Jeremy Cooper/Oliomedia.

Figure 2.14 Personal behaviour at the Vietnam Veterans Memorial. Photo: Jeremy Cooper/Oliomedia.

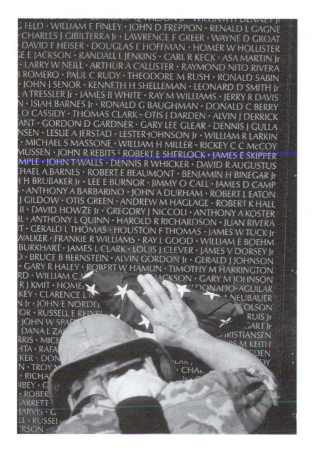

Figure 2.15 Personal behaviour at the Vietnam Veterans Memorial. Peter Marlow/Magnum.

> There is an energy there that is unreal ... I knew he knew that I was trying to reach out and let him know that I'm okay. He knows that I'm worried about him ... I wanted him not to worry about me ... I really didn't think anyone was going to read my letter. I got out a pencil and just wrote. I felt a lot better. I can't express the feeling I had after writing it ... When I set it down and stood up and I wiped my tears, I knew, either alive or dead, he knew that I had just made contact with him.
>
> (Quoted in Palmer, 1987, p.49)

Another visitor explained that it was the one place in the world where she felt as if she had the opportunity to communicate with her father and tell him how much she loved him and wished they could have shared a life together (cited in Palmer, 1987, p.95). In the present context, it is instructive to compare such comments with those of the Englishman, Tim Pain, as he tried to make sense and explain the significance of visiting his grandfather's name, located on a panel high on the Menin Gate. It is also hardly surprising that the Wall has been described as 'a kind of spirit medium' (Berdahl, 1994, p.98).

Beyond the Wall itself, the Vietnam Veterans Memorial has also become the subject and focus of a considerable literature, both scholarly and popular. In many ways it is the popular literature that is most significant in the present context.[7] Books dedicated to the letters and messages left at the wall, such as *Shrapnel in the Heart* (Palmer, 1987) and books of photographs of the Wall, of people at the Wall, and of things left at the Wall, such as *The Wall* (Lopes, 1987), *The Vietnam Veterans Memorial* (Katakis, 1988), and *Hunger of the Heart* (Powell, 1995), have become almost an extension of the memorial itself. Just as visits to the Wall may be described as acts of pilgrimage, so the tone of books such as these may appropriately be said to resemble works of devotion or spirituality. They seek, above all, to evoke and to celebrate the Wall itself and the rituals that are associated with it.

On the Internet, meanwhile, a variety of web sites refer to the Vietnam Veterans Memorial. These include 'The Vietnam Veterans Memorial Wall Page' which is run by an organization for Vietnam Veterans and is dedicated to the Wall as a living memorial. The subsections of this web site include, for example, details of those on the Wall whose date of birth corresponds to the date of the visit to the web site; the possibility of an 'electronic rubbing' of a name from the Wall; literary items such as poems, meditations, tributes or recollections; galleries of photographs; and a message centre, plus links to other relevant sites. The official web site of the Vietnam Veterans Memorial Fund similarly provides information about the history of the Wall, the annual activities that take place there, and the various educational and memorial initiatives and activities that are sponsored by the Fund. It also provides a link to a site entitled 'The Virtual Wall'. This is an interactive database concerning the Wall and the details of every individual named on it. It is possible to view the Wall and to focus on individual panels and individual names. Visitors to the site can post their own messages of remembrance, search for messages of remembrance left by others, or read the electronic messages left at the site on any particular day since the initiative began in 1998. An electronic 'rubbing' of a name can be made. The site is linked in turn to another site – 'The Wall That Heals' – dedicated to the history and activities of the half-scale travelling replica of the Vietnam Veterans Memorial, created and run by the Vietnam Veterans Memorial Fund, which has been taken to over 100 American cities since it was unveiled on Veterans Day 1996. The images of the 'Travelling Wall'

---

[7] For references to many of the scholarly and academic discussions of the Vietnam Veterans Memorial, see the reference lists at the end of this and the following chapter.

Figure 2.16 The 'Travelling Wall', half-size replica of the Vietnam Veterans Memorial. Associated Press/Wide World Photos/Steve Cutri.

replicate the images of the rituals that are characteristic of the actual Wall in Washington: people touch the names on the Travelling Wall and leave gifts and letters in front of it.[8]

It may or not be true that the Vietnam Veterans Memorial is the only 'really alive war memorial in any western nation' (Mosse, 1990, p.224). It is certainly the case, however, that this particular memorial is remarkably alive in its continuing impact on American conscious-ness at the beginning of the twenty-first century. As the next chapter will explore, the relationship between the Vietnam Veterans Mem-orial and 'American civil religion' is, in many ways, complex and ambiguous. But what is not in doubt is that the Wall constitutes – with whatever complexity and ambiguity – one of the major shrines of contemporary American civil religion. It does so, moreover, because of its popular appeal, because it is a site of popular pilgrimage. It has been observed that American civil religion has no formal equivalent of church attendance to measure its strength or popularity. Thus, it is in informal and popular ways that American commitment to civil

[8] There have, in fact, been mobile replicas of the Wall since 1984, for which see Wagner-Pacifici and Schwartz (1991, p.413) and Berdahl (1994, p.113).

religion is often revealed, one of the most common manifestations being the elevation of a particular place to the status of a 'shrine' of civil religion by virtue of mass pilgrimage to it (Sellars and Walter, 1993, p.179). Measured against this criterion, the *New York Herald* was right to call the Vietnam Veterans Memorial a 'sacred place', a 'hallowed national shrine'.

Conclusion: civil religion and the personal

This chapter has been concerned with the ways in which individuals express or seek to resolve their private griefs and perplexities over the deaths of relatives or friends in war by visiting official war cemeteries and memorials. The making of such a visit, it has been argued, is often appropriately described or characterized as an act of personal 'pilgrimage'. Civil religions, however, according to the concise working definition of a civil religion proposed by Richard Pierard and Robert Linder, are primarily concerned with providing beliefs, values, rituals and ceremonies that unite communities and societies, providing a shared sense of history and destiny, and linking them to some sense of absolute meaning (Pierard and Linder, 1988, pp.22–3). Working with that definition, the previous chapter argued that, in the UK and the USA at least, remembrance of those killed in the wars of these two nations constitutes a major element in the rituals and ceremonies by which their civil religions are maintained. Self-evidently, war cemeteries and memorials are in turn central elements of the rituals of remembrance of both British and American civil religion.

But the phenomena with which this chapter has been concerned are personal rather than collective, individual rather than communal. Granted, pilgrimages run by, for example, the Royal British Legion may possess a collective, communal quality. Similarly, some of the visits to the Vietnam Veterans Memorial by groups from particular communities or veterans' associations also exhibit such character-istics. But the focus and interest of this chapter has been firmly on the responses of individuals, or at most families, to the encounter with war graves, war cemeteries and war memorials.

Can such visits and responses be described, in any meaningful sense, as a dimension of 'civil religion'? There is, perhaps, a parallel to be drawn with the way in which, in major religious traditions, 'official' belief and practice coexists with 'popular' belief and practice. It is not unusual – indeed it is very common – for ordinary believers in various religions to adapt their personal beliefs and practices to their own religious and spiritual needs, even if in so doing they go beyond the norms and rituals officially prescribed by their religion and its spokespersons. Something similar may be seen in personal pilgrimages to war graves and memorials.

For example, the theme of talking to the dead, of leaving them messages or gifts, and of believing that, in some way, however incoherently understood or articulated, the dead are aware of this process, is not a part of the official civil religious rituals of remembrance in either the UK or the USA.[9] The official rituals remember, honour and celebrate the sacrifice of those killed in war. Beyond this, however, they tend to be highly unspecific and generalized, not least because they seek to unite nations and communities in remembrance, and too great a specificity might tend to divide rather than to unite. They are also less intense and less overwhelmingly emotional than the experiences recorded by many pilgrims to graves and memorials. The actions of individuals in their encounter with war graves and memorials can therefore be seen as supplying a depth – a degree of personal 'devotion' or even 'spirituality' – to the overall processes of remembrance. Moreover, it is arguable that such intense personal experiences constitute compelling evidence that the remembrance of those killed in war in British and American civil religion is far more than a simplistic or narrowly nationalistic or patriotic phenomenon. On the contrary, the power of war graves and war memorials – or at least some war memorials – to prompt such intense reactions among visitors suggests that the themes which civil religion seeks to address in rituals of remembrance are both profound and personal. And if the emotions and experiences involved – such as the stubborn conviction that in some way the dead and the living interact – are not strictly rational or explicable, this surely should not count against their being treated seriously. Although unsupported by sophisticated and detailed theological frameworks and justifications, it is by no means clear that such convictions and beliefs are any less credible or rational than many of the beliefs held by the adherents of a variety of religious traditions.

It was argued in the previous chapter that, in the context of national rituals of remembrance, it remains an open question whether such rituals constitute a way in which British and American civil religions connect their respective societies with 'a realm of

---

[9] The significance of the apparently widespread conviction that there is thus some communication between the living and the dead is explored further in the following chapter, especially pages 120–3.

absolute meaning'. It was suggested, however, that at the very least, national rituals of remembrance connect British and American society with profound reflection on the meaning – or lack of it – of the human sacrifice, suffering and loss that are a consequence of war.[10] Accounts of personal pilgrimages to war graves and memorials and the impact of personal encounters with individual graves, whole cemeteries and other memorials tend to enhance rather than diminish the sense of the act of remembrance connecting people with 'a realm of absolute meaning'.

Writing of the significance of contemporary visits to the battlefields of the American Civil War, the American historian Richard Sellars posed the question of what, apart from a sense of 'the fumbling march of armies to victory or defeat', visitors may gain from the experience. His answer was that 'Civil War battlefields and memorials may still evoke deep feelings of empathy within those visitors who are able to grasp the appalling tragedy and grief engendered by these conflicts' (Sellars, 1986, p.21). The same is surely true of many, if not most, of those who visit the cemeteries of the two world wars of the twentieth century and the Vietnam Veterans Memorial. Certainly it is reflected in the personal experiences referred to in this chapter. It has been observed that, both in relation to pilgrimages to British war cemeteries and to the Vietnam Veterans Memorial, one of the most profound realizations is that these are memorials, not only to what happened in the past, but also to what might have been but never was. They are memorials to lost futures and to subsequent individual lives and relationships that did not happen (Walter, 1993, p.70; Sutherland, 1995, p.x.)

The cemeteries and memorials discussed here are therefore also places that provocatively and profoundly juxtapose intense individuality and the reality of mass death. On the one hand, there is the awful reality of thousands of names listed together: whether on the panels of the Thiepval, Menin Gate or Tyne Cot memorials in northern Europe (to cite only memorials referred to in this chapter), or on the polished black marble panels of the Vietnam Veterans Memorial. In each case – as in the experience of visiting 'row, upon row, upon row of headstones', recorded in John Schwartz' taped diary with which this chapter began – it is the sheer number of names that initially prompts empathy, reflection, and humility in the face of the evidence of such loss. But beyond the impact of the numbers, it is usually the encounter with individual names that focuses most effectively both attention and emotion, and that symbolizes most profoundly, because most personally, the whole point of remembrance of those

---

[10] See especially pages 51–2 of Chapter 1.

killed in war. The encounter with individual names may take any number of particular forms: the repeated journey to the particular grave where the visitor will finally 'choke up'; the discovery of a grandfather's name, on a panel, high on a memorial to thousands never found; the discovery by a schoolboy of his namesake in a book of the dead commemorated in a particular graveyard; the finding of a name on a black marble wall that prompts the finder to write a letter or perform a personal ritual. The common feature is the encounter with individual human mortality within the context of personal loss and the search for meaning despite that loss.

Towards the end of his seminal article on American civil religion – written as controversy over the Vietnam War grew in the USA of the late 1960s, and intended as a contribution to that controversy – Robert Bellah expressed the hope that one day American civil religion might become simply one part of a 'new civil religion of the world' (Bellah, 1967, p.19). It was, perhaps, an essentially Utopian hope – and one that was curiously coloured by the optimism of the radical protest movements of the 1960s. But if such a broader concept of a world civil religion were ever to emerge, then the role of war cemeteries and war memorials – experienced and interpreted not as commemorations of national pride or military glory, but as monuments to human loss and grief – might prove a strangely effective element of such a religion. That this thought is not merely the stuff of academic speculation but might have a wider resonance is suggested by the remarks of John Peel, the presenter of the *Home Truths* radio programme, at the end of the audio-diary item by John Schwartz recounting his visit to his friends' graves. Peel – himself a prominent figure in the radical and alternative youth culture of the 1960s – rounded off the item by saying:

> For anyone tempted to come and spray-paint the *Home Truths* office because they think we're glorifying war, I think that John's diary, like the Cenotaph, does exactly the opposite. I've always thought of the Cenotaph as a sort of collective tombstone for all of the people who died in all wars, regardless of what side they were on, or whether they were soldiers or civilians.
>
> (*Home Truths*, BBC Radio 4, 20 May 2000)

References

Allen, L. (1995) 'Offerings at the Wall', *American Heritage*, 46, pp.92–103.

Barker, P. (1998) *Another World*, London: Viking.

Barker, P. (1999) 'How did Uncle Edmund die?', *Observer* 'Review', 7 November, p.2.

Bellah, R. (1967) 'Civil religion in America', *Daedalus*, 96, pp.1–21.

Berdahl, D. (1994) 'Voices at the Wall: discourses of self, history and national identity at the Vietnam Veterans Memorial', *History and Memory*, 6, pp.88–124.

Carlson, A. and Hocking, J. (1988) 'Strategies of redemption at the Vietnam Veterans Memorial', *Western Journal of Speech Communication*, 52, pp.203–15.

Evans, M. and Lunn, K. (eds) (1997) *War and Memory in the Twentieth Century*, Oxford: Berg.

Faulks, S. (1994) *Birdsong*, London: Vintage.

Foote, K. (1997) *Shadowed Ground: America's Landscapes of Violence and Tragedy*, Austin: University of Texas Press.

Gregory, A. (1994) *The Silence of Memory: Armistice Day 1919–1946*, Oxford: Berg.

Harbutt, C. (1995) 'The things they leave behind', *New York Times*, 12 November, section 6, p.38.

Hass, K. (1998) *Carried to the Wall: American Memory and the Vietnam Veterans Memorial*, Berkeley: University of California Press.

Inglis, K. (1992a) 'The homecoming: the War Memorial Movement in Cambridge, England', *Journal of Contemporary History*, 27, pp.583–605.

Inglis, K. (1992b) 'War memorials: ten questions for historians', *Guerres Mondiale et Conflits Contemporains*, 167, pp.5–21.

Inglis, K. (1993) 'Entombing unknown soldiers: from London and Paris to Baghdad', *History and Memory*, 5, pp.7–31.

Jackman, B. (1998) 'The lost boys', *Sunday Times* 'Travel', 8 November, p.5.

Katakis, M. (1988) *The Vietnam Veterans Memorial*, New York: Crown Publishers.

King, A. (1998) *Memorials of the Great War in Britain: The Symbolism and Politics of Remembrance*, Oxford: Berg.

Lloyd, D. (1998) *Battlefield Tourism: Pilgrimage and Commemoration of the Great War in Britain, Australia and Canada*, Oxford: Berg.

Longworth, P. (1985) *The Unending Vigil: A History of the Commonwealth War Graves Commission*, London: Leo Cooper/Secker & Warburg.

Lopes, (S.) (1987) *The Wall: Images and Offerings from the Vietnam Veterans Memorial*, New York: Collins.

Marling, K. and Wetenhall, J. (1989) 'The sexual politics of memory: the Vietnam Women's Memorial Project and "The Wall"', *Prospects*, 14, pp.341–72.

Moriarty, C. (1991) 'Christian iconography and First World War memorials', *Imperial War Museum Review*, 6, pp.63–75.

Moriarty, C. (1995) 'The absent dead and figurative First World War memorials', *Transactions of the Ancient Monument Society*, 39, pp.7–40.

Mosse, G. (1990) *Fallen Soldiers: Reshaping the Memory of the World Wars*, Oxford: Oxford University Press.

Norman, M. (1987) 'Introduction', in S. Lopes, pp.15–19.

Pain, T. (1990) 'Say goodbye to Grandad', *Guardian* 'Weekend', 3–4 November, p.28.

Pierard, R. and Linder, R. (1988) *Civil Religion and the American Presidency*, Grand Rapids: Zondervan.

Palmer, L. (1987) *Shrapnel in the Heart: Letters and Remembrances from the Vietnam Veterans Memorial*, New York: Vintage Books.

Powell, L. (1995) *Hunger of the Heart: Communion at the Wall*, Dubuque Iowa: Islewest Publishing.

Reader, I. and Walter, T. (eds) (1993) *Pilgrimage in Popular Culture*, London: Macmillan.

Rowlands, M. (1999) 'Remembering to forget: sublimation as sacrifice in war memorials', in A. Forty and S. Küchler (eds) *The Art of Forgetting*, Oxford: Berg, pp.129–45.

Scruggs, J. and Swerdlow, J. (1985) *To Heal a Nation: The Vietnam Veterans Memorial*, New York: Harper & Row.

Sellars, R. (1986) 'Vigil of silence: the Civil War memorials', *History News*, 41, pp.19–23.

Sellars, R. and Walter, T. (1993) 'From Custer to Kent State: heroes, martyrs and the evolution of popular shrines in the USA', in I. Reader and T. Walter (eds) pp.179–200.

Sutherland, C. (1995) 'Preface', in Powell, pp.ix–xi.

Sweeney, J. (1999) 'Day trip to hell gives young a lesson in war's folly', *Observer*, 7 November, p.14.

Wagner-Pacifici, R. and Schwartz, B. (1991) 'The Vietnam Veterans Memorial: commemorating a difficult past', *American Journal of Sociology*, 97, pp.376–420.

Walter, T. (1990) *Funerals and How to Improve Them*, London: Hodder & Stoughton.

Walter, T. (1993) 'War grave pilgrimage', in I. Reader and T. Walter (eds) pp.63–91.

Winter, J. (1995) *Sites of Memory, Sites of Mourning: The Great War in European Cultural History*, Cambridge: Cambridge University Press.

Internet sources consulted

http://www.vvmf.org – the official web site of the Vietnam Veterans Memorial Fund, with links to the Virtual Wall and to other relevant sites.

http://www.thewall-usa.com – the web site of the Vietnam Veterans Memorial Wall Page run by the Vietnam Veterans Association.

http://www.britishlegion.org.uk – the official web site of the Royal British Legion, including information on visits and pilgrimages to war cemeteries.

http://www.cwgc.org – the official web site of the Commonwealth War Graves Commission.

CHAPTER 3

'To heal a nation'? Civil religion and the Vietnam Veterans Memorial

The Vietnam War divided the USA. Between the deaths of the first Americans killed in the conflict in 1959 and the evacuation of the American embassy as Saigon fell in 1975, over 58,000 Americans were killed. Militarily it was a defeat. The aims and objectives of American involvement were never achieved. Moreover, long before it ended, the USA had become deeply and bitterly divided by the moral issue of the war. From the mid-1960s onwards, a passionate anti-war movement opposed American policy and involvement in Vietnam. Equally passionate supporters of the war regarded the anti-war movement as unpatriotic and un-American. Between 1965 and 1971, mass protests, marches and demonstrations against the war were organized in American cities and on college and university campuses. Particular highpoints included a gathering of over 100,000 protesters against the war in the nation's capital, Washington DC, in October 1967, and nationwide demonstrations in October and November 1969 that involved over two million Americans. In early May 1970, four student protesters against the war were killed and nine others wounded at Kent State University, Ohio, when National Guardsmen opened fire on anti-war protesters. Ten days later two more students were killed and another twelve wounded at Jackson State College, Mississippi.

Within a month protests were held at over 1,350 colleges and universities, involving perhaps half the nation's students. In Washington, in response to the shootings at Kent State, a protest organized in only a week resulted in a crowd of over 100,000 people. Newspapers suggested that the USA had become as deeply divided as it had been at any time since the Civil War just over 100 years earlier (Wells, 1994, p.428). By the early 1970s even veterans of the Vietnam

War were becoming prominent among those protesting against it. In April 1971, 1,000 veterans of the war, together with the parents and widows of soldiers killed in Vietnam, demonstrated in Washington. They tried to hold a memorial service in Arlington National Cemetery and were at first refused permission to do so. The next day they returned and succeeded. Then, as the symbolic climax to the demonstration, the veterans threw their medals on to the steps of the Capitol building in Washington. As one observer recalled: 'This was a big event in their lives. This was no small matter ... to throw away their medals. There was no bullshit, there was no joking.' As one of the veterans recalled: 'It was like two hours before I could stop crying. It was very, very, very heavy' (quoted in Wells, 1994, p.496).[1]

In the context of such deep division, it is hardly surprising that, when the war eventually ended, there was no national initiative or even any widespread desire to commemorate it or those who fought in it. The experience had been deeply scarring for both sides in the controversy over the war and the nation remained bitterly divided by the issues involved. Any attempt at commemoration would almost certainly have revived these controversies and divisions. Instead, there was a general desire to forget the war. However, in April 1979, a group of veterans decided to campaign for the erection of a memorial to the Americans who had served in Vietnam. Funding the project entirely through charitable donations and without government financial assistance, they formed the Vietnam Veterans Memorial Fund, and secured approval for the memorial to be located in Washington, in the heart of the nation's capital city.

The design of the memorial was decided in an open competition, judged by an official jury of architects, landscape architects, sculptors and critics. Despite fierce controversy over the chosen design, the memorial was completed and officially dedicated on 13 November 1982 – just three and a half years after the initial decision to seek such a memorial. The memorial was immediately popular with the American people. It quickly became – and remains – one of the most visited sites in Washington. It has generated a literature – both scholarly and popular – that recognizes the memorial as a place of pilgrimage for veterans, families of the dead, and other Americans who seek to address the still unresolved tensions and contradictions of the Vietnam War. The memorial is now commonly described in religious language. It is a 'holy place', a 'shrine', 'hallowed ground', 'a

---

[1] For a detailed history of the domestic conflict within the USA over the Vietnam War, see Wells (1994). For a brief survey of the origins, conduct and history of the war, together with a summary of the domestic controversies and conflicts, see Edmonds (1998).

national healing shrine'. It is said to possess a reverential atmosphere. It is commonly described as a place of healing and reconciliation.

The first part of this chapter will review the history of the building of the Vietnam Veterans Memorial, including the principal controversies that surrounded the project. The second part will examine a number of subsequent interpretations of the memorial by scholars and academics. A final section will then briefly consider the relationship between the memorial and the concept of an American civil religion.

Finding a commemorative form: the controversies over the design of the Vietnam Veterans Memorial

In October 1980, the Vietnam Veterans Memorial Fund, the official organization formed to establish a national memorial to the Americans who served in Vietnam, announced a national competition to select a design for the proposed memorial. It had already obtained the agreement of the US Congress that two acres of land would be assigned to the memorial in Constitution Gardens, a large area, known as the Mall, situated on Constitution Avenue. The site was located on the part of the Mall between the Lincoln Memorial and the Washington Monument, two defining memorials to American presidents. It had been agreed that the memorial was to be financed entirely by private donations and without the help of public funds. It was further understood that the final design would have to be approved by the National Capital Planning Commission, the Commission of Fine Arts, and the Department of the Interior.

The rules of the competition for the design of the memorial were simple, yet also very ambitious. The memorial was to be 'reflective and contemplative' in character. It was to harmonize with its surroundings and relate sensitively to the Lincoln Memorial and the Washington Monument that would be nearby; it was to include the names of all of the Americans who had died in Vietnam; and it was not to make any 'political statement regarding the war or its conduct' (quoted in Howett, 1985, p.4). The competition attracted over 1,400 entries and the jury of architectural and sculptural experts and critics who were appointed to judge these announced the winning entry in May 1981. The jury made their decision without knowing the identities of the designers. Unanimously they chose a design by a 21-year-old Chinese-American woman from Ohio, Maya Ying Lin, who was an architecture student at Yale University.

Figure 3.1 The Vietnam
Veterans Memorial, the
Washington Monument
reflected in it. Vietnam
Veterans Memorial Fund.
Photo: Jan Scruggs, President
of the Fund.

Figure 3.2 The Vietnam
Veterans Memorial. Vietnam
Veterans Memorial Fund.

Figure 3.3 The Vietnam
Veterans Memorial at night.
Erich Hartmann/Magnum.

Her design consisted of two long walls composed of panels of black polished marble. The walls were to be set into the ground in a wide 'V' shape, each arm of the 'V' tapering from a foot high at its outer edge to a height of ten feet at the point of the 'V' where the arms met. A sloping path would lead down to the point of the 'V' and the panels of the wall were to be engraved with the names of the Americans killed in the Vietnam War. The order of the names was not to be alphabetical or according to military unit or rank; it was to be in simple chronological order of the deaths of those commemorated. The two arms of the 'V' of the memorial, which were to be set at an angle of 125 degrees, were to point east towards the Washington Monument, and south-west towards the Lincoln Memorial. The jurors who chose the design subsequently explained that one of the principal things they had liked about it was the way that Maya Ying Lin's design avoided conventional symbolism. One of them remarked that, 'in a heterogeneous society symbols don't work; they arrest thought rather than expanding it'. Yet at the same time the jury members said in an official statement that they believed the memorial would create 'an eloquent place where the simple meeting of earth, sky and remembered names contains messages for all who will know this place' (quoted in Howett, 1985, pp.3–4). Subsequently Maya Ying Lin explained that:

> I felt a memorial should be honest about the reality of war and be for the people who gave their lives ... I didn't want a static object that people would just look at, but something they could relate to as on a journey, or a passage, that would bring each to his own conclusions ... I had an impulse to cut open the earth ... an initial violence that in time would heal ... It was as if the black-brown earth were polished and made into an interface between the sunny world and the quiet dark world beyond that we can't enter. The names would become the memorial. There was no need to embellish.
>
> (Quoted in Berdahl, 1994, p.92)

Perhaps inevitably, given the profound and bitter divisions caused by the Vietnam War and its legacy, the design caused intense contro-versy. In general, the reception from artists, architects and critics was favourable. But a vociferous and politically well-connected minority of traditionally patriotic veterans – including some who had been important early supporters of the Vietnam Veterans Memorial Fund – together with prominently placed and politically right-wing sup-porters, launched a bitter attack on the design. According to this group, Maya Ying Lin's design was a betrayal of those who had died in Vietnam. The black colour proposed for the memorial and the fact that it was to be dug into the ground symbolized, for them, defeat and shame, instead of honouring and glorifying those who gave their lives. 'Black', it was argued by a leading opponent of the design, was the 'universal colour of shame, sorrow and degradation in all races, all societies worldwide'. It was 'a degrading ditch'. It was an 'insulting and demeaning memorial' to the experience of Vietnam veterans. The monument should be white and should include a prominently displayed American flag. The proposed design was unheroic: it should have included representations of American soldiers as a central feature. Instead of showing them as deaths in a cause, the chronological listing of names made them individual deaths: 'they might as well have been a traffic accident', the proposed ordering was 'a malicious random scattering'. The design was criticized because the names lacked ranks or service designations; the word 'Vietnam' did not appear on the original design; and the 'V' symbolized the peace sign made by the anti-war protesters. To these critics the entire ethos of the winning design represented an implicit endorsement of the anti-war movement and its left-wing and liberal opinions and values. It would become a 'wailing wall for anti-draft demonstrators'. It was a 'tribute to Jane Fonda' – a reference to the fact that the actress had been prominent in the anti-war movement, visiting the North Vietnamese capital and thereby acquiring the nickname 'Hanoi Jane'. Most memorably, in a phrase that the media picked up and repeated frequently, one of the leading spokesmen for the opposition to Maya Ying Lin's design called it 'a black gash of shame' (Howett, 1985, pp.6–7; Scruggs and Swerdlow, 1985, pp.80–4; Hess, 1987, pp.265–6; Wagner-Pacifici and Schwartz, 1991, pp.394–5).

Despite such opposition, however, the overwhelming majority of the members and supporters of the Vietnam Veterans Memorial Fund approved of the design. Veterans' associations such as the Veterans of Foreign Wars, the Vietnam Veterans of America and the American Legion – organizations that were generally patriotic and conservative, not liberal in opinion – continued to support the Vietnam Veterans Memorial Fund and its efforts. The organizers of the Fund issued a Fact Sheet rebutting the charges made against the design by its opponents. Far from being associated with the anti-war movement, the Vietnam Veterans Memorial Fund was run predominantly by veterans of the war, by the relatives of Americans still officially classified as missing in action, and by the parents and families of others who had died in the war. They believed that the location of the memorial below ground level was not to denote shame, but to provide a clear line of sight to the Washington Monument and the Lincoln Memorial and to allow everyone to have access to all the names. The 'V' shape was not an echo of the anti-war movement but was also a means of locating the memorial in relation to the

Washington Monument and the Lincoln Memorial. The absence of military ranks and units emphasized that all the dead were, equally, Americans and had made an equal sacrifice. The chronological sequence of the names would mean that veterans and families would be able to read the memorial and find their friends and relatives commemorated in a panel that corresponded to their particular time – and the time of their death – in Vietnam.[2] Most war memorials lacked flags. The word 'Vietnam' would, in fact, appear on the memorial. The colour black was not a symbol of shame or defeat; it was the means of rendering the names clearly readable, even in bright sunlight (Howett, 1985, pp.7–8; Scruggs and Swerdlow, 1985, pp.80–4 and 100).

The particular issue of the colour of the memorial was eventually brought to a decisive conclusion in a public meeting in 1982 by the intervention of a retired senior officer who was black. 'Black', he observed, 'is not a colour of shame. I am tired of hearing it called such by you. Colour meant nothing on the battlefields of Korea and Vietnam ... Colour should mean nothing now' (quoted in Scruggs and Swerdlow, 1985, p.100). The complaint that the memorial would not include a reference to Vietnam was answered by the two inscriptions that it had subsequently been agreed would be added to the original design. These consisted of a simple prologue and epilogue. The former stated:

> In honour of the men and women of the armed forces of the United States who served in the Vietnam War. The names of those who gave their lives and of those who remain missing are inscribed in the order they were taken from us.

The latter read:

> Our nation honours the courage, sacrifice and devotion to duty and country of its Vietnam Veterans. This memorial was built with private contributions from the American people.

[2] Initially some of the veterans on the Vietnam Veterans Memorial Fund had resisted Maya Ying Lin's chronological listing of the names and had urged an alphabetical one. When they examined the Defence Department's two-inch thick list of casualties, however, they changed their minds. With over 600 'Smiths' and 16 'James Jones', individual identities would have become lost in a kind of engraved telephone book. The veterans therefore accepted Maya Ying Lin's chronological listing. Subsequent experiences of veterans visiting the completed memorial bore out Lin's contention that the chronological ordering would relate each name to its particular place in the war. Thus, particular veterans would find a name or group of names and relate them to the specific incidents in which their friends had been killed (Scruggs and Swerdlow, 1985, pp.78–9 and 148).

The Vietnam Veterans Memorial Fund insisted on using the word 'war', rather than the more politically charged 'police action' or 'conflict', because this reflected the reality of the scale and intensity of the Vietnam War. But they also insisted on not using phrases such as 'fight for freedom' or 'never again', because of the overtly political meanings that might be attached to these. Similarly, in keeping with the requirements for the original design competition, they chose not to make the lettering of the inscriptions larger or more elaborate than the lettering of the names of the dead (Scruggs and Swerdlow, 1985, pp.79–80).

The response of the Vietnam Veterans Memorial Fund to the criticisms and objections of opponents of Maya Ying Lin's design proved effective, and it became clear that the original winning design would not be rejected. Opponents of the design therefore shifted their ground and argued that an American flag and a figurative statue portraying soldiers should be added to the memorial. It became clear that opponents of the design had sufficient political support among key figures in Washington to make a compromise necessary.[3] In order to avoid prolonged delay and the risk of a continuing public debate in which support for the design might be eroded, it was agreed that a flag and figurative statue would be added. The flag, it was provisionally agreed, would be placed at the top of the wall, where the two arms met at the point of the 'V'. A figurative statue portraying veterans would be placed at the foot of the wall, also where the arms met. If they had been completed, such additions would have had the effect of reducing Maya Ying Lin's design to a 'frame' for the realistic figurative sculpture and flag. In fact, after ongoing controversy during 1982, and while the building of the original design proceeded, both the Commission of Fine Arts and the National Capital Planning Commission – two bodies that had to give final approval to the additions to the design – ruled that the flag and figurative statue should not be located at the point of the 'V' of the wall. Instead, they were to be located in a grove of trees at the south-west corner of the memorial site, 120 feet from the wall, as part of an entranceway. It is likely that the sheer impact of the original design even under construction played a significant part in the final decision

---

[3] Specifically, the Secretary of the Interior, James Watt, a supporter of the opponents of the design, had the power to prevent the beginning of the construction of the monument unless a compromise was reached. One of the ironies of the campaign against Maya Ying Lin's design is that it was sustained principally by the political 'New Right' and a minority of veterans, while the majority of veterans and veterans' associations supported the design and favoured the emphasis on individual casualties (Howett, 1985, p.7; Scruggs and Swerdlow, 1985, pp.87 and 102–7; Hess, 1987, p.266).

not to place the flag and statue at the wall itself. Thus, for example, a nationally prominent journalist who had supported the war in Vietnam, visited the construction site, and described the experience:

> Gradually the long walls ... came into view. Nothing I had heard or written had prepared me for the moment. I could not speak. I wept ... This memorial has a pile driver's impact. No politics. No recriminations. Nothing of vainglory or of glory either. For twenty years I have contended that these men died in a cause as noble as any cause for which war was ever waged ... Never mind. The memorial carries a message for all ages: this is what war is all about ... On this sunny Friday morning, the black walls mirrored the clouds of a summer's ending and reflected the leaves of an autumn's beginning, and the names – the names! – were etched enduringly on the sky.
>
> (Quoted in Scruggs and Swerdlow, 1985, pp.129–30)

Similarly, an influential veteran wrote:

> I must admit that when I first viewed the artist's sketch, I was not impressed. In fact, I did not like the design, and sat at my desk to write a protest ... Last week I was in Washington on business and was fortunate enough to visit the construction site of the memorial. Although it is only half completed, its size and strength are awesome. One cannot comprehend the reality of this memorial by looking at artist's sketches. Nor can one feel the many emotions that arise on viewing the names.
>
> (Quoted in Scruggs and Swerdlow, 1985, p.130)

The memorial was completed and dedicated on 11 November 1982 in a ceremony that was attended by over 150,000 people and was marked by an intensity of emotion unusual in public events of this kind (Scruggs and Swerdlow, 1985, pp.151–5; Griswold, 1986, p.688).

The figurative statue was finally installed at the Vietnam Veterans Memorial two years later in November 1984. The work of the sculptor Frederick Hart, the statue consists of a portrayal of three young American servicemen, dressed in the combat uniforms that were characteristic of American forces in Vietnam and carrying weapons and ammunition. One is clearly white, another is black. The racial identity of the third is not made clear, but is probably intended to be Hispanic. The origins of the statue lay in a desire by conservative groups to secure a more conventional and heroic element within the Vietnam Veterans Memorial. Ironically, however, the resulting statue and its relationship to the Wall proved much more ambiguous than was intended or anticipated. The expression on the faces of the three men has been described as 'somewhat peculiar; they look stunned – more bewildered than heroic' (Hess, 1987, p.268). Another article observed, 'Here, then, is the realism that critics of the wall's

Figure 3.4 The dedication of the Vietnam Veterans Memorial in November 1982. Susan Meiselas/Magnum.

Figure 3.5 The Frederick Hart statue of three soldiers at the Vietnam Veterans Memorial. Vietnam Veterans Memorial Fund.

abstraction desired. Here is life – as opposed to the wall's expression of death – but it is life exhausted and confused' (Wagner-Pacifici and Schwartz, 1991, p.399). Moreover, the final location that was agreed for the statue – a location with which Hart agreed, recognizing that the Wall and his statue would clash if placed close together – resulted in an unanticipated element of pathos. The figures appear just to have emerged from the trees and to be contemplating the names on the wall. Maya Ying Lin – who, not surprisingly, had been deeply opposed to the proposal to place a flag and figurative statue in close proximity to her original design – observed of the final juxtaposition of the Wall and the statue that: 'In a funny sense, the compromise brings the memorial closer to the truth. What is also memorialised is that people still cannot resolve that war, nor can they separate the issues, the politics, from it' (quoted in Scruggs and Swerdlow, 1985, p.133; and in Hass, 1998, p.20).

The same ambiguity is even echoed in the inscription at the base of the flag. The inscription reads: 'This flag affirms the principles of freedom for which [the Vietnam Veterans] fought and their pride in having served under difficult circumstances.' The expression 'under difficult circumstances' is remarkable, for it is clear that it refers to the political context and moral disagreements over the war, even though this part of the memorial was added in response to demands for a more conventionally patriotic monument (Wagner-Pacifici and Schwartz, 1991, p.399). Writing in 1997, an architectural historian noted that most discussions of the Vietnam Veterans Memorial pay very little attention to the figurative statue. He then followed this precedent in his own discussion of the memorial, having concluded that 'interaction with these sculptures is largely peripheral to the fundamental experience of the Vietnam Veterans Memorial' (Ochsner, 1997, p.157).

A further figurative statue was added to the Vietnam Veterans Memorial in November 1993. After almost ten years of work to raise the funds and secure support – and after a prolonged struggle to secure approval from the relevant government agencies and the Commission of Fine Arts – the Vietnam Women's Memorial was dedicated. The names on the Wall include those of eight American women service personnel killed in Vietnam. Situated three hundred feet from the Wall in a grove of eight trees, the Women's Memorial portrays three women assisting a wounded soldier. One of the women chiefly responsible for the campaign to secure the addition of the Women's Memorial explained that, had Maya Ying Lin's original design stood alone, she would not have sought the addition of a further memorial specifically dedicated to women. It was the addition of the figurative statue of three servicemen that prompted her to

Figure 3.6 The Women's Memorial at the
Vietnam Veterans Memorial. Vietnam
Veterans Memorial Fund.

campaign for a memorial to focus and commemorate the particular
alienation experienced by women veterans of the Vietnam War[4]
(Hess, 1987, pp.275–6; Wagner-Pacifici and Schwartz, 1991, p.409;
Hass, 1998, pp.18–20).

Evaluating ambiguity: interpreting 'the Wall'

After all the controversies over its design, once it was dedicated in
November 1982 it was immediately clear that the Vietnam Veterans
Memorial was not merely extremely popular with the American
people, but was also a site of remarkable emotional and spiritual
power. As the discussion in the previous chapter demonstrated, 'the
Wall' – as the memorial quickly and affectionately came to be known

[4] On the particular types of alienation experienced by women who served in
Vietnam, see, for example, Palmer (1987, pp.125–31), Marling and Wetenhall
(1989), and Sturkin (1991, pp.130–1).

– rapidly established itself not merely as one of the most visited sites in Washington, but also as a place of personal pilgrimage, healing and reconciliation. Veterans and the families and friends of those named on the Wall devised their own personal rituals of remembrance and commemoration: touching the wall; leaving messages to the dead; leaving gifts of the most varied kinds.[5] The Wall has continued to function in these ways to the present, while the language of the 'sacred place', the 'shrine', and the 'hallowed' and 'reverential' space is commonly associated with the memorial. On the Internet, meanwhile, a 'Virtual Wall' offers visual access to any one of the marble panels and to the details of any one of the names recorded on the Wall. The same site offers the opportunity to read the personal remembrances and electronic messages left by individuals on any day since the inauguration of the Virtual Wall in 1998. And the literally thousands of personal responses to the Wall have given rise to published collections of messages, personal reminiscences and photographs. In addition to 'popular' anthologies such as these, however, the Wall has inspired an impressive number of academic studies and interpretations of its significance.[6]

Although particular interpretations inevitably differ in their details, it is a common feature of many scholarly studies of the Vietnam Veterans Memorial that the Wall surprises the visitor by its impact, draws the visitor into its space, and confronts the visitor with the need to respond at a personal and profound level. Thus, academic commentators on the Wall, no less than ordinary individuals making their personal pilgrimages to the Wall, tend to speak of the memorial in strikingly personal and intimate terms. One early academic commentator on the Wall began his analysis of the Vietnam Veterans Memorial with the autobiographical explanation that his reflections were provoked by a visit to Washington in which he had 'happened on' the Memorial 'almost by accident', only to find himself 'reduced to awed silence' (Griswold, 1986, p.688). Another scholar characterized the experience of visiting the memorial thus:

> For first-time visitors, even those who have no direct personal relationship to anyone whose name is on the wall, the power of the Vietnam Veterans Memorial usually comes as a surprise. One can

[5] For more detailed examples and discussion of the possible significance(s) of such personal rituals and actions, see the previous chapter, especially pages 86–96.

[6] The list of academic and scholarly articles and books on the Vietnam Veterans Memorial is both extensive and highly interdisciplinary. This chapter makes no attempt to survey or summarize the entire field. The examples chosen for consideration here are, however, broadly representative of the range and variety of scholarly interpretations of the memorial.

come on it almost without warning and then be led into its space. Because the path along the wall is paved only to a width of ten feet, one walks along the memorial, experiencing it sequentially and taking in the names only gradually. As the path descends, the number of names grows, however. For each visitor, there seems to be a point at which the immensity of more than fifty-eight thousand names becomes apparent. Suddenly, it seems that the distant abstraction of so many dead and missing has become very real. Here are fifty-eight thousand individual names – every one different, every one a real person who lived and died. Some visitors have probably heard about the peculiar power of the Vietnam Veterans Memorial from friends who have been there, yet no-one seems prepared for the way in which the memorial subverts the kind of distant attention that visitors bring to familiar tourist sites. At some point along our descent into the space, it is as if we are 'caught' by the memorial – or perhaps we suddenly catch on to what the memorial is about.

(Ochsner, 1997, p.161)

A third academic interpreter of the Wall observed that:

... each panel is longer than the last and cuts more deeply into the ground, so that you walk downhill towards the apex, at which point the black panels tower three or four feet above your head. At the centre you are half buried in a mass of names; pulled toward the black granite, you see yourself and the open lawns of the mall behind you reflected in the memorial. The centre of the monument is a strangely private, buffered public space. Literally six feet into the hillside you are confronted simultaneously with the names and with yourself. The black granite is so highly reflective that even at night visitors see their own faces as they look at the Wall ... This brilliant element of the design asks for a personal, thoughtful response ... The power of the design lies in the overwhelming presence of individual names, which represent complicated lives cut short. This attention to individual lives lost would not, however, be as potent if it were separated from the black expanse of all the names together, the effect of which is so overwhelming that it both foregrounds the individual names and hides them.

(Hass, 1998, pp.14–15)

But how do such academic interpreters of the Vietnam Veterans Memorial develop their understanding of the Wall and its significance? For the first of the scholars cited above, the principal functions of the memorial are simultaneously therapeutic and challenging. Thus, Charles Griswold argues that the memorial is therapeutic for individuals, for the community of veterans and the families of those killed, and for the American people as a national community. For individuals – whether veterans in search of dead comrades or families and friends in search of their own dead – the therapeutic function is clear, as the discussion of personal pilgrimage in the previous chapter showed. The finding of the name, the touching, the leaving of messages, the sense of communion, the sense of renewed contact with the dead, and of the dead finally having 'come home': all of these point clearly to the personal healing that may be found at the Memorial. For the community of veterans and families and friends of the dead, meanwhile, the Vietnam Veterans Memorial is therapeutic in its recognition and honouring of all the Americans who fought in the Vietnam War – as both the inscriptions on the Wall and the formal title of the memorial indicate. The original impulse behind the campaign to build a memorial to the Americans who fought in Vietnam was precisely the sense that, in the aftermath of a war that had bitterly divided the nation and ended in defeat, those who fought in Vietnam had never been properly recognized by the nation or welcomed home. Rather, they had been ignored or explicitly rejected as inconvenient reminders of an episode in American history that it was still too painful to recall and address. The Vietnam Veterans Memorial provided – and still provides – belated recognition of the service and suffering of the American men and women whose lives were transformed by the Vietnam War. The memorial is not heroic. It speaks principally of pain and of loss. Yet, without making any political or moral claim about the war, it also honours all those who served in it[7] (Griswold, 1986, pp.708–9).

Perhaps somewhat surprisingly, therefore, at the level of the national community Griswold also sees the Vietnam Veterans Memorial as a place where it is possible for Americans to rediscover a sense of patriotism. The memorial, he suggests, has an ability to engender declarations of patriotism. The dedication of the memorial in November 1982, which he attended, was in his view overwhelmingly patriotic in sentiment. Similarly, as even the briefest acquaintance with images of the gifts left at the Wall will amply confirm, among the thousands of highly varied items left there, American flags are prominent. The memorial, therefore, may facilitate expressions of belief in America and the values that individuals associate with their nation. And in recognizing and honouring the service and sacrifice of the *individuals* who served in Vietnam – without commenting on the rightness or wrongness of the war and its conduct – the memorial provides a point of national unity even for those who may still radically disagree about the Vietnam War. Indeed, it is precisely the

[7] On the depth of the sense of rejection and isolation experienced by Vietnam veterans on their return to the USA, and the extent to which the dedication of the Vietnam Veterans Memorial proved a decisive moment in the recognition and reversal of this process, see Scruggs and Swerdlow (1985, especially pp.139–56).

fact that the memorial is neutral about the merits or otherwise of the war itself that makes it possible for the service, sacrifice and suffering of individuals to become a source of patriotic sentiment (Griswold, 1986, p.712).

But for Griswold, the patriotism that the Vietnam Veterans Memorial makes possible – and indeed may even inspire – is also a critical patriotism, 'informed by the healthy willingness to question the decisions of the politicians of the day about where and when Americans should die for their country' (Griswold, 1986, p.713). Thus, the Vietnam Veterans Memorial is not merely therapeutic but also challenging – indeed, its therapeutic, healing potential is surely partly dependent on the way in which the memorial challenges and demands a response from those who encounter it. The questions it implies are, in Griswold's words, 'terrible questions: Did these individuals die in vain? Was their death in keeping with our nation's best traditions as symbolised by the nearby monuments [to Presidents Washington and Lincoln]? For what and when should Americans die in war?' (Griswold, 1986, p.711). Arguably, it is precisely because the Wall insistently poses these questions, but equally insistently refuses to offer its own explicit answers, that it functions so effectively as a means of healing at both the personal and the communal level. Thus, the essential ambiguity and openness of the Vietnam Veterans Memorial and its deeply-rooted refusal to 'tell viewers and visitors what to think' have also been noted by other scholarly commentators and interpreters (Foss, 1986; Carney, 1993).

Writing a decade and a half after the dedication of the Wall, Jeffrey Ochsner offers another consistently positive interpretation of the Vietnam Veterans Memorial. Ochsner addresses the questions of how and why the memorial engages the visitor, how it so insistently prompts active responses, and how its ability to touch the visitor should be understood. In answer to these questions, he argues that the memorial is a powerful example of 'a space of absence', a place 'in which we have the simultaneous experience of both the absence and the presence of the dead' (Ochsner, 1997, p.156).

Like Griswold, Ochsner recognizes that the memorial performs a vital healing process for the American people as well as for individuals. After the collective denial that accompanied the end of the war and the refusal to engage with the experiences and sufferings of veterans, the construction of the memorial in the heart of the capital, close to the Lincoln Memorial – itself a symbol of national reconciliation after the Civil War in the mid-nineteenth century – was a powerful symbol of recognition of the Vietnam veterans. The location of the memorial implied that it was to be a site of shared public mourning as well as of private grief. It affirmed that, in public and national life, as well as in thousands of personal lives, these deaths would not be forgotten (Ochsner, 1997, p.159). The building of the memorial thus performed the function of a national rite of passage. It was the equivalent of a national, collective, funeral or memorial service. Or, to borrow the language of popular horror films – though doing so to make an entirely serious point – by allowing America to confront the 'ghosts' of the Vietnam War, who had 'haunted' American consciousness because their deaths had never been properly acknowledged, the Vietnam Veterans Memorial integrated the 'living dead' into the historical memory, providing a proper burial and the mourning they were owed (Ochsner, 1997, p.160).

Thus it is that the names of the dead on the Wall are again identified as central to the power of the memorial. In particular, Ochsner focuses on the interaction between the intense individuality of each name – their 'quirkiness' and uniqueness – and the impact of the relentless number of names on the memorial: the realization that there are so many of them. 'The experience of incomprehensibility of the immense number of names against which the individuality of each is suddenly perceived is difficult to describe.' The abstract figures heard about in books, films and discussions of the Vietnam War are suddenly made concrete and the reality of the cost of human conflict is brought to life (Ochsner, 1997, p.161). At the same time, Ochsner suggests, the Vietnam Veterans Memorial creates 'a space of absence', a place whose 'overwhelming message is the absence of the dead person, no longer with us in life and yet somehow present within the aura of the monument'. Such places, he argues, may stimulate and rekindle the memories that keep the dead alive in the minds of those who mourn them, even to the extent that the dead may be experienced as, in some sense, alive again and present. Ochsner characterizes such experiences as 'the felt presence of the other' (Ochsner, 1997, p.163).

The design of the Vietnam Veterans Memorial facilitates such experiences, he argues, because it includes the unexpected and does not impose an explicit meaning on the visitor – again affirming the importance of ambiguity, of openness and of not telling the visitor what to think. The visitor to the Wall descends into a space set apart from the surrounding mall and monuments. Within that space apart, the intensely reflective polished black surface of the Wall exercises a crucial effect:

> Through the reflective surface we first find others and then ourselves in the wall. The simultaneity of vision of the names of the dead and missing, first with images of unknown others and then with ourselves,

could not be more direct in establishing an inter-personal connection
... We understand, not abstractly but rather directly, the common
human nature of those who are named and those who read the names.
The directness of proper names connects us; the reflective surface
superimposes our images on the names. Indeed, we not only see
ourselves superimposed on the names, we also see ourselves gazing
out from within the wall.

(Ochsner, 1997, p.164)

From this experience, the argument continues, there emerges a sense
of the connection between the living and the dead. The desire to
touch the Wall – and the reflection of one's own hand as the touching
is completed – further heighten and intensify the experience. Hence,
Ochsner concludes, the desire arises either to take a rubbing of one of
the names or to leave something at the Wall – or to do both. The
intensity of the encounter and the sense of connectedness with the
dead named on the Wall gives rise to the desire to express that
connection – that sense of the 'felt other' – and to preserve it in some
way. Even those who did not personally know anyone named on the
Wall may feel moved to make a rubbing on leave something behind[8]
(Ochsner, 1997, pp.165–6).

This particular theory of why the Vietnam Veterans Memorial
functions so effectively and powerfully may or may not prove
persuasive for any given reader. It is striking, however, that in at least
two respects it potentially illuminates – and perhaps goes some way
to explaining – characteristic aspects of the personal experiences of
many of those who visit war graves and memorials, whether as
pilgrims, as tourists who become 'accidental pilgrims', or as part of an
educational trip. As the previous chapter noted, two responses
commonly recur in attempts to describe the impact of personal
encounters with war cemeteries or memorials. On the one hand,
there is the same complex interaction between the awful weight of
accumulated names and the insistent individuality of particular
names that, for whatever personal reason, attract and focus the
attention of the visitor and make real the cost of human conflict. And
on the other hand, there is the frequently experienced desire to
communicate in some way with the dead, and the stubborn and

[8] This interpretation and explanation of the desire to communicate with the dead,
to take rubbings of names, or to leave gifts does not necessarily conflict with the
suggestion that the prevalence of such activities at the Wall derives partly from the
influence of Native American, African American, Italian American and Mexican
American traditions of mourning and commemoration, in which speaking with the
spirits of the dead and leaving items at graves are not uncommon (Hass, 1998,
pp.77–83 and 88). Both proposed processes might well contain an element of truth
and would, in that case, be likely to prove mutually supportive and interactive.

Figure 3.7 Visitors reflected in the Wall of the Vietnam Veterans Memorial. Susan Meiselas/Magnum.

persistent sense that, in some perplexing way, the dead are aware of this.[9] Perhaps, therefore, the Vietnam Veterans Memorial is by no means unique in its ability to create a 'space of absence', but is rather a most effective example of a more widespread phenomenon and experience.

Other scholarly and academic interpreters of the Vietnam Veterans Memorial have adopted a more negative tone in their response to the ambiguity of the memorial and are less persuaded by many of the positive claims made on its behalf. It is possible, for example, to reverse the argument about the deliberate refusal of the Vietnam Veterans Memorial to provide specific and explicit answers to the questions that it poses. Thus, in his study of the role and function of monuments to all kinds of incidents of violence in American history, Kenneth Foote emphasizes the limited nature of the national compromise achieved in the Vietnam Veterans Memorial. Writing a decade and a half after the dedication of the memorial, he concedes that it is 'one of the most evocative shrines ever erected by Americans', and that it has served an 'important cathartic, healing function' for its hundreds of thousands of visitors and for the nation as a whole. But he sees the memorial, nevertheless, primarily as a symbol of the still unresolved meanings of the Vietnam War, rather

[9] See the previous chapter, especially pages 77–9 and 89–96.

than as a focus for a broader reconciliation based precisely on acceptance of the inevitable ambiguity and unresolved tension over the war, mixed with agreement to honour and remember the individuals who died in Vietnam (Foote, 1997, pp.314–17).

This theme had previously been explored at some length both in an article by sociologists Robin Wagner-Pacifici and Barry Schwartz, published in 1991, and also in another by historian Daphne Berdahl, published in 1994. The former article drew attention to the degree of conflict and ambivalence that was involved in almost every aspect of the Vietnam Veterans Memorial and its history. It emphasized, for example, the way in which the deliberate attempt to honour the dead but avoid comment on the cause for which they died simply perpetuated American divisions over the Vietnam War. Noting that the dedication ceremony for the memorial had included the invocation, 'Let the Memorial begin the healing process and forever stand as a symbol of our national unity', the authors remarked that this rhetoric in fact expressed an ideal, not a reality (Wagner-Pacifici and Schwartz, 1991, p.378). They noted, for example, that among the thousands of items left at the Wall, the object most frequently left is a small American flag beneath a name that the visitor wishes to mark. 'Through this offering', the authors assert, 'visitors uttered a political statement that was not supposed to be made. They asserted their patriotism, their loyalty to a nation.' The authors go on to note that almost a third of the objects left at the Wall are military in origin – insignia, dog-tags, bits of uniform and medals, for example. These too, they argue, constitute a clearly political and patriotic statement:

> Designed to draw attention to the individual and away from the nation and its cause, the Memorial's wall turns out to be a most dramatic locus of patriotic feeling. The wall's use moved it toward that traditional war monument genre that opponents and supporters alike once believed it deviated from.
>
> (Wagner-Pacifici and Schwartz, 1991, p.405)

Yet, the authors continue, the memorial does still transcend the traditional war monument because patriotism is not the only response that it excites. It also functions as 'a kind of debating forum – a repository of diverse opinions about the very war that occasioned its construction'. The letters, poems and messages left at the Wall articulate diverse reactions to and opinions about the war. More than half of these are classified by the authors as 'ambivalent or negative'. The specific examples that they cite include such items as a note from a veteran (classified as 'an obviously alienated correspondent') which reads simply, 'Still don't know why? Think you guys may be better off.' Another example cited was a letter from a soldier

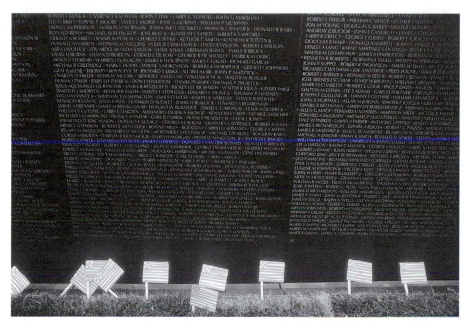

Figure 3.8 American flags left at the Vietnam Veterans Memorial. Susan Meiselas/Magnum.

written from Vietnam in 1968. All the news, he said, was bad. He hoped that if he made it through his remaining 71 days in Vietnam he would never go back there. The letter was left with a note of the location of the soldier's name on the Wall (Wagner-Pacifici and Schwartz, 1991, pp.405–6).

For these two interpreters, therefore, the Vietnam Veterans Memorial remains essentially a paradox. It is the war memorial that is most visited and revered by Americans; but it is a memorial to those who fought in the least prestigious and most controversial of America's wars. Americans, therefore, assemble at the Vietnam Veterans Memorial 'with more gravity than is displayed at shrines commemorating any other war', yet the rituals 'do not resolve historical controversies; they only articulate them, making their memory public and dramatic'. The Vietnam Veterans Memorial, on this view, is essentially an expression of contradiction, not of unity (Wagner-Pacifici and Schwartz, 1991, pp.407 and 416–17).

A similar emphasis on the unresolved and still contested nature of the Vietnam Veterans Memorial and its significance characterizes the analysis of the memorial by Daphne Berdahl. She begins by acknowledging that the memorial has come to be understood as 'a national healing shrine', which prompts a multitude of personal responses to its 'stark, haunting beauty'. She affirms the power of the names and of Maya Ying Lin's design, and she reviews the controversies over the design and its realization (Berdahl, 1994, pp.88–94). She then focuses on the diversity revealed in the responses to the Wall. The dedication of the memorial, Berdahl argues, marked the beginning of 'an explosion of personal narratives' and established the 'centrality of individual histories in the memorial's discourse' (Berdahl, 1994, pp.94–6). She recognizes – and cites moving examples of – the range and variety of personal narratives that are played out at the Wall, either in ritual actions or in the leaving of gifts and messages. She accepts that such actions and acts of remembrance possess deeply personal and healing significances for the individuals involved. In addition, however, Berdahl argues that the individual narratives and voices that are articulated at the Wall collectively constitute a popular history of the national experience of the Vietnam War and its significance. She notes that the items left have become more carefully prepared. They are meant to be kept and preserved. The National Park Service increasingly receives enquiries from people who want to make sure that their offerings have been added to the collection. Similarly, the characteristic actions of people at the Wall frequently show signs of conforming to established patterns, precedents and rituals. The process of visiting and experiencing the memorial may be said to have developed an almost 'liturgical' quality. The memorial and the experience of visiting it have become associated with a particular range of ritual actions and reactions, a process fostered by the widespread and continuing media interest in the Wall and its status as a national shrine (Berdahl, 1994, pp.105–6 and 114–17).

If, however, narratives and voices articulated at the Wall constitute a popular history of the national experience of the Vietnam War, both the national experience involved and the history that is articulated remain sharply contested. For Berdahl, the Vietnam Veterans Memorial is a fundamentally contested site – because the personal narratives told there are so divided and contradictory. Through the thousands of personal stories that it prompts and attracts, the memorial quickly became – and still remains – a 'site of resistance' that contests any single official interpretation of the war and its meaning. Far from producing a 'fixed consensual memory of Vietnam', the variety of individual histories and biographies articulated at the Wall 'construct and reconstruct public memory and history of the Vietnam War and its aftermath in the United States' (Berdahl, 1994, pp.107–11 and 117). As a particular example of the unresolved contradictions in the opinions expressed at the Wall, Berdahl cites the tenth anniversary of the dedication of the memorial in 1992 – an occasion that produced such a multiplicity of opinions and contrasting styles of behaviour that it has been described as 'a deeply schizophrenic public event' (Hass, 1998, p.108). Held on Veterans Day 1992, the event included music that ranged from 'New Age' to popular patriotic songs, country songs, bagpipes and military bands. Veterans were prominent among those present and there were many American flags – but some veterans also carried banners or wore T-shirts that protested over the issue of prisoners still believed to be held in Vietnam and ignored by the American government, or about the effects on veterans of Agent Orange, a defoliant used widely in the Vietnam War that has subsequently damaged or destroyed the health of many veterans. The speeches given ranged from affirmation of the enduring value and worth of the war, despite the defeat, to condemnation of the war as senseless and brutal. The characteristic response of the crowd was to applaud both interpretations. There were, therefore, no clear codes about what it meant to be a veteran, to be patriotic or to stand by your nation. There was as much rage at the government as there was pride. There was certainly patriotism – but it was often a complicated, 'conflicted' patriotism that affirmed the veterans, perhaps even the war, yet protested against the government (Hass, 1998, pp.108–12).

Scholarly discussion of the Vietnam Veterans Memorial thus ranges from a celebration of its ability to provide a focus of healing for individuals, for groups and for the American people within the context of a self-critical patriotism, to the insistence that the memorial is essentially an expression and focus of the continuing disunity within the USA concerning the Vietnam War and its legacy. In the present context, however, it remains to ask how the Wall and these varying interpretations of its role and function for contemporary Americans relate to the concept of 'civil religion'?

The Vietnam Veterans Memorial and civil religion in America

It is clear that the Vietnam Veterans Memorial is fundamentally ambiguous and ambivalent about the Vietnam War. It offers no official political statement about the war or its meaning – or lack of meaning. It was always intended as a memorial to those who served in the war, not to the war itself. Indeed, the founder of the Vietnam Veterans Memorial Fund, himself a veteran of the war, has even conceded that:

> ... the memorial is kind of an anti-war statement. It is not an anti-Vietnam War statement, but a kind of universal statement on war. I think it really focuses on the tragedy of the loss of individual lives. I do not think, nor have I ever thought, that the memorial makes a political statement about that particular war.
>
> (Quoted in Berdahl, 1994, pp.93–4)

Similarly, a Park Service volunteer who works at the Wall summed up the statement made by the memorial: 'The memorial says: this is the price we pay. It doesn't say whether it was right, it doesn't say whether it was wrong, it doesn't say whether it was worth it or not. It simply says "this is the cost of war"' (quoted in Berdahl, 1994, p.94).

At the same time it is quite clear that the memorial *is* a place that evokes patriotic sentiment and feeling. And it is also a place that prompts the expression of a wide variety of feelings and opinions about the war. It is less clear that a simple line can be drawn between 'patriotism' and 'protest'. Former anti-war activists have left messages at the Wall expressing respect for the individuals whose names are engraved on it. Conversely, veterans of the war have echoed the view that it is an 'anti-war memorial' – such as the man who attended a Veterans Day ceremony holding a sign that read: 'I am a Vietnam veteran. I like the memorial. And if it makes it more difficult to send people into battle again, I'll like it even more' (quoted in Hass, 1998, p.17).

It is also surely too simple to view military items, such as identity tags, medals, insignia or old uniforms, as straightforwardly or unambiguously 'patriotic'. To do so ignores the possibility that they may imply other more subtle meanings as well. To leave such an item may represent a leaving behind – a letting go – of the past; it may be an expression of solidarity with an ex-comrade, yet without patriotic overtones; or it may even be a laying down and relinquishing of a once patriotically regarded symbol. As one commentator on the possible significance of items left at the Wall observed, 'Perhaps relinquishing these reminders of war is a means of release or maybe a gesture of appreciation for a fallen comrade. According to one veteran, leaving something at the Wall was a way to connect with his friends whose names he found there' (Powell, 1995, p.9). The leaving of American flags is also open to more than a simplistically patriotic interpretation. It is surely conceivable that a flag left at the Wall may be essentially a mark of respect or remembrance, expressed through the nation's flag, yet without implying uncritical acceptance of the nation's policies and actions in the Vietnam War. Unless the concept of a 'critical patriotism' is regarded as an impossibility, surely an American flag placed at the foot of the Vietnam Veterans Memorial is open to interpretation primarily as an act of personal remembrance, or an affirmation that there are still national values worthy of respect *despite* the nation's past policies.

If such a concept is allowed, however, then the Vietnam Veterans Memorial may plausibly be interpreted as a striking contemporary expression of 'American civil religion'. Measured against the characteristics of a civil religion proposed by Richard Pierard and Robert Linder,[10] the Vietnam Veterans Memorial arguably emerges as an expression of American civil religion that is at once subtle and powerful. Despite the continuing divisions within the USA over the Vietnam War and its legacy, and despite the fact that the Vietnam Veterans Memorial provides a focus for the continuing expression of those divisions, the memorial also, in fact, fosters a widespread acceptance of a shared sense of the nation's history and destiny in relation to the Vietnam War. What is shared is a sense of loss and pain. What is also shared is the very sense of division over the war. The memorial provides a place where a shared history of bitter division and national trauma can at last be addressed in the context of a 'national healing shrine' – even if the divisions are not yet resolved (or perhaps ever will be). The memorial also relates the American experience of Vietnam to what Pierard and Linder call 'a realm of absolute meaning'. The almost 60,000 names on the Wall insistently pose to Americans the question of the value of individual lives measured against the values and causes for which their nation chooses to go to war.

Perhaps most importantly, however, the Vietnam Veterans Memorial provides a symbol of unity – supported by a 'sacred place' and a set of popularly devised rites, rituals and symbols – that transcends internal conflicts and fosters a larger unity. Despite the continuing diversity of the responses to the Vietnam War expressed at the Wall and reflected in the particular messages left there, the overwhelming fact remains that, once built and dedicated, the Vietnam Veterans Memorial immediately became a place of popular pilgrimage for millions of Americans. The intense and bitter controversies that preceded the building and dedication of the memorial did not continue. That it does not impose a single meaning on those who visit it does not therefore mean that it cannot and does not function as a unifying symbol. As one of the early interpreters of the memorial observed, the monument serves 'the vital function of getting people "to remember together"; the remembering alone, because it is shared by the group, affirms a kind of social unity beneath the manifold diversities of contemporary communities' (Howett, 1985, p.9).

[10] See the Introduction, pages 5–6.

It is also worth reflecting once again that when Robert Bellah explored the concept of an 'American civil religion' in 1967, he did so in the context of the Vietnam War and the rise of American opposition to that war. Bellah sought and hoped for a prophetic form of American civil religion that would provide the basis for the criticism of American values and policies, not merely the celebration of them (Bellah, 1967). His original article was an attempt to show that the values and principles of American civil religion required opposition to the war in Vietnam. Bellah subsequently withdrew from the discussion of the concept of American civil religion, frustrated by those who insisted that 'civil religion' was by definition uncritical and idolatrous in its endorsement of the state. But the Vietnam Veterans Memorial does not glorify the war that it commemorates. It does not impose a particular, official meaning or interpretation of the war on those who visit it. Instead, it invites and inspires the expression of diverse interpretations and evaluations of the Vietnam War. Indeed, it has even been suggested that 'the immense sorrow of the place ... enables other private rituals, of repentance. It is one of the few war memorials ... that allows, yet does not force, repentance for our part in the war as well as honour for those who died' (Sellars and Walter, 1993, p.189). In the light of such comment, it is, perhaps, not entirely fanciful to see in the Vietnam Veterans Memorial a belated expression of the critical, prophetic style of civil religion that Bellah advocated.

Whether, in the long term, the Vietnam Veterans Memorial will continue to play such a remarkable role as a 'national shrine' and prompt so much comment and attention from scholars and academics is necessarily an open question. As the authors of one of the more critical and questioning analyses of the memorial have commented,

> A day will come when the names that appear on the Vietnam Memorial's wall are known to few living persons ... the intensity of feeling evoked by the wall will be less acute; the flags and objects that decorate the wall will be less dense; the solemnity that now grips those who enter the Memorial site will be diluted by an air of casualness; the ritual relation that now links shrine and pilgrim will become a mundane relation that links attraction and tourist.
>
> (Wagner-Pacifici and Schwartz, 1991, pp.417–18)

Perhaps this will happen, although the evidence of the extent to which, over 80 years after the end of the conflict, the memorials and cemeteries of the First World War continue to exercise a fascination and influence that exceeds mere tourism, might suggest that this judgement may one day require qualification. It is possible that the Vietnam Veterans Memorial will also exhibit a similar capacity to transmit its haunting questions and its reverential quality across generations. It is also possible, however, that the remarkable intensity of the reactions to 'the Wall' during the first two decades of its existence will prove, after all, to have been a peculiar feature of the years in question.

Should this indeed prove to be so, it is possible that the reasons will not be limited solely to the particular intensity of the national processes of mourning and healing that were prompted by the dedication of the Wall in 1982, or to the fact that such processes were initially suppressed for so long. It may also be the result of the further transformation of the area of the Mall in Washington. There is little doubt that part of the impact of the Vietnam Veterans Memorial lies in its location in the long area between the Lincoln Memorial and the Washington Monument. The very success of the Vietnam Veterans Memorial, however, prompted calls for the introduction of other war memorials in the Mall. In July 1995, on the forty-second anniversary of the armistice that ended the war in Korea between 1950 and 1953, a Korean War Veterans Memorial was dedicated. Later that year, on Veterans Day, a site on the Mall was also dedicated for the construction of a national memorial to all Americans who served in the Second World War. The groundbreaking for the construction of the National World War II Memorial was begun in a ceremony on Veterans Day 2000.

The Korean War Veterans Memorial combines realistic statues of American servicemen in Korea with a polished black granite wall that reflects the statues and displays faces – taken from actual photographs of unidentified servicemen in Korea – etched into its surface. A Pool of Remembrance, encircled by trees, completes the memorial. Numbers of killed, wounded, missing and prisoners-of-war are etched in a nearby stone, opposite which is another granite wall with the inlaid words, 'Freedom Is Not Free' (Highsmith and Landphair, 1995). Two acres in size – as is the Vietnam Veterans Memorial – the Korean War Veterans Memorial is relatively discreet and does not fundamentally transform the Mall.

By contrast, the design for the National World War II Memorial is far more ambitious and will have a much greater impact and presence on the Mall. It has been allocated a seven and a half acre site – almost four times the size of the other two war related memorials on the Mall. It will be situated prominently, 'below' and 'in front' of the Washington Monument, facing towards the Lincoln Memorial at the other end of the Mall. It will thus stand at the east end of the long Reflecting Pool that runs the length of the section of the Mall between the Washington Monument and the Lincoln Memorial. Indeed, the proposed design of the National World War II Memorial will involve the redesign of the east end of the Reflecting Pool and its incorporation within the new memorial. The National World War II Memorial will also be highly traditional and classical in design. It will share the white marble and classical appearance of the Lincoln Memorial and the Washington Monument, and it will evoke the architectural style of the Memorial Amphitheatre in Arlington National Cemetery (where the Tombs of the American Unknown Soldiers are located) rather than the less conventional designs of the memorials to the Korean and Vietnam veterans. Supporters of the design argue that, given the size of the Mall as a whole, the National World War II Memorial will not significantly affect the overall appearance of the area. Critics of the design complain that it will be one of the largest monuments in the city and that it will fundamentally change the ethos and appearance of the Mall. It will also include an unambiguous affirmation of the moral rightness of America's participation in the Second World War. The explanation of the design states that it will be 'An inviting and welcoming place to celebrate the American spirit that brought victory of democracy over tyranny, light over darkness. It will also be a place for quiet contemplation of the sacrifices made in a common and just cause.' As to the specific location of the memorial, the same source explains that there is no more appropriate place to recognize 'the triumph of democracy over tyranny than directly in line with the other national symbols of our democratic ideals: the Capitol, the Washington Monument, and the Lincoln Memorial'.[11]

When the National World War II memorial is completed, the Mall will have become the site of three major memorials to the wars that America fought in the middle decades of the twentieth century. It will no longer contain a single ambiguous and ambivalent memorial to the cost of one particular, controversial war. Will the peculiar critical and questioning impact and the remarkable therapeutic healing function of the Vietnam Veterans Memorial retain their power when 'the Wall' is only one among three war memorials, the largest of which will be strikingly conventional in appearance and design? Will the Wall still be a unique 'hallowed national shrine', which expresses American civil religion in a critical, prophetic manner — its effect

---

[11] This quotation is taken from the 'Design' section of the web page devoted to the National World War II Memorial. It may well be thought entirely appropriate that a memorial dedicated to those who served in the Second World War should be characterized in this way. In the present context, however, the utterly unambiguous nature of the intended meaning of the memorial and its explicit association with the Washington Monument and the Lincoln Memorial stand in particularly stark contrast to the deliberate and calculated ambiguity of the design and meaning of the Vietnam Veterans Memorial.

perhaps even enhanced by the contrast with the other memorials? Or will that effect be blunted and dulled, and the transition from shrine to tourist attraction hastened, by the inclusion of the Vietnam Veterans Memorial within a larger complex of monuments and memorials that collectively celebrate an American civil religion of a more conventional and less critical kind?

References

Bellah, R. (1967) 'Civil religion in America', *Daedalus*, 96, pp.1–21.

Berdahl, D. (1994) 'Voices at the Wall: discourses of self, history and national identity at the Vietnam Veterans Memorial', *History and Memory*, 6, pp.88–124.

Carney, L. (1993) 'Not telling us what to think: the Vietnam Veterans Memorial', *Metaphor and Symbolic Activity*, 8, pp.211–19.

Edmonds, A. (1998) *The War in Vietnam*, Westport, Connecticut: Greenwood Press.

Foote, K. (1997) *Shadowed Ground: America's Landscapes of Violence and Tragedy*, Austin: University of Texas Press.

Foss, S. (1986) 'Ambiguity as persuasion: the Vietnam Veterans Memorial', *Communication Quarterly*, 34, pp.326–40.

Griswold, C. (1986) 'The Vietnam Veterans Memorial and the Washington Mall: philosophical thoughts on political iconography', *Critical Inquiry*, 12, pp.688–719.

Hass, K. (1998) *Carried to the Wall: American Memory and the Vietnam Veterans Memorial*, Berkeley: University of California Press.

Hess, E. (1987) 'Vietnam: memorials of misfortune', in R. Willimas (ed.) *Unwinding the Vietnam War: From War into Peace*, Seattle: The Real Comet Press, pp.262–80.

Highsmith, C. and Landphair, T. (1995) *Forgotten No More: The Korean War Veterans Memorial Story*, Washington DC: Chelsea Publishing.

Howett, C. (1985) 'The Vietnam Veterans Memorial: public art and politics', *Landscape*, 28, pp.1–9.

Marling, K. and Wetenhall, J. (1989) 'The sexual politics of memory: the Vietnam Women's Memorial Project and "the Wall"', *Prospects*, 14, pp.341–72.

Ochsner, J. (1997) 'A space of loss: the Vietnam Veterans Memorial', *Journal of Architectural Education*, 50, pp.156–71.

Palmer, L. (1987) *Shrapnel in the Heart: Letters and Remembrances from the Vietnam Veterans Memorial*, New York: Vintage Books.

Powell, L. (1995) *Hunger of the Heart: Communion at the Wall*, Dubuque Iowa: Islewest Publishing.

Scruggs, J. and Swerdlow, J. (1985) *To Heal a Nation: The Vietnam Veterans Memorial*, New York: Harper & Row.

Sellars, R. and Walter, T. (1993) 'From Custer to Kent State: heroes, martyrs and the evolution of popular shrines in the USA', in I. Reader and T. Walter (eds) *Pilgrimage in Popular Culture*, London: Macmillan, pp.179–200.

Sturken, M. (1991) 'The Wall, the screen, and the image: the Vietnam Veterans Memorial', *Representations*, 35, pp.118–42.

Wagner-Pacifici, R. and Schwartz, B. (1991) 'The Vietnam Veterans Memorial: commemorating a difficult past', *American Journal of Sociology*, 97, pp.376–420.

Wells, T. (1994) *The War Within: America's Battle over Vietnam*, Berkeley: University of California Press.

Internet sources consulted

http://www.nps.gov/kwvm/home.htm – the official web site of the United States National Park Service, Korean War Veterans Memorial page.

http://www.thewall-usa.com/ – a site dedicated to the Vietnam Veterans Memorial run by the Vietnam Veterans Association. It offers access to a variety of commemorative activities and sites.

http://www.vvmf.org/ – the official web site of the Vietnam Veterans Memorial Fund.

http://www.wwiimemorial.com/ – the official web site of the organization dedicated to the construction of the American National World War II Memorial.

http://www.themovingwall.org./ – the web site of the group who first began taking a moving replica of the Vietnam Veterans Memorial around America in 1984.

CHAPTER 4

'Dedicated to the Virgin': civil religion and Sienese devotion to the Madonna

The Italian city of Siena is located in southern Tuscany, some 50 kilometres south of Florence. Contemporary Siena has a population of between 65,000 and 70,000 people. The city – and the population – is divided internally into seventeen distinct and clearly defined districts or neighbourhoods, called '*contrade*'.[1] Each *contrada* carefully cultivates a sense of its own history and identity. The members of each *contrada* share personally in this sense of identity and are fiercely loyal to their own *contrada* as well as to the city of Siena as a whole. It is the seventeen *contrade* that compete in the Palio – the twice-yearly festival that culminates in a horse race around the central piazza of Siena and for which modern Siena has become famous. In the following chapters, it will be argued that the Palio constitutes a vibrant modern and contemporary expression of Sienese civil religion. Such contemporary Sienese civil religion has its roots, however, in much older traditions and versions of Sienese civil religion, dating back as far as the thirteenth century, and centred on a centuries-long Sienese devotion to the Virgin.

The aim of this chapter is to explore the status and significance of the Virgin in Sienese civil religion. It will do so in four stages. First, it will examine the origins and history of Sienese devotion to the Virgin from the twelfth century onwards, including successive dedications of the city to the Virgin between the thirteenth and sixteenth centuries. Second, it will examine the most recent rededication of the city to the Virgin in June 1944, locating this within the context of the deliberate and self-conscious revival of many aspects of Sienese civil

---

[1] A list of the Sienese words and terms that are used in this and the following chapters, together with brief definitions, appears on pages 273–4.

religion during the early decades of the twentieth century. The third section of the chapter will focus on the bronze door – known as the 'Porta della Riconoscenza' – which was donated to Siena cathedral in 1946 in thanks for the city escaping destruction during the Second World War. It will be shown that the door is both a modern expression of Sienese civil religion and a celebration of the history of Sienese civil religion in past centuries. The concluding section of the chapter will consider the role of the Sienese *contrade* and the Palio in relation to this particular expression of modern Sienese civil religion and its commemoration since the 1940s.

The 'myth of Montaperti' and the development of Sienese civil religion

The civil religion of modern and contemporary Siena is, of course, by no means the same as the civil religion of Siena in the medieval, renaissance or early modern periods. Inevitably, Sienese civil religion – like any other religious tradition – has changed over the centuries of its existence. At the same time, one of the most remarkable characteristics of modern and contemporary Sienese civil religion is precisely the extent to which it deliberately and self-consciously draws on the traditions of earlier eras. Indeed, it is no exaggeration to say that in many ways – as both this chapter and Chapter 6 will seek to show – it is impossible to understand many of the details of contemporary Sienese civil religion without first understanding the development of Sienese civil religion from the thirteenth to the early eighteenth centuries. Therefore this section will outline the development of Sienese civil religion during these centuries.

The existence of a special devotion to the Virgin on the part of the Sienese can be traced securely to at least the twelfth century. By then the high altar of the cathedral in Siena was dedicated to the Virgin – a dedication that may well have continued a tradition first established in the early tenth century. In the early thirteenth century, the entire cathedral then became dedicated to the Virgin of the Assumption (van der Ploeg, 1993, p.66; Norman, 1999, pp.3 and 215). From as early as 1200, the cathedral was the location for an annual procession – known as the Corteo dei Ceri e dei Censi ('The Procession of Candles and Tributes') – in which the Sienese brought candles in tribute to the Virgin on the feast dedicated to the tradition of her bodily assumption into heaven. At the same feast, the subject territories of the Sienese state also brought candles, banners and other tributes, both to demonstrate their own devotion to the Virgin and to renew their submission to, and acceptance of, Sienese rule (Falassi and Catoni, 1982, p.60; Webb, 1996, p.256; Norman, 1999, p.3). In 1252, moreover, an image of the Virgin appeared on a new Sienese civic seal, together with an inscription expressing the wish that she should preserve the city (Webb, 1996, pp.255 and 269; Norman, 1999, pp.4 and 215). Clearly, therefore, the roots of a special relationship between the people and community of Siena and the Virgin lie firmly in the period before the dramatic events that surrounded the battle of Montaperti in 1260.

It was the events of early September 1260, however, that transformed the already existing Sienese devotion to the Virgin into a fully-fledged civil religion centred on the Virgin and the belief in a special relationship between her and Siena. The accounts of the events of 2–4 September 1260, given in Sienese chronicles of the fourteenth and fifteenth centuries, are both detailed and dramatic.[2] They are also crucial for the subsequent development of Sienese civil religion, while the story of Montaperti is one to which the Sienese repeatedly return in later moments of their history. Indeed, it is no exaggeration to say that the myth of Montaperti provides the foundation of subsequent Sienese civil religion. For this reason it is essential to know the traditional narrative of Montaperti in some detail.

The longstanding rivals of Siena, the Florentines, had gathered a large army, far outnumbering that of Siena, and had advanced deep into Sienese territory. They presented the Sienese with an ultimatum calling for the immediate surrender of their city and the acceptance of Florentine rule. The ruling council of Siena met in the church of San Cristoforo and resolved to fight. They agreed to elect a leader who would have full power over Sienese affairs for the duration of the crisis and chose for this office a man of renowned good character called Buonaguida Lucari. While the secular authorities debated in the church of San Cristoforo, the bishop of Siena assembled the local

---

[2] The principal chronicles concerned are: Cronaca senese di autore anonimo del secolo XIV; Cronaca senese conosciuta sotto il nome di Paolo di Tommaso Montauri; and La Sconfitta di Montaperti secondo il manoscritto di Niccolò di Giovanni Francesco Ventura. The first two are available in printed form in Lisini and Iacometti (1931–9), and the latter in Porri (1844). Early printed histories by Sienese antiquarians also provide important testimony to the way in which the Sienese recalled and commemorated Montaperti, notably those by Malavolti, originally published in 1599; Tommasi, originally published in 1625–6; and Gigli, originally published in 1717 and 1723. For details of modern editions of these works see the references for this chapter. The history and authenticity of the chronicles are very complex issues – as will be discussed, briefly, below on pages 139–41. For a recent summary and interpretation of the various chronicle accounts in greater detail, see Koenig (1998).

clergy in the cathedral and called on them to pray to the Virgin and the saints that Siena might be saved from the Florentines. The bishop then led the clergy, barefooted, in procession around the cathedral, singing psalms and prayers.

Lucari, meanwhile, addressed the council and the crowd of Sienese gathered in the square outside the church. He called on them to give themselves, their goods, their city and their territory to the Virgin. He then stripped to his shirt, placed a rope around his neck, and led a procession, bareheaded, barebacked and barefoot, through the streets to the cathedral, praying to the Virgin as they went. At the cathedral they joined the bishop and the clergy. Lucari and the bishop knelt before the high altar, on which stood a painted image of the Virgin, while the people continued to pray and lament. Lucari, standing in front of the image of the Virgin, addressed her as 'Queen of Heaven', 'Mother of Sinners' and 'Aid of the Afflicted', and proclaimed: 'I, most miserable and unfaithful of sinners, give, donate, and concede to you this city of Siena and all its *contado* [territory], with all its rights and jurisdictions, and as a sign of this, I place the keys of the city of Siena on this altar.' Lucari asked the Virgin to accept the keys of the city and in return to protect Siena from all who would occupy, oppress or destroy it. The bishop then preached a sermon in which he called on the Sienese to unite and forgive each other, to confess their sins, take communion, commend their city to the Virgin, and join the clergy in a great procession. The resulting procession – led by a large, much-venerated wooden cross and an image of the Virgin – visited the main sites of the city and ended once more at the cathedral. Here the bishop blessed the keys of the city and returned them to Lucari, who gave them back them to the civic officials.

The next day, the Sienese army left the city to prepare to confront the Florentines. They chose as their principal battle standard the banner of the section of Siena called 'Camollia'. This was a huge banner of white silk, which the Sienese regarded as a symbol of the Virgin's pure white cloak with which she traditionally shielded those who sought her protection. Meanwhile, the bishop led those who remained in the city in further devotions to the Virgin for her help and protection, processing through the city, stopping at all the shrines and churches, and carrying relics from the cathedral and other churches. The Sienese army camped opposite the Florentines near the hill of Montaperti, just to the north-east of Siena. According to the chronicle accounts, during the night of 3–4 September, a white cloud was seen over the Sienese camp. Among the Florentines there was disagreement as to the nature of the cloud: some said it was the smoke of the Sienese campfires, others that it was the cloak of the Virgin. For the Sienese there was no such doubt or debate: it was, indeed, a miraculous expression of the Virgin's favour and protection. On 4 September, the Sienese won a remarkable and overwhelming victory over the Florentines, defeating them so completely that they captured the Florentine *carroccio* – the huge war cart on which the Florentine standards were placed – and took thousands of prisoners. The following day the victors returned to Siena in triumph, bringing with them the Florentine *carroccio* and prisoners.

For historians, the principal difficulty with the various accounts of the events of Montaperti is that they all date from periods long after the events that they purport to describe. Although it is entirely possible that these chronicles may have drawn on much earlier – perhaps even contemporary – sources, the actual texts on which the myth of Montaperti is based date from the late fourteenth and the first half of the fifteenth centuries (Webb, 1996, p.253). By this time the events had already assumed a mythic status for the Sienese and had become much more than merely an important moment in Sienese history. According to Sienese tradition, they already constituted the defining moment for the continuing Sienese belief in the special relationship that existed between themselves, their city and the Virgin.

It is clear that the various chronicle accounts of the myth of Montaperti should not be read uncritically or simply taken at face value. The narratives become increasingly detailed and specific the further removed from the events they are – a circumstance that, in itself, should give rise to an appropriate scepticism concerning the accuracy of many of the more specific details in the later accounts (Raveggi, 1995, p.89; Webb, 1996, p.253). Some historians even suggest, therefore, that it should be assumed that most of the story surrounding the battle of Montaperti – and certainly most of the detail of that story – was made up or extensively elaborated in the fourteenth and fifteenth centuries, including the account of the donation of the keys of the city to the Virgin (Garrison, 1960a; 1960b; Heal, 2000). Similarly, it has been suggested that later authors deliberately increased the role assigned to the Virgin in 1260, and that the decisive growth in the civic cult of the Virgin occurred in the early fourteenth century rather than in the decades immediately after Montaperti (Heal, 2000).

Other historians have been much less sceptical and have simply accepted that, however uncertain many of the details may be, the battle of Montaperti was, at the very least, the occasion for a new and special dedication of the city to the Virgin (Bowsky, 1981, pp.160 and 274–5; Waley, 1991, p.139). Yet others have recently re-examined various aspects of the historical records surrounding the myth of Montaperti, and have subjected the sources to careful critical scrutiny.

Taken together, their work suggests that a persuasive case can, indeed, be made for there having been a special donation and dedication of the city to the Virgin in 1260, thus initiating a new phase in the development of Sienese civil religion – even if many of the precise details of the story remain questionable. For example, on 8 September 1260, just four days after the battle, the inhabitants of Montalcino – a town to the south of Siena that had set aside its allegiance to Siena and sided with the Florentines at Montaperti – made an act of resubmission to Siena. The Montalcinese assembled in the Campo – the main piazza in Siena – in front of the victorious Sienese *carroccio,* to make their re-submission, and the document recording this act refers to 'Mary ever Virgin, who is defender and governor of this city'. But the terms 'defender' and 'governor' were not applied to the Virgin in earlier texts recording the submissions of subject cities to Siena – thus suggesting that the events before Montaperti had involved an increase in, and an enhancement of, the Virgin's official status and role in relation to Siena. Moreover, unlike the chronicle accounts of Montaperti, the document describing the submission of the Montalcinese is a contemporary one (Webb, 1996, pp.259–60).

Similarly, a number of requirements in the official Sienese government statutes issued in 1262 – just two years after the battle – reflect the commemoration of Montaperti and link this to honouring the Virgin. These statutes required the city government to pay for a lamp to burn day and night in front of the victorious Sienese *carroccio* – 'in honour of God and the blessed Virgin Mary' – and for two large candles to burn continuously in front of the altar of the Virgin in the cathedral. In addition, the city government undertook to provide a site for a chapel in honour of God, the Virgin, and the saints on whose day the victory of Montaperti had been won (Hook, 1979, p.126; Webb, 1996, p.257). New coins issued by the Sienese government after 1260 also suggest the attribution of a new status and role for the Virgin in relation to Siena. Thus the traditional inscription on Sienese coins since the late twelfth century, SENA VETUS ('Ancient Siena'), was replaced by coins bearing the inscription 'SENA VETUS CIVITAS VIRGINIS' ('Ancient Siena, City of the Virgin') (Koenig, 1998, pp.27 and 58).

The historical credibility of the chronicle narratives has been assessed positively by comparing the accounts of the various processions, acts of penitence and pleas for the Virgin's assistance recorded in these narratives with similar accounts found in the histories of other medieval cities and communities. The specific rituals, processions, actions, prayers, and even modes of dress, of both the clergy and the laity of Siena – and of both men and women –

as described in the principal chronicle accounts of Montaperti, can be shown to resemble closely similar rituals described elsewhere in medieval Italy when communities sought deliverance from particular crises (Koenig, 1998). Finally, the history of the sequence of paintings of the Virgin that were placed, successively, on the high altar of Siena cathedral during the late thirteenth and early fourteenth centuries points, yet again, to the importance of the events of 1260.

There is a broad – though not complete – consensus among art historians that the painted image of the Virgin that was on the altar in 1260 was a panel showing a somewhat austere portrayal of the Virgin in a frontal pose, with the Christ Child on her lap (van Os, 1984, pp.12–17; Norman, 1999, pp.28–9). Known as the *Madonna degli occhi grossi* ('Madonna of the Big Eyes'), this painted panel can now

Figure 4.1 Early thirteenth century, *Madonna degli occhi grossi*, Museo dell'Opera del Duomo, Siena. Foto Lensini, Siena.

Figure 4.2 Guido da Siena, *c.*1270s, *Madonna del Voto*, Siena cathedral. Foto Lensini, Siena.

be seen in the museum located next to Siena cathedral. There is a similar consensus that, sometime after the battle of Montaperti, probably in the late 1260s or early 1270s, the *Madonna degli occhi grossi* was replaced on the high altar of the cathedral by a new image of the Virgin. By then, the cathedral had been substantially redesigned and a new high altar installed – thus a new, more contemporary and less austere painting of the Virgin would have been an appropriate addition, as well as a further expression of thanks and celebration for the victory of Montaperti. The new painting, attributed to the Sienese artist Guido da Siena, again showed the Virgin holding the Christ Child, but it presented a more human and emotional image (van Os, 1984, pp.17–19; Norman, 1999, pp.29–30). The new painting was known as the *Madonna del Voto* ('Madonna of the Vow') and, as we shall see, became the focus for further rededications of the city to the Virgin in later moments of crisis. Today the *Madonna del Voto* can still be seen in the Cappella del Voto, a chapel in the cathedral built in the mid-seventeenth century especially to house this image.

The *Madonna del Voto* remained on the high altar of Siena cathedral until 1311, when it was replaced by a huge and double-sided altarpiece by the Sienese painter Duccio di Buoninsegna. The front face of Duccio's new altarpiece portrayed the Virgin, seated on a throne and with the Christ Child on her lap, surrounded by saints and angels. In the foreground there appeared four saints – Ansano, Savino, Cresenzio and Victor – who were Siena's subsidiary patron saints. They were portrayed on the altarpiece kneeling before the Virgin and gesturing towards her in prayer on behalf of Siena. On the step beneath the Virgin's throne appeared the painted inscription: 'Holy mother of God be the cause of peace for Siena' (Norman, 1999, pp.21–5, 37–41). Nor was this altarpiece the only such image of the Virgin painted for the Sienese at this time. Within five years, one wall of the room in the Palazzo Pubblico – the Sienese town hall – in which the ruling council of medieval Siena met was decorated by a fresco painting by Simone Martini of the Virgin similarly enthroned and surrounded by saints, with Siena's four subsidiary patron saints again placed prominently in the foreground and appealing to the Virgin (Norman, 1999, pp.48–58).[3]

Taken together, therefore, the evidence – the language used in the official resubmission of Montalcino to Siena, the provisions of the Sienese statutes of 1262, the new inscriptions on Sienese coins, the details of the rituals and prayers in the accounts of the events before Montaperti, and the appearance of the sequence of paintings that adorned the high altar of the cathedral – strongly supports the view that the Sienese indeed intensified their relationship with the Virgin on the eve of the battle of Montaperti. However, it is also clear that the myth of Montaperti and the enhanced place of the Virgin in medieval Sienese civil religion did not immediately assume its full stature in 1260. On the contrary, it was consciously developed and elaborated by the Sienese over the succeeding decades and centuries. In particular, it has been pointed out, it was between the mid-fifteenth and the mid-sixteenth centuries that the Sienese self-consciously retold and fully developed the myth of Montaperti, and similarly developed the image of the Virgin as the heavenly protectress of Siena in their works of art. Thus, it was in the mid-fifteenth century

---

[3] Most of the surviving parts of the high altarpiece by Duccio can be seen today in the Museo dell'Opera del Duomo, situated next to Siena cathedral. The fresco by Simone Martini remains on the wall of the room now known as the Sala del Mappamondo in the Palazzo Pubblico.

Figure 4.3 Duccio di Buoninsegna, *c.*1308–11, *Maestà*, Museo dell'Opera del Duomo, Siena. Foto Lensini, Siena.

Figure 4.4 Simone Martini, c.1315–21, *Maestà*, Sala del Mappamondo, Palazzo Pubblico, Siena. Foto Lensini, Siena.

that Niccolò di Ventura composed his influential chronicle version of the events surrounding Montaperti and added painted illustrations to his text. It was also in this period that the image of the Virgin, in the act of protecting the city, became a frequent subject for the elaborate painted covers that were made for the annual account books of the Sienese government (Webb, 1996, pp.264–5; Borgia *et al.*, 1984). Moreover, the Sienese repeated the dedication of their city and the donation of its keys to the Virgin on no less than four occasions between 1483 and 1555. However, it is significant that this was precisely the period during which Siena's power and influence steadily declined to the point at which its existence as an independent city state was first threatened and then came to an end (Webb, 1996, pp.263–8 and 310–12).

Figure 4.5 Painted cover for Sienese civic accounts, 1480: the Virgin commends Siena to the care of Jesus. Foto Lensini, Siena.

By the mid-fifteenth century, Siena had begun a period of slow but inexorable decline. The balance of political and economic power within Tuscany had already shifted decisively towards Florence, which enjoyed the economic advantage of being on a major river, whereas Siena was not. Florence, moreover, determinedly pursued a policy of aggressive territorial expansion. Siena, meanwhile, suffered from increasing internal divisions and rivalry between factions and thus from political instability. At the same time, the city and its territories were regularly threatened and weakened by the attacks of powerful bands of mercenary soldiers (Hook, 1979, pp.160–3 and 172–9; Pertici, 1995; Caffero, 1998). The first rededication of Siena to the Virgin and redonation of the keys of the city to her occurred in 1483, and reflected these circumstances. With the city facing a particularly acute political crisis, the civic authorities went in procession to the cathedral. In the presence of the archbishop, they rededicated their city to the Virgin and placed the keys of the city on an altar in the south aisle of the cathedral, on which stood the *Madonna del Voto*. By the mid-fifteenth century, this altar had become a popular shrine, although popular tradition had by then confused the *Madonna del Voto* with the image that had been on the high altar in 1260 for the original dedication of the city to the Virgin. As a result, the *Madonna del Voto* had assumed great status in popular devotion as the image that had saved Siena at Montaperti. The rededication of 1483 was commemorated in the scene depicted on the painted cover for the Sienese city accounts for that year (Borgia *et al.*, 1984, p.184; Webb, 1996, p.310).

The second rededication of the city and redonation of the keys to the Virgin took place in 1526, when Siena was threatened with conquest by the combined armies of Florence and the Pope which had advanced to the northern city gate, the Porta Camollia. Again, the city authorities processed to the cathedral and repeated the gift of the keys to the Virgin in front of the *Madonna del Voto*. Subsequently, the Sienese defeated the attacking armies in a battle that came to be seen as a 'second Montaperti', and in which, according to Sienese legend, the Virgin again cast her cloak over Siena in the form of a cloud (Heywood, 1899, pp.77–8). The act of rededication and the subsequent victory were again commemorated on painted covers for the city accounts (Borgia et al, 1984, pp.226–9).

Within a quarter of a century, however, Siena faced a new and greater crisis. In 1550, the circumstances of Italian and European power politics resulted in Siena being occupied by Spanish troops of the Holy Roman Emperor, who began to build a fortress to dominate the city. Again, the civic authorities repeated the now familiar ritual, processed to the cathedral and rededicated the city to the Virgin in

Figure 4.6 Painted cover for Sienese civic accounts, 1483: the offering of the keys of Siena to the Virgin in the cathedral to save Siena from internal divisions. Foto Lensini, Siena.

front of the *Madonna del Voto* – which on this occasion had been brought from its altar in the south aisle of the cathedral and placed once more on the high altar. On this occasion, the Sienese had to wait until 1552 before they regained the independence they desired, for only then did the Spanish forces leave after a successful rebellion by the Sienese. In 1554, however, the imperial forces returned, supported by the Florentines. Thus began the final epic siege that was to end Siena's existence as an independent republic. Towards the end of the siege, in March 1555, the Sienese again rededicated their city to the Virgin according to the established ritual. This time, however, the deliverance that they sought did not come about. The

Figure 4.7 Painted cover for Sienese civic accounts, 1526: the offering of the keys of Siena to the Virgin in the cathedral of Siena before the battle of Camollia. Devonshire Collection, Chatsworth. Reproduced by permission of the Duke of Devonshire and the Chatsworth Settlement Trustees. Photographic Survey Courtauld Institute of Art.

Figure 4.8 Painted cover for Sienese civic accounts, 1526: the Sienese victory at the battle of Camollia. Foto Lensini, Siena.

Figure 4.9 Painted cover for Sienese civic accounts, 1552: the Virgin blesses the demolition of the fortress built at Siena by the Spanish. Foto Lensini, Siena.

city was forced to surrender in April 1555 – although a group of Sienese retreated to the south and set up a Sienese republic in exile at Montalcino which lasted until 1559.[4] The Sienese explained the Virgin's failure to protect them this time by referring to the incident of 'the useless mouths'. In order to save food for the defenders as the siege tightened, the Sienese had sent women and children out of the city. The besieging forces had killed them. The Virgin, the Sienese rationalized, had withdrawn her favour and protection because of this act (Heywood, 1899, pp.79–95; Hook, 1979, chapter 9; Landi, 1994; Pellegrini, 1995).

After the fall of Siena – and despite the failure of the Virgin to save them during the siege – the Sienese remained devoted to the Virgin. Indeed, within 40 years of the final defeat of the independent republic, the Sienese had added a new popular cult of the Madonna to the annual cycle of their devotion to the Virgin. For many years, a terracotta bust of the Virgin, located between two windows of a

---

[4] For the way in which this republic in exile is still commemorated in the historic parade before each Palio, see Chapter 5, p.198.

house in Via dei Provenzani, had been regarded popularly as possessing miraculous powers. The bust was, according to popular legend, originally set up in the fourteenth century by Saint Catherine of Siena. In 1594, Siena was threatened by both famine and plague, and the Sienese once again proposed to seek the protection of the Virgin through renewed devotion to the image of the *Madonna del Voto*. But on this occasion they were unable to do so, because the current archbishop was in conflict with the other cathedral authorities, and access could not be gained to the *Madonna del Voto* within the cathedral. So the city authorities processed, instead, to the terracotta Madonna of Provenzano. The cult of the Madonna of Provenzano now became so popular that it was agreed to build a new church to house this revered bust of the Virgin. The project was begun in 1594–5 and completed in 1611, when the Madonna of Provenzano was installed above the high altar of the new church of Santa Maria di Provenzano, where it remains to this day. The flowering of this new cult, from the civic procession of 1594 to the installation of the bust in the new church in 1611, was again portrayed in a series of painted covers for Sienese civic accounts dating from these years (Borgia *et al.*, 1984, pp.286–7, 294–5, 300–1 and 304–5; Leoncini, 1994, pp.156–8; Bonelli, 1999). The feast of the Madonna of Provenzano was celebrated on 2 July each year, the date that became – and still remains – the occasion of the July Palio, the rituals of which are closely connected with the cult and church of Provenzano.[5]

Alongside the rise of the cult of the Madonna of Provenzano, however, the Sienese remained devoted to the image of the *Madonna del Voto*, and in the mid-seventeenth century a new chapel was built in the cathedral specifically to house this revered image. The altar in the south aisle of the cathedral on which the *Madonna del Voto* had stood for many decades was destroyed in a reorganization of the cathedral, and between 1659 and 1662, a new chapel was built in the right transept. Designed to house the *Madonna del Voto*, it was paid for by Alessandro Chigi, a member of a prominent and wealthy Sienese family, who had become Pope in 1655, taking the papal name of Alexander VII (Proto Pisani, 1979, pp.49–52; Butzek, 2001). In 1699, the new chapel was the location for another act of civic devotion to the Virgin, when the civic authorities presented the archbishop of Siena, Leonardo Marsili, with a silver

---

[5] For the place of the July Palio within the history and traditions of the Palio as a whole, see Chapter 5.

Colour Plate 1 Drappellone *for the Palio of 5 September 1954. Won by the Contrada del Leocorno. Foto Lensini, Siena.*

Colour Plate 2 Drappellone *for the Palio of 4 September 1960. Won by the Contrada della Civetta. Foto Lensini, Siena.*

Colour Plate 3 Drappellone *for the Palio of 2 July 1962. Won by the Contrada della Selva. Foto Lensini, Siena.*

Colour Plate 4 Drappellone *for the Palio of 16 August 1996. Won by the Contrada del Bruco. Foto Lensini, Siena.*

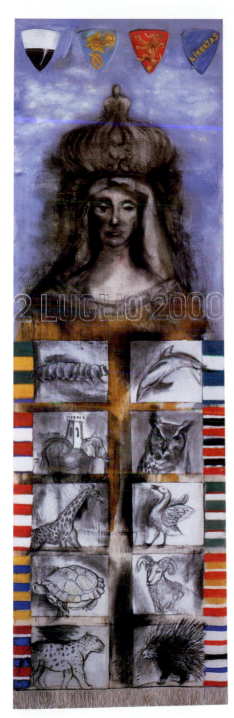

Colour Plate 5 Drappellone *for the Palio of 2 July 2000. Won by the Contrada dell'Istrice. Foto Lensini, Siena.*

Colour Plate 6 Drappellone *for the Palio of 16 August 2000. Won by the Contrada del Leocorno. Foto Lensini, Siena.*

Colour Plate 7 Drappellone *for the Palio of 9 September 2000. Won by the Contrada della Selva. Foto Lensini, Siena.*

Colour Plate 8 The banner of the Magistrato delle Contrade. Foto Lensini, Siena.

Colour Plate 9 The church of the Contrada della Lupa. Foto Lensini, Siena.

Colour Plate 10 The Sala della Vittoria of the Contrada del Nicchio. Foto Lensini, Siena.

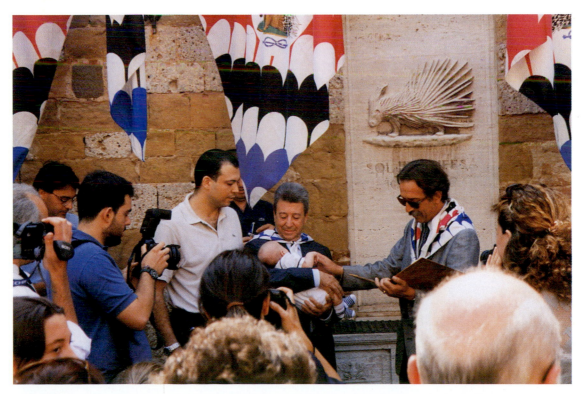

Colour Plate 11 A moment during the annual contrada *baptism in the Contrada dell'Istrice. Photo: Gerald Parsons.*

Colour Plate 12 *A detail from the Corteo Storico. The* tamburino *of the* Contrada di Valdimontone *leads the* comparsa *of his* contrada *in the Campo. Foto Lensini, Siena.*

Colour Plate 13 *A detail from the Corteo Storico. The* paggio maggiore *of the* Contrada della Pantera *with the banner of his* contrada. *Foto Lensini, Siena.*

Colour Plate 14 *A detail from the Corteo Storico. The two* alfieri *of the Contrada di Valdimontone performing a display with their* contrada *flags. Foto Lensini, Siena.*

Colour Plate 15 A detail from the Corteo Storico. The carroccio carrying the drappellone around the Campo at the end of the historic parade. Foto Lensini, Siena.

Colour Plate 16 The winning jockey of the Palio of September 2000 is carried from the Campo on the shoulders of members of the victorious Contrada della Selva. Foto Lensini, Siena.

Colour Plate 17 The rejoicing moments after the end of the Palio of July 1997. The flags of the victorious Contrada della Giraffa as well as flags of other contrada are waved in celebration – some because their rivals did not win, others because they are allied to the Giraffa. Foto Lensini, Siena.

Colour Plate 18 A celebration in Siena cathedral after the victory of the Contrada del Bruco in the Palio of August 1996. Foto Lensini, Siena.

Colour Plate 19 The drappellone *for the Palio of August 2000 on display in Siena cathedral after being blessed. Photo: Gerald Parsons.*

Colour Plate 20 A drappellone *for the Palio of August 1998 next to the altar in the church of the victorious Contrada del Nicchio in the days after the Palio. Photo: Gerald Parsons.*

Figure 4.10 Painted cover for Sienese civic accounts, 1592–5: the civic authorities of Siena kneel before the image of the Madonna of Provenzano and vow to build a church for the image. Foto Lensini, Siena.

Figure 4.11 Painted cover for Sienese civic accounts, 1601–4: the bust of the Madonna of Provenzano, venerated by saints Bernardino and Catherine of Siena. Foto Lensini, Siena.

Figure 4.12 Painted cover for Sienese civic accounts, 1610–13: the translation of the Madonna of Provenzano into the new church of Santa Maria di Provenzano. Foto Lensini, Siena.

statue of the Virgin and Saint Ansano,[6] who was holding the city in his hands. The statue was a votive offering in thanksgiving to the Virgin for having saved Siena from a series of devastating earthquakes which had threatened the city between mid-September and mid-December 1697. The earthquakes had stopped just short of the Porta Camollia.

In 1704 the civic authorities again reaffirmed Sienese devotion to the Virgin by introducing another annual celebration of her role as patron and protectress of Siena. Henceforth, every 22 September, the feast of the 'Madonna del Patrocinio' was to be celebrated in the fifteenth-century chapel inside the Palazzo Publicco (Falorni, 2000, pp.131–2). In the early seventeenth century, the works of the Sienese scholar Girolamo Gigli also provided both a catalogue and a celebration of Sienese devotion to the Virgin. In *La Città diletta di Maria* (1716), Gigli described in great detail the many different Marian devotions of the Sienese, past and present. In his 'Diary',

[6] Saint Ansano was an early Chistian martyr who, according to tradition, had first converted the Sienese to Christianity.

Figure 4.13 The Cappella del Voto. Foto Lensini, Siena.

meanwhile, published in 1723, the year after his death, Gigli listed the
religious devotions and festivals associated with each day of the year
in Siena, thereby drawing attention to the sheer number and variety
of annual Sienese celebrations of the Virgin.

Sienese devotion and dedication to the Virgin thus survived the
trauma of their defeat and loss of independence in the mid-sixteenth
century. It was not until the mid-twentieth century and the crisis of
the Second World War, however, that a further rededication of the city
took place.

Civil religion reaffirmed: June 1944

In late May and June 1944, Siena faced an imminent and formidable crisis. After the fall of Monte Cassino, north of Naples, to the Allied forces on 17/18 May, and the Allied entry into Rome in early June, the front line between the retreating German army and the advancing Allied armies moved inexorably closer to Siena, bringing with it the threat of the possible destruction of much of the city, either by aerial bombardment or as a result of fighting within Siena itself. The Sienese fear of such destruction was by no means unreasonable. To the north of Siena, the cities of Pisa and Florence and the towns of Empoli and Poggibonsi had already suffered severe damage and casualties as a result of Allied bombing (Paoletti, 1994, pp.20–1, 25, 36 and 47). Moreover, Siena had suffered air raids by American bombers in January, February and April 1944. In the first – and the worst – of these, on 23 January, twenty-four people were killed, and the fifteenth-century church of the Osservanza, located on the north-eastern outskirts of Siena on a hill overlooking the city, was destroyed in a raid probably aimed at the railway station (Ciabattini, 1991, pp.200–1; 1997, pp.75–9; Paoletti, 1994, pp.26–7 and 32; Socini Guelfi, 1994, pp.6–7).

Strenuous efforts had been made by a variety of authorities to save Siena from destruction by securing for the city the status of an agreed 'hospital city', recognized by all parties to the conflict and thus mutually respected as a non-military location which would neither be defended nor attacked. These initiatives were principally the work of the archbishop of Siena, Mario Toccabelli, the mayor of Siena, Luigi Socini Guelfi, and the Fascist head of the province of Siena, Giorgio Alberto Chiurco, but they also received the support of Gerhard Wolf and Ludwig Heydenreich, respectively the German Consul in Florence and the German official responsible for the protection and preservation of the artistic patrimony of Tuscany. However, despite all such efforts and the diplomatic activity of the papacy and the Vatican – with which Archbishop Toccabelli enjoyed close and influential contacts – Siena never received formal or official recognition as a 'hospital city' either from the Allies, the Germans, or the continuing Italian Fascist government in the north (Paoletti, 1994; Ciabattini, 1997; Parsons, 2001, pp.154–6).

June 1944 was a month of great anxiety and fear for the Sienese. Further Allied bombs fell on Siena on the evenings of the 8th, 9th and 12th of the month, causing several deaths, destroying the glass in the church of San Francesco and damaging the nearby seminary and other buildings (Giorgio, 1985, p.24; Socini Guelfi, 1994, p.15). As the

German and Italian Fascist forces retreated, moreover, the fear arose that fighting might occur within Siena or that the city might yet be defended by the Germans and consequently bombarded by the Allies. In the end, this did not occur. As the Fascist authorities left the city, the mayor, in co-operation with the local Committee for National Liberation, organized the formation of a civil guard to maintain order in the city until the arrival of the Allied forces, and successfully negotiated the final stages of the withdrawal of the remaining German troops (Paoletti, 1994, pp.52–6; Socini Guelfi, 1994, pp.10–19; Ciabattini, 1997, pp.145–80). Thus, when French colonial troops entered Siena from the south by the gateway known as the Porta San Marco at dawn on 3 July 1944, they discovered the city to be undefended. By 7.30 that morning, Allied forces had occupied the city and the Sienese had welcomed them into the Campo with the flags of the *contrade*. The *contrade* also displayed their flags at the boundaries of their territories, rang the bells of their churches, and celebrated with dancing and singing until late into the night (*Il Campo*, a local Sienese newspaper, 1–2 July 1945, pp.2–3; Lucchini, 1987, p.267).

It was during the final days before the liberation of Siena that the Sienese once again formally dedicated their city to the Virgin. In addition to his diplomatic endeavours on behalf of Siena through his contacts with the Vatican, Archbishop Toccabelli had continued to exercise his pastoral and spiritual oversight of Siena during the critical period between the declaration of the armistice between Italy and the Allies on 8 September 1943, and the liberation of Siena in early July 1944. Indeed, as early as 1 August 1943, as the annual celebration of the festival of the Assumption of the Virgin approached, Archbishop Toccabelli had called on the Sienese to make a special renewal of their devotion to the Virgin. On the front page of *Il Popolo di Siena*, the local Catholic weekly newspaper, he invited the Sienese to reaffirm their devotion and piety, to commit themselves to saying the rosary together as families every day until the end of the war, and to renew their dedication to the Virgin by writing their names on pages that would be bound into a book. The book would then be placed in the Cappella del Voto – as the seventeenth-century chapel built by Pope Alexander VII had become known – by the altar above which hung the image of the *Madonna del Voto*. The entire appeal appeared beneath the dramatic headline, 'O Maria, la tua Siena difendi' ('O Mary, defend your Siena'), the first line of the chorus of a popular Sienese hymn to the Virgin.

In suggesting that the Sienese should rededicate themselves to their traditional patron saint, Toccabelli was building on a broader revival of Sienese civil religion that had been actively promoted since the 1920s both by successive archbishops of Siena and also by the civic authorities of the city. In the 1920s, Toccabelli's predecessor as archbishop, Prospero Scaccia, had sought to foster traditional Sienese religious devotions and, in particular, had encouraged renewed celebration of the feasts of saints Ansano, Catherine of Siena and Bernardino[7]. Archbishop Toccabelli continued this strategy, which culminated in June 1939 with the proclamation of Catherine of Siena as patron saint of Italy. After the entry of Italy into the Second World War in 1940, Toccabelli regularly issued pastoral letters to the Sienese, dedicated to saints Catherine, Bernardino and Ansano. He also reintroduced devotion to the cult of the right arm of John the Baptist (a much prized relic in the possession of the Sienese church) and regularly emphasized renewed devotion to the cult of the *Madonna del Voto* (Bocchini Camaiani, 1994, pp.75–7 and 86–7). The civic authorities and the *contrade* of Siena also contributed to this process by assisting in the restoration of two traditional rituals of Sienese civil religion which had been abandoned in the 1860s, after the unification of Italy, as the Sienese celebrated their place within the new national state. Thus, in 1924, the traditional Corteo dei Ceri e dei Censi (see pp.136–7) was reintroduced as part of the celebration of both the feast of the Assumption and the Palio of mid-August, having been in abeyance since 1864 (Grassi, 1972, vol.1, pp.39–40, vol.2, p.36; Mirizio, 1993, pp.648–9; Parsons, 2001, p.164).[8] Similarly, in 1928, the mayor of Siena, Fabio Bagagli Petrucci, reintroduced the annual celebration of the feast of the Patrocinio di Maria, held in the fifteenth-century chapel in the Sienese town hall each 22 September. This annual event had also been in abeyance since the 1860s (Falorni, 2000, pp.131–2).

It was also the civil authorities that, in June 1944, made the specific proposal for a formal rededication of the city to the Virgin. Archbishop Toccabelli recorded in his diary on 13 June 1944 that, as the situation in Siena became increasingly critical following the bombing that month, the mayor suggested that it would be an

---

[7] Catherine of Siena was a local saint of the mid-fourteenth century; Bernardino was a local saint of the early fifteenth century.

[8] For a further summary of the significance of this annual procession in the history of Sienese devotion to the Virgin and in the history of the Palio, see also Chapter 5, pp.194–6.

opportune time to rededicate Siena to the Virgin, again consigning the keys of the city to her, as had been done in previous crises in the city's history (article in *La Voce del Popolo*, 22 September 1974, p.4).[9] For some time Toccabelli had been celebrating mass each morning in the cathedral in front of the *Madonna del Voto*, and each evening he led public Marian devotions in the Cappella del Voto, at which he informed those present of the latest news of the war. He now readily agreed to the mayor's suggestion and devised an order of service for the proposed rededication, which was to take place five days later on the evening of Sunday 18 June, after the regular evening devotions in the Cappella del Voto (*La Voce del Popolo*, 25 August and 22 September 1974; Mori, 1994). Meanwhile, on 17 June, the mayor issued notices announcing the intention of the civic authorities to follow the example of their forerunners and renew both their vows and the donation of the keys of the city to the 'Venerable Image of the Madonna del Voto, Queen of Siena' (Ciabattini, 1997, p.159; Mumm, 2002, reading 3.12.

The rededication duly took place. The mayor and other civic authorities, with civic banners and trumpets, accompanied by the Rector of the Magistrato delle Contrade,[10] Count Guido Chigi Saracini, the Priors of the seventeen *contrade* together with pages carrying the flags of the *contrade*, and a large crowd of ordinary Sienese citizens, processed from the Palazzo Pubblico to the cathedral, carrying with them a small wooden urn containing the symbolic keys of the city. At the cathedral, the archbishop led a litany to the Virgin, after which the mayor read out an 'Act of Donation' rededicating Siena to the Virgin. The mayor placed the urn containing the symbolic keys of the city (and also containing a copy of the Act of Donation (see Figure 4.18) on the altar of the *Madonna del Voto*, and the ceremony closed with a Marian prayer, the singing of the traditional Sienese Marian hymn 'Maria, Mater Gratiae',[11] and a

---

[9] Archbishop Toccabelli's diary has not yet been published in a full edition. Extensive extracts were, however, published in the Sienese catholic newspaper *La Voce del Popolo* in 1974, in celebration of the thirtieth anniversary of Toccabelli's role in the preservation of Siena during 1944. The full text of the diary remains in the archives of the Sienese archdiocese.

[10] The Magistrato delle Contrade is the organization that represents the collective interests of all seventeen of the Sienese *contrade*.

[11] The hymn in question is popularly referred to as a 'Te Deum', but this is not literally the case. A 'Te Deum' is a Latin hymn to God, whereas the hymn sung by the Sienese is a Latin hymn to the Virgin, called, from its first line, 'Maria Mater Gratiae'. It has, however, been called 'the true Te Deum of the Sienese' (Falassi, 1996, p.107). The text and music of 'Maria Mater Gratiae' are reproduced in De Cristofaro (1988, pp.7 and 24–5).

blessing by the archbishop. After the official ceremony, the assembled crowd sang – according to one source, 'at first softly and then vigorously' – the popular Sienese hymn to the Virgin:

> Volgi un guardo, celeste Regina,
> Alla nostra città a Te diletta ...
> O Maria, la Tua Siena difendi,
> Per lei prega benigna il Signor!
> [Direct a look, heavenly Queen,
> At our city that delights You ...
> O Mary, defend Your Siena,
> Pray benignly to the Lord for her!][12]

The archbishop's diary entries for the next few days contain frequent references to continuing expressions of Sienese devotion to the *Madonna del Voto* – notably through pilgrimages to the Cappella del Voto by different parishes and sections of the city (*La Voce del Popolo*, 6 and 27 October 1974). On 3 July he recorded the liberation of the city.

Civil religion commemorated: the Porta della Riconoscenza

In the entries in his diary in the days and weeks immediately following the liberation of Siena, Toccabelli referred more than once to proposals to embellish the cathedral with bronze doors in thanksgiving for the salvation of the city. On 23 July, he recorded his own proposal that, in order to express their personal gratitude, all the Sienese should put an image of the *Madonna del Voto* in their houses. He then noted that the side entrance to the cathedral, located beneath the campanile – and hence near to the Cappella del Voto which housed the image of the *Madonna del Voto* – was to be given a bronze door donated by a wealthy and influential Sienese aristocrat, Count Guido Chigi Saracini (*La Voce del Popolo*, 12 January and 16 March 1975).

Progress on the proposed door was rapid. In his diary entry for 5 August 1944, Toccabelli recorded that, at 5.30 in the evening, he went to see the model for the door with Chigi Saracini, Vico Consorti, the sculptor chosen for the project, Professor Pèleo Bacci, the recently retired Superintendent of Sienese Artistic Monuments who had

[12] The principal accounts of the rededication are found in *La Voce del Popolo* (22 September 1974, p.4), Socini Guelfi (1994, pp.13–14), and the text of the Act of Donation itself. For the detail concerning the singing of 'Maria, la tua Siena difendi', see Tailetti (1972, p.80).

Figure 4.14 Siena cathedral, showing the façade and Porta della Riconoscenza beneath the campanile. Foto Lensini, Siena.

advised on the historical context and details of the door, and Piero Valiani, a senior official of the influential Sienese bank, the Monte dei Paschi (*La Voce del Popolo*, 1 June 1975). Two years later, on 16 August 1946, the bronze door was installed. Replacing the old wooden door to the entrance to the south aisle of the cathedral, near to the Cappella del Voto, the Porta della Riconoscenza – as the new door came to be called – was formally inaugurated and blessed by Archbishop Toccabelli, in the presence of representatives of the civic authorities and the *contrade*, and in front of a crowd that included many who had been present two years earlier at the rededication of the city to the Virgin (*La Voce del Popolo*, 15 and 24 August 1946; Tailetti, 1972, p.84; Falassi, 1992, p.8).

The Porta della Riconoscenza (literally 'the door of gratitude' or 'the door of thankfulness') consists of four main rectangular panels. Each panel depicts an occasion on which the Virgin was believed to have shown her favour to Siena and saved the city in a moment of crisis and danger. Above each main panel appears a smaller oblong panel showing an allegorical scene relevant to the particular threat facing Siena at the time of the scene depicted immediately below. Beneath the main panels are four more oblong panels, each of which displays a date, in Roman numerals, which refers to the scene

Figure 4.15 Vico Consorti, the Porta della Riconoscenza, Siena cathedral, 1946. Foto Lensini, Siena.

Figure 4.16 Vico Consorti, *The Dedication of Siena to the Virgin before Montaperti*, detail of the Porta della Riconoscenza, Siena cathedral, 1946. Foto Lensini, Siena.

depicted in the main panel to which it is related. Across the entire width of the top of the door, there is an inscription indicating that the donor was Guido Chigi Saracini, while on the left- and right-hand sides of the door, a sequence of Chigi Saracini coats of arms and emblems, together with the family motto, form a tall and narrow border framing the whole door (Parsons, 2001, p.163).

The first main panel in the sequence, on the top left-hand section of the door, portrays the story of the first donation of the keys of Siena to the Virgin before the battle of Montaperti in September 1260. Following the version of the events surrounding the battle recorded in the mid-fifteenth century chronicle by Niccolò di Ventura, the panel shows the figure of Buonaguida Lucari approaching the high altar of the cathedral and presenting the keys of the city to an image of the Virgin. Lucari, barefoot, barebacked and with a rope around his neck in penitence, is surrounded by soldiers. The bishop of Siena appears on the left, next to the altar. On the altar is an image of the Virgin which is clearly intended to be a depiction of the *Madonna degli occhi grossi* (see pp.141–2). Above this scene, the smaller allegorical panel shows the hill of Montaperti – with its distinctive modern appearance, surmounted by a circle of cypress trees – together with a representation of the struggle between good and evil, in the form of an angel, hovering protectively above Montaperti, and a dragon recoiling from the angel (Bacci, 1946, pp.25–8). The depiction of the hill of Montaperti on the allegorical panel may echo a detail in the decoration at the top of the 'Act of Donation' read out by the mayor at the rededication of June 1944. The main feature of the decoration on the Act is a detailed depiction of Siena, viewed from the south – as it would have appeared to the advancing Allied forces. Just to the right of the city, and thus notionally to the east and therefore mirroring the geographical location of Montaperti, appears a hill, crowned with cypresses, which may be intended as a reference to this location.

The portrayal of an angel confronting a dragon may also refer to a detail in the myth of Montaperti. The traditions surrounding Montaperti – both in the later chronicle accounts and in more

Figure 4.17 Vico Consorti, *Allegory of the Struggle between Good and Evil*, detail of the Porta della Riconoscenza, Siena cathedral, 1946. Foto Lensini, Siena.

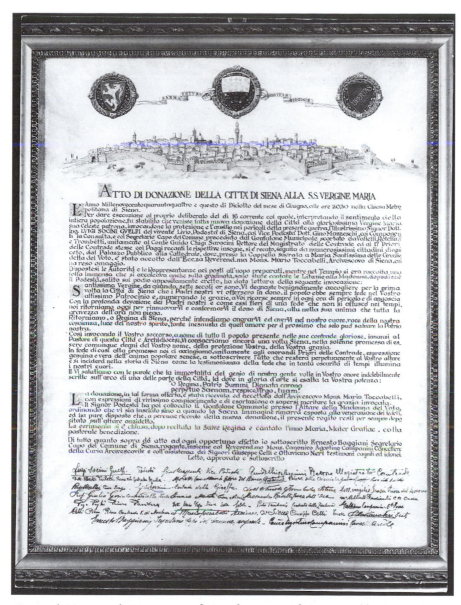

Figure 4.18 Atto di Donazione [Act of Donation], June 1944. Foto Lensini, Siena.

contemporary documents – include references to Saint George and his invocation by the Sienese and a group of German mercenary troops who fought for them at Montaperti. The same chronicles claim that, after the battle, the mercenaries built a church in Siena dedicated to Saint George, and that for many years the Sienese held a festival outside the church in which Saint George fought a dragon, the festival subsequently being transferred to the Campo when the area in front of the church became too small for the crowd that wished to watch the ritual confrontation. The presence of the dragon in the allegorical panel above the portrayal of the dedication of the city to the Virgin in 1260 may also imply a reference to the traditional role of Saint George at the battle of Montaperti, as well as to the victory of good over evil. That this popular tradition certainly remained alive in Sienese consciousness was subsequently demonstrated by the *drappellone* (banner) painted for the 'extraordinary' Palio run on 4 September 1960 in celebration of the 700th anniversary of the battle of Montaperti. The *drappellone* was dominated by the figure of Saint George, broken lance in hand, and slain dragon beneath his feet with scenes of Siena, the battle, and the hill of Montaperti in the background.[13]

After Montaperti, the Sienese resolved to offer two candles each year on the feast of Saint George at the church built by the mercenary troops. The church in question, San Giorgio in Via Pantaneto – on the route out of the city taken by the Sienese forces on the eve of Montaperti – still retains popular associations with the traditions surrounding the battle. Thus, popular Sienese tradition asserts that the 48 windows of the campanile – which is all that remains of the original thirteenth-century church – correspond to the number of Sienese military companies at Montaperti (Nannini, 1953, p.24; Torriti, 1988, p.338; Webb, 1996, pp.265–6). The church of San Giorgio is also the venue for the start of the annual Corteo dei Ceri each August.

The second main panel, on the top right-hand side of the Porta della Riconoscenza, portrays the thanksgiving of the Sienese for the Virgin's protection of the city from a severe outbreak of the plague in 1486. Periodically subject to such outbreaks – in the fifteenth century alone Siena had already suffered particularly severe recurrences of plague in 1420, 1430 and 1448 – that of 1486 infected almost the entire city. According to government documents, it prompted the Sienese to carry 'the panel of the Virgin' in solemn procession through the city and to release a number of debtors from prison, in honour of the Virgin, on the feast of the Assumption (Bacci, 1946, pp.29–33). The scene on the second main panel depicts the gratitude of the Sienese to the Virgin for her protection from the plague on this occasion. In the centre of the panel, a single citizen, representing all the Sienese, approaches an image of the Virgin, while around him are gathered a group of prisoners who are to obtain their liberty. The image of the

[13] This *drappellone* is illustrated in Colour Plate 2, and is discussed in more detail in Chapter 6, page 228. Chapters 5 and 6 also explain and analyse the importance of Palio *drappelloni* within Sienese civil religion.

Figure 4.19 Vico Consorti, *Thanksgiving for Deliverance from the Plague*, detail of the Porta della Riconoscenza, Siena cathedral, 1946. Foto Lensini, Siena.

Virgin in front of which they are depicted is clearly a portrayal of the *Madonna del Voto* as it would have appeared in the late fifteenth century, housed in a chapel in the south aisle of the cathedral. The smaller allegorical panel associated with this scene shows an angel, sent by the Virgin, to restore life to a young victim of the plague whose body is held by his mother.

The third main panel, on the bottom left-hand side of the door, recalls the events of 1697 when Siena was threatened by a series of earthquakes, beginning with a major tremor on 20 September (see pp.150–2). The panel on the Porta della Riconoscenza shows the occasion, two years later, when the civic authorities brought a silver votive statue of the Virgin and Child accompanied by Saint Ansano to the cathedral, and presented it to the archbishop in front of the Cappella del Voto. The portrayal of the ornate façade and the altar of the Cappella del Voto is highly accurate, including the image of the *Madonna del Voto*, complete with the crowns on the Virgin and

Figure 4.20 Vico Consorti, *Allegory of the Restoration of Life to a Victim of the Plague*, detail of the Porta della Riconoscenza, Siena cathedral, 1946. Foto Lensini, Siena.

Figure 4.21 Vico Consorti, *Thanksgiving for Deliverance from an Earthquake*, detail of the Porta della Riconoscenza, Siena cathedral, 1946. Foto Lensini, Siena.

Christ Child with which, by this time, the image had been adorned and which it retains to this day. In the left foreground of the panel, Archbishop Marsili is shown seated, just outside the chapel. In the centre foreground a page presents the votive statue to him, while in the right foreground five other figures represent the Sienese government. The allegorical panel associated with this scene depicts two angels – arms raised expressively as if fending off blows – in front of the entrance to Siena, shielding the city to assist the Virgin in preventing the earthquake from reaching it (Bacci, 1946, pp.34–8). The entrance portrayed is identifiable as the outer gate (*antiporto*), to the north of Siena, which can still be seen today.

Finally, the main panel on the bottom right-hand side of the door depicts the events of the evening of 18 June 1944. Set within the Cappella del Voto – with the *Madonna del Voto* clearly visible – Archbishop Toccabelli appears on the right, in the act of receiving the symbolic keys of the city. These are carried on a cushion by a page accompanied by a group of figures on the left-hand side of the panel. Within this group three figures predominate, each of them, like the figure of Toccabelli, clearly identifiable from contemporary photo-

Figure 4.22 Vico Consorti, *Allegory of Deliverance from an Earthquake*, detail of the Porta della Riconoscenza, Siena cathedral, 1946. Foto Lensini, Siena.

Figure 4.23 Vico Consorti, *Rededication of Siena to the Virgin in June 1944*, detail of the Porta della Riconoscenza, Siena cathedral, 1946. Foto Lensini, Siena.

graphs as accurate representations of their subjects. Immediately beside the page appears the mayor, Luigi Socini Guelfi, and between him and the altar appears the tall figure of Guido Chigi Saracini, his head bowed and his hands clasped in prayer. Further to the left appears a figure dressed in medieval costume and carrying a banner on which is the insignia 'Magistrato delle Contrade'. He is identifiable as Lorenzo di Fabbri, nicknamed 'Pappio', who was a member of the Contrada del Drago and had been responsible for carrying the banner of the Magistrato delle Contrade at official ceremonies in the 1930s and 1940s (Giannelli, 1997, pp.29–30). He had thus been present and prominent at the rededication of June 1944.

Between the figures of Socini Guelfi, Chigi Saracini and di Fabbri there also appears a representation of a bronze statue of a young woman in the act of presenting a votive lamp. The actual statue stands in the Cappella del Voto, to the left of the entrance and facing the altar. Itself called *La Riconoscenza*, it was the work of the Sienese sculptor Arturo Viligiardi, and had been donated to the chapel in 1918 by Guido Chigi Saracini in thanks for his recovery from a serious illness contracted while on military service during the First World War. The final allegorical panel above this entire scene shows a schematic depiction of Siena viewed – as it is also portrayed on the Act of Donation – from the south, as it would have appeared to the approaching Allied forces. Two angels, kneeling and in profile, look upwards to the sky and hold a protective cloak over the city – an ingenious reflection of the particular Sienese fear, in 1944, that their city would suffer aerial bombardment (Bacci, 1946, pp.40–1).

At one level, it would be easy to interpret the Porta della Riconoscenza as essentially no more than a particularly striking modern expression of the familial patronage of a community's churches that was characteristic of Italian civic culture in earlier eras. The door was the gift of Guido Chigi Saracini, and it bears his family mottoes and insignia. His family antecedents are celebrated through the portrayal of the chapel founded by his seventeenth-century ancestor, Fabio Chigi. Moreover, the personal and familial signifi-

Figure 4.24 Vico Consorti, *Allegory of the Protection of Siena from Aerial Bombardment*, detail of the Porta della Riconoscenza, Siena cathedral, 1946. Foto Lensini, Siena.

cance of the door is further attested by the inscriptions that appear above it and on the marble facing of the entrance passageway. However, the Porta della Riconoscenza is far more than merely an intensely personal and familial act of religious and artistic patronage. It is also a celebration and commemoration of Sienese civil religion.

Collectively, the four scenes portrayed in the main panels may be read as an evocation of the history of a key aspect of Sienese civic devotion and civil religion. They relate not only sequentially and chronologically but also diagonally. The top left-hand and bottom right-hand scenes portray the first and last donations of the keys of the city to the Virgin, while the top right-hand and bottom left-hand scenes depict moments of thanksgiving to the Virgin for deliverance from particular threats. At the same time, read in their chronological order, the four scenes rehearse the principal stages in the history of the particular images of the Virgin to which the Sienese have had a special devotion and, in addition, focus increasingly closely on the place within the cathedral which has become the focal point of Sienese devotion to the Virgin. Thus, the scene commemorating the first donation of the keys of the city to the Virgin in 1260 portrays the first image of the Madonna to which the Sienese became devoted, the *Madonna degli occhi grossi*, on the high altar of the cathedral. The next scene, for the year 1486, shows the *Madonna del Voto* on the altar in the south aisle of the cathedral where it was located from at least the mid-fifteenth century until the mid-seventeenth century. The third scene, commemorating Siena's escape from the earthquakes of 1697, shows the *Madonna del Voto*, now adorned with golden crowns, on the altar of the Cappella del Voto – though the image and the chapel are viewed from outside. Finally, the last scene of the rededication of the city in June 1944 again shows the *Madonna del Voto*, but this time from inside the chapel. The history of Sienese devotion to these two images of the Virgin is thus summarized in visual form, culminating in the chapel that remains, to this day, the principal focus for the personal devotion of many Sienese.[14]

The Porta della Riconoscenza, therefore, is both an expression of Sienese civil religion – because it was an offering in thanksgiving for the 'salvation' of the city in 1944 – and, at the same time, a celebration and commemoration of the history of Sienese civil religion and devotion to the Virgin.

---

[14] The wall immediately outside the chapel on the right remains the location for a rich variety of personal votive offerings placed there by ordinary Sienese in thanksgiving to the *Madonna del Voto*. Significantly, the original copy of the Act of Donation of June 1944 is now displayed in a case situated immediately to the left of the Cappella del Voto.

Conclusion: *contrade*, Palio and the memory of 1944

For students of recent Sienese history, it is notable that the main sources for the story of the Porta della Riconoscenza and its origins are studies of the Palio and the *contrade* of Siena (Tailetti, 1967; 1972; Falassi, 1992; Giannelli, 1997). But contemporary guidebooks and histories of Siena say little, if anything, about this striking monument to Sienese civil religion. There are at least two factors that may explain this pattern: namely, the political context of the origins of the Porta della Riconoscenza; and the role and prominence of the *contrade* and the Palio in the contemporary expression and preservation of Sienese civil religion.

As the account of the origins of the Porta della Riconoscenza given above clearly demonstrates, while Guido Chigi Saracini was the central figure in the project, Archbishop Toccabelli and the Sienese church authorities also played a significant part in its realization. As recent studies of the history of Siena in the twentieth century have pointed out, in the political crises and realignments of the period after the Second World War, Toccabelli and the local Catholic Church sided decisively with the political right. Siena as a whole, however, has consistently proved to be a stronghold of the political left in the post-war era (Barzanti, 1997, pp.345–6; Bocchini Camaiani, 1998). Moreover, Archbishop Toccabelli and the local Catholic authorities had shown marked sympathy and support for the Fascist regime during the mid- and late 1930s and early 1940s. Similarly, even before the end of the war, it was already clear that the opposition of Toccabelli and the Sienese Catholic Church to the political left was to become a dominant theme within the Sienese church in the post-war era (Bocchini Camaiani, 1994, pp.81–90). Given such circumstances, it is perhaps understandable that the Porta della Riconoscenza does not feature prominently in most accounts of Siena and its recent history.

Conversely, there are good reasons for the preservation of the memory of the Porta della Riconoscenza and its origins in literature that is primarily devoted to the history of the Palio and the *contrade*. As the next chapter will argue, in modern Siena it is the Palio and the *contrade* that are the principal means by which the distinctive character of Sienese life and culture is still preserved. Above all, it is the seventeen *contrade* and their passionate commitment to the Palio and its traditions that sustain the highly self-conscious awareness of their history that is characteristic of the Sienese and their culture. Each of the seventeen *contrade* fiercely preserves its own identity, not least through its own museum, archives and publications relating to its history. In so doing, the *contrade* also contribute to the preservation of the collective memory and identity of the Sienese and the cultivation of *Senesità* – the personal understanding and expression of what it is to be Sienese. Thus, despite their intense individuality and rivalry, the *contrade* are also the source of unity within Sienese life as a whole. The cultivation of such 'unity in diversity', together with a deep affection for the diverse local histories of the Sienese, make the *contrade* a natural source for the preservation of popular traditions and memories – such as those surrounding the events of 1944 and the origins of the Porta della Riconoscenza – which might well remain relatively neglected or forgotten in other sources. Nor should it be forgotten that the *contrade* were all participants in the events of 18 June 1944 and that the Prior of each *contrada* signed the Act of Donation, as did Guido Chigi Saracini in his capacity as Rector of the Magistrato delle Contrade – a post that he was to hold for almost 40 years, from 1927 until 1964, the year before his death, when he was succeeded as Rector by one of the other leading figures in the events of June 1944, Luigi Socini Guelfi.

It is, then, hardly surprising that it is in the history and recollection of *contrada* life and of the Palio that the Porta della Riconoscenza is best remembered. In the twice-yearly festival of the Palio – each of which also celebrates the Virgin and her special relationship with Siena – there is a natural connection between the civil religion of the medieval Sienese and the necessarily different, but arguably no less intense, expression of contemporary Sienese civil religion. And if, like their contemporaries elsewhere in Italy, the modern Sienese are far from being uniformly committed to the norms and requirements of official Catholic belief and practice, yet in Siena popular devotion to the Virgin remains intense, even if it is often expressed more through the rituals of Palio and *contrada* than it is through more conventional means of Marian devotion. Thus, one recent commentator on Sienese religious and devotional life has observed that it is the Palio that is the truest and greatest development of the Marian faith of the Sienese (De Cristofaro, 1988, p.300). At the same time, as the next chapter will argue, the Palio and its traditions may also be interpreted as a modern expression – perhaps, indeed, the principal modern expression – of the civil religion of the Sienese.

In one particular annual ritual of the *contrade*, popular Marian faith, Sienese civil religion, and the memory and echo of June 1944 come together. Each year, in each *contrada*, one of the main rituals in the annual celebration of the festival of the *contrada*'s patron saint is the service of Solenne Mattutino, held in the church of the *contrada* on the eve of the principal day in the celebration of the patronal festival (Ceccherini, 1995, pp.21–2; Falassi, 1996, p.107). The service characteristically concludes with the singing of the Latin hymn to the Virgin, 'Maria Mater Gratiae' and the popular hymn, 'Volgi un guardo', with its chorus, 'O Maria, la tua Siena difendi'. For those who have witnessed such moments and heard the emotion with which the hymn is still sung, it is not difficult to imagine the intensity that must have accompanied its singing in Siena cathedral on the evening of 18 June 1944. Nor is it difficult to understand why it is mainly in the literature of the Palio and the *contrade* that the Porta della Riconoscenza is best remembered.

References

Bacci, P. (1946) *La porta di bronzo che mena alla cappella detta del Voto fondata del Papa Alessandro VII Chigi*, Siena: Arte Graffiche Lazzeri.

Barzanti, R. (1997) 'Dalla ricostruzione a ieri', in R. Barzanti, G. Catoni and M. De Gregorio (eds) *Storia di Siena III*, pp.339–66.

Barzanti, R., Catoni, G. and De Gregorio, M. (eds) (1995) *Storia di Siena I: dalle origini alla fine della repubblica*; (1996) *Storia di Siena II: dal granducato all'unità*; (1997) *Storia di Siena III: l'età contemporanea*, Siena: Edizioni Alsaba.

Bocchini Camaiani, B. (1994) 'Devozione e cristianità. Chiesa e cattolici a Siena nel periodo fascista', *Passato e Presente*, 12, pp.69–90.

Bocchini Camaiani, B. (1998) '"È l'ora di Dio! Dio lo vuole". Contrapposizioni politiche e ripercussioni ecclesiali nell'azione pastorale di Mons. Toccabelli a Siena e nella provincia senese', *Rivista di Storia e Letteratura Religiosa*, 34, pp.279–304.

Bonelli, V. (1999) 'L'origine del culto della Madonna di Provenzano', *Istituto Storico Diocesano Siena Annuario 1998–1999*, pp.142–280.

Borgia, L. *et al.* (1984) *Le Biccherne: tavole dipinte dell magistrature senesi secoli*, Rome: Le Monnier.

Bowsky, W. (1981) *A Medieval Italian Commune: Siena under the Nine, 1287–1355*, Berkeley: University of California Press.

Butzek, M. (2001) 'La Cappella Chigi nel Duomo di Siena', in A. Angelini, M. Butzek and B. Sani (eds) *Alessandro VII Chigi (1599–1667): Il Papa Senese di Roma Moderna*, Siena: Protagon Editore Toscani.

Caferro, W. (1998) *Mercenary Companies and the Decline of Siena*, Baltimore: Johns Hopkins University Press.

Ceccherini, D. (1995) *Gli oratori delle contrade di Siena: storia, architettura, arte*, Siena: Betti Editrice.

Ciabattini, P. (1991) *Siena fra la scure e la falce e martello: cronaca e memorie dal 1926 al 1950*, Sovicille: I Mori A.G. Ticci.

Ciabattini, P. (1997) *Quando i Senesi salvarono Siena: Siena città ospedaliera*, Rome: Edizioni Settimo Sigillo.

De Cristofaro, R. (1988) *Siena: I canti del popolo*, Siena: Edizioni Cantagalli.

Falassi, A. (1992) 'Un quarto di secolo', in L. Betti (ed.) *Pallium: evoluzione del drappellone dalle origini ad oggi. Volume 3: dal dopoguerra alla conquista della luna*, Siena: Betti Editrice, pp.7–15.

Falassi, A. (1996) 'Le contrade', in R. Barzanti, G. Catoni and M. De Gregorio (eds) *Storia di Siena I*, pp.95–108.

Falassi, A. (1998) *Palio: The Colors of Siena*, Siena: Comune of Siena.

Falassi, A. and Catoni, G. (1982) *Palio*, Milan: Electa Editrice.

Falorni, M. (2000) *Arte cultura e politica a Siena nel primo novecento: Fabio Bargagli Petrucci (1875–1939)*, Siena: Il Leccio.

Garrison, E. (1960–62) *Studies in the History of Medieval Painting. Volume 4*, Florence, L'Impronta.

Garrison, E. (1960a) 'Towards a new history of the Siena cathedral madonnas', in E. Garrison, pp.5–22.

Garrison, E. (1960b) "Sienese historical writings and the dates 1260, 1221, 1262, applied to Sienese paintings', in E. Garrison, pp.23–58.

Giannelli, E. (1997) 'Lorenzo Fabbri detto Pappio', in *Barbareschi: una vita per il Palio*, Siena: Alsaba, pp.29–33.

Gigli, G. (1716) *La Città diletta di Maria*, Rome: Francesco Gonzaga.

Gigli, G. (1854) *Diario Senese*, 3 volumes, Bologna: Arnaldo Forni Editore (originally published 1723).

Giorgio, E. (1985) *Guerra e pace a Montepulciano: Diario autentico di un testimone oculare*, Montepulciano: Edizioni de l'Araldo Poliziano.

Grassi, V. (1972) *Le contrade di Siena e le loro feste – il Palio attuale*, 2 volumes, Siena: Edizioni Periccioli.

Heal, B. (2000) '"Civitas Virginis"? The significance of civic dedication to the Virgin for the development of Marian imagery in Siena before 1311', in J. Cannon and B. Williamson (eds) *Art, Politics and Civic Religion in Central Italy 1261–1352*, Aldershot: Ashgate, pp.295–305.

Heywood, W. (1899) *Our Lady of August and the Palio of Siena*, Siena: Enrico Torrini.

Heywood, W. (1904) *Palio and Ponte: An Account of the Sports of Central Italy from the Age of Dante to the XXth Century*, London: Methuen.

Hook, J. (1979) *Siena: A City and Its History*, London: Hamish Hamilton.

Koenig, J. (1998) 'Wartime religion: the pre-Montaperti Sienese supplication and ritual submission', *Bullettino Senese di Storia Patria*, 105, pp.7–62.

Landi, F. (1994) *Gli ultimi anni della Repubblica di Siena 1525–1555*, Siena: Edizioni Cantagalli.

Leoncini, A. (1994) *I tabernacoli di Siena: arte e devozione popolare*, Siena: Nuovo Immagine Editrice.

Lisini, A. and Iacometti, F. (eds) (1931–9) 'Cronache senesi', in *Rerum Italicarum Scriptores*, new series 15, 6, Bologna.

Luchini, L. (1987) *Palio XX secolo: una città fra realtà e leggenda*, Siena: Tipografia Senese Editrice.

Malavolti, O. (1982) *Dell'historia di Siena*, Bologna: Arnoldo Forni (originally published 1599).

Mirizio, P. (1993) *I Buoni Senesi: cattolici e società in provincia di Siena dall'Unità al Fascismo*, Brescia: Editrice Morcelliana.

Mori, L. (1994) 'La Liberazione: sette secoli dopo Montaperti', *La Voce del Campo*, 7 July 1994, p.14.

Mumm, S. (ed.) (2002) *Religion Today: A Reader*, Aldershot: Ashgate.

Nannini, G. (1953) 'La Torre di S. Giorgio in Pantaneto', *Terra di Siena*, 7, part 4, p.24.

Norman, D. (1999) *Siena and the Virgin: Art and Politics in a Late Medieval City State*, New Haven and London: Yale.

Os, H. van (1984) *Sienese Altarpieces 1215–1460: Form, Content, Function. Volume 1: 1215–1344*, Groningen: Bouma's Boekhuis BV.

Paoletti, P. (1994) 'La vicenda diplomatica del riconoscimento di Siena "città aperta": tra il falso storico della "città ospedaliera" e la verità oggettiva del centro ospedaliero', in P. Paoletti, C. Biscarini and V. Meoni, *1943–1944: vicende belliche e resistenza in terra di Siena*, Siena: Nuova Immagine Editrice, pp.9–58.

Parsons, G. (2001) '"O Maria, la tua Siena difendi": the Porta della Riconoscenza of Siena', *Zeitschrift für Kunstgeschichte*, 64, pp.153–76.

Pellegrini, E. (1995) 'L'assedio e la capitolazione', in R. Barzanti, G. Catoni and M. De Gregorio (eds) *Storia di Siena I*, pp.453–68.

Pertici, P. (1995) 'La furia delle fazioni', in R. Barzanti, G. Catoni and M. De Gregorio (eds) *Storia di Siena I*, pp.383–94.

Ploeg, K. van der (1993) *Art, Architecture and Liturgy: Siena Cathedral in the Middle Ages*, Groningen: Egbert Forsten.

Porri, G. (ed) (1844) *Miscellanea storica senese: due narrazioni sulla sconfitta di Montaperto tratte da antichi manoscritti*, Siena: Onorato Porri.

Proto Pisani, R. (1979) 'Il Tesoro della Cappella del Voto nel Duomo di Siena', *Bullettino Senese di Storia Patria*, 86, pp.49–99.

Raveggi, S. (1995) 'La vittoria di Montaperti', in R. Barzanti, G. Catoni and M. De Gregorio (eds) *Storia di Siena I*, pp.79–94.

Socini Guelfi, L. (1994) 'Nel cinquantenario del passaggio della guerra da Siena', *Miscellanea Toscana di Elzeviri Storico-Archivistici*, 3, pp.3–20.

Tailetti, A. (1967) *Anedotti Contradaiolo*, Rome: Olimpia.

Tailetti, A. (1972) 'Cronistoria del Palio dal 1938 al 1972', in V. Grassi, vol.2, pp.67–134.

Tomassi, G. (1973) *Dell'historie di Siena*, Bologna: Arnoldo Forni Editore (originally published 1625–26).

Torriti, P. (1988) *Tutta Siena: contrada per contrada*, Florence: Bonechi.

Waley, D. (1991) *Siena and the Sienese in the Thirteenth Century*, Cambridge: Cambridge University Press.

Webb, D. (1996) *Patrons and Defenders: The Saints in the Italian City-States*, London: Taurus.

CHAPTER 5

'Unity in diversity': civil religion and the Palio of Siena[1]

As noted in the introduction, the concept of a 'civil religion' has been explored extensively in relation to the USA and, to a lesser degree, the modern UK. In both countries, it is argued, there exist clusters of beliefs concerning national values and national identity which are, in turn, sustained, nurtured and reiterated by a variety of national rituals. In each case, the resulting 'civil religion' sustains the widespread acceptance by a people of a shared sense of their nation's history and destiny; relates their society to a realm of absolute meaning; enables them to look at their society and community as in some sense special; provides a vision that ties the nation together as an integrated whole; and provides a collection of beliefs, values, rites, ceremonies and symbols which, taken together, give sacred meaning to the life of the community and thus provide an overarching sense of unity that transcends internal conflicts and differences (Pierard and Linder, 1988, pp.22–3).

However, as pointed out in the introduction, the concept of a civil religion is by no means exclusively modern and Anglo-Saxon in origin. In late medieval and renaissance Italy, for example, the distinctive identities and particular values of individual city states were also frequently expressed in civic rituals amounting to a form of civil religion. Such medieval and renaissance civil religions, it was noted, were closely associated with the festivals of a city's patron saints, with the celebration of the Virgin Mary as a particular protectress of the city in question, or with other religious festivals adopted as the focus of civic identity and devotion. The rituals usually culminated in elaborate civic processions in which the various constituent parts of the community honoured their designated

---

[1] An earlier version of this chapter first appeared in *The Italianist* (1997, 17). I am grateful to the editors of *The Italianist* for permission to re-use the substance of the original article here.

heavenly protector and patron with gifts of candles and banners. They were also, in most cases, an important annual reassertion and reconfirmation of the intimate relationship that existed between a late medieval Italian city and the subject towns and territories of its surrounding possessions. In general, however, from the late sixteenth century onwards, both the relationships between Italian cities and their subject territories and the civic rituals in which those relation-ships were celebrated and confirmed went into decline, to the point at which many civic festivals and rituals disappeared altogether. Two factors in particular were central to these changes. On the one hand, from the mid-sixteenth century onwards, the Catholic Church increasingly sought to emphasize the specifically religious signifi-cance of patronal and Marian festivals, at the expense of the civic roles that they also performed. On the other hand, most of the independent Italian city states were gradually conquered by more powerful neighbours or absorbed into larger regional states which controlled whole areas of Italy (Chittolini, 1990).[2]

In some cases, the civic rituals of Italian medieval city states have survived, though in a modified and reduced form, even to the present day. In the Tuscan city of Siena, such rituals have not only survived but have become closely associated with the Palio – a twice-yearly festival which culminates in a horse race around the Campo, the famous shell-shaped central piazza of Siena. The Palio and the traditions that surround it exhibit many of the characteristics commonly associated with the 'civil religions' of the modern UK and USA. Indeed, it will be the central argument of this chapter that the remarkable and pervasive significance of the Palio within Sienese life constitutes a striking example of a modern civil religion – but one that also has roots in the medieval period, and in the civil religion of medieval and renaissance Siena. The Palio, it will be argued, includes a compelling range of rituals, rites, ceremonies and beliefs which collectively sustain a distinctive Sienese identity, and a corresponding set of values amounting to a specific and definable Sienese world-view. In presenting this thesis, the chapter will begin by providing a brief summary of the Palio and a review of conventional assessments of its significance for the Sienese. It will then examine the overtly

---

[2] For other recent studies of the role of civil religion in the city states of medieval and renaissance Italy in general see, for example, Vauchez (1993, pp.153–68); and Webb (1993 and 1996). For recent detailed case studies of the development of such medieval civil religion in the Umbrian cities of Perugia and Orvieto, and the Tuscan cities of Cortona, Pisa, Arezzo and Siena, see Dickson (1998); Cannon and Vauchez (1999); and Cannon and Williamson (2000). For broader overviews of the same process in medieval and renaissance Siena, see Bowsky (1981, chapter 7); Kempers (1994); Webb (1996, chapters 6–8); and Norman (1999).

religious associations and aspects of the Palio, and further features of this phenomenon which point to its function as a civil religion. The final section will summarize the ways in which the Palio and its traditions conform to the key elements in the definition of a civil religion.

The Palio and its significance in Sienese life

Twice a year, on 2 July and 16 August, ten horses, ridden bareback by jockeys representing ten of the *contrade* (or districts) into which Siena is divided, race three times around the Campo. For these events the Campo is transformed into a racetrack. Earth is laid around the edge of the piazza to form the track, and stands are erected around the outside, while barriers are placed on the inside enclosing the large central area. A crowd numbering up to 60,000 packs into the Campo, occupying every space both in the centre and around the perimeter. The race, which lasts approximately 90 seconds, is preceded by a two-hour historical parade, in medieval and renaissance costumes, of the civic authorities and representatives of each of the seventeen *contrade* of Siena. Both the race and the parade are, in turn, the climax of four days of festival, beginning with the selection of the horses and their assignment to particular *contrade*, proceeding through a series of six *prove* – preliminary 'races' prior to the Palio itself – and including the blessing of each horse in the church of the *contrada* for which it will run.

The winning *contrada* receives a large rectangular banner made of painted silk – also called a 'palio', but popularly referred to by the Sienese as the *drappellone* (the 'big banner'), or even, in local slang, *il cencio* (the 'rag') – the central feature of which is a depiction of the Virgin. Amid scenes of intense emotion, the winning *contrada* processes either to Siena cathedral (in August) or to the church of Santa Maria di Provenzano (in July) to sing a hymn to the Virgin in thanks for the victory. In the days that follow, only the flags and emblems of the winning *contrada* remain on display in the streets of Siena, as members of the winning *contrada* celebrate their victory by parading through the streets with the newly won *drappellone* – which they now refer to as *il cittino* ('the little citizen') or *il neonato* ('the newborn') – by holding suppers in the streets of their own section of the city, and by making fun of their rivals. They will also speak of the rebirth of their *contrada* and may well express their personal sense of that rebirth by wearing a baby's bottle (often filled with wine) or a

Figure 5.1 The Campo, Siena. Foto Lensini, Siena.

Figure 5.2 The Campo prepared for the Palio. Foto Lensini, Siena.

Figure 5.3 Members of the Contrada dell'Oca celebrate their victory in the July Palio, 1998, outside the church of Santa Maria di Provenzano. Foto Lensini, Siena.

dummy attached to their *contrada* scarf – a colourful garment, portraying the symbols and colours of the *contrada*, which all members proudly possess and wear whenever they wish to advertise and display their identity.

The four days of the Palio in July and August each year are, however, the culmination of an entire annual sequence, amounting to an alternative calendar, centred on and structured around the Palio, which determines the rhythm of the year for each *contrada* and, consequently, for Siena itself. Thus, between April and September, each *contrada* will celebrate the festival of its patron saint, during which its members will parade through the city with flags and drums. The Palio will be a constant theme during such celebrations, both through the recollection of past Palii and in the anticipation of the next Palio in which the *contrada* will participate. At the heart of the Sienese year are the two annual Palii. Approximately a month before each Palio, the final identity of the ten *contrade* that will compete is determined by the drawing of lots in a ceremony in the Palazzo Pubblico, the Sienese town hall which

Figure 5.4 *Contrada* members parading and wearing dummies and babies' bottles after winning the Palio. Foto Lensini, Siena.

Figure 5.5 Members of the Contrada del'Istrice celebrate their victory in the Palio of July 2000. Note the homemade '*drappellone*', made from a newspaper poster of the *drappellone*, announcing the arrival of the 'newborn citizen'. Photo: Gerald Parsons.

faces the Campo.[3] From that point on, the various *contrade* will begin the complex negotiations and intrigues that precede every Palio. The reality of this 'alternative calendar' is clearly attested by the fact that the Sienese readily speak of the '*anno contradaiolo*' – 'the *contrada* member's year' – and even recognize that it has an official starting date on 1 December, the feast day of Saint Ansano (see Chapter 4, footnote 6). On this day the *contrade* participate, together with the civic authorities of Siena, in a service in the cathedral in honour of Saint Ansano (Falassi and Catoni, 1982, p.52; Cairola, 1989, pp.291–2).

The culmination of the preparation for each Palio is the laying of the track. Lorry-loads of yellow earth are brought to the Campo for this purpose and, with the return of '*la terra in piazza*' ('the earth in the piazza') the sense of the imminence of the Palio increases. The local papers begin to speak of the Palio being 'in the air' and of the Campo being dressed in its 'Palio clothes'. In the evenings, Sienese of all ages visit the Campo to walk on the track and 'tread on the earth in the piazza', thereby personally associating themselves with the festival (Dundes and Falassi, 1975, pp.53–4; Falassi and Catoni, 1982, p.55). Both the genuinely popular nature of this ritual and also the intensity of the feelings associated with it are well illustrated by the opening paragraph on the first page of one of the local weekly newspapers in July 1996:

> The return of the earth in the piazza is always an emotional moment. The passing of the years does not diminish the sentiments that the Sienese feel at the moment when they walk down through one of the historic alleyways that take them into the sacred place where the ritual of the festival is renewed. To tread on the earth in the piazza is a rite that no *contrada* member will miss. If they do not manage to do this *contrada* members will feel regret, as if the failure mortified them like a sin. When they do so again, it is a liberation.
>
> (*Il Campo di Siena*, 3 July 1996; author's translation)

---

[3] The identity of the *contrade* that will run in each Palio is determined in the following way. Each July and August the seven *contrade* that did not run in the corresponding Palio the previous year run 'by right', the remaining three being chosen by lot. The two 'cycles' of the July and August Palii are separate: thus, a given *contrada* may run twice in one year or not at all. It may also run in a sequence of years if fortunate enough to be drawn repeatedly by lot. Conversely, the system ensures that no *contrada* will be absent from the Palio for more than a single year – unless suspended for disciplinary reasons, having contravened the regulations at a previous Palio. The results of the drawing of lots are indicated to the large and excited crowd in the Campo by the display of the flags of the chosen *contrade* from the windows of the Palazzo Pubblico.

Six or seven days before the Palio, the *drappellone* for which the race will be run is presented to the public at a crowded ceremony held in the evening in the courtyard of the Palazzo Pubblico. The precise design and iconography of each *drappellone* is eagerly awaited by the Sienese. If a particular *drappellone* is popular, and especially if it is felt to show a genuine understanding of *Senesità* (roughly, 'what it means to be Sienese'), it will elicit great applause and enthusiasm when it is presented to the public. But if it is deemed to lack sufficient respect for, or understanding of, Siena and its traditions, then it may attract whistles and other expressions of open disapproval. Immediately the *drappellone* will become the subject of intense debate among the Sienese regarding its design, its style and the interpretation of its details. Such debates are conducted in the local daily and weekly newspapers, but are also to be overheard in the streets, in shops and on buses – another clear indication of the pervasive and popular nature of Sienese enthusiasm for the Palio.

On the fourth morning before the running of the Palio, ten horses are selected from perhaps thirty or more that have been presented for consideration by their owners. The ten selected are assigned – again by drawing lots – to the ten *contrade* competing in this particular Palio. From this point on, until the running of the Palio itself, the whole attention of Siena focuses on the rhythms and rituals of the

Figure 5.6 The presentation of the *drappellone* in the courtyard of the Palazzo Pubblico, July 2000. Foto Lensini, Siena.

Figure 5.7 An assignment of the horses for the Palio – the mayor announcing the lots as they are drawn. Foto Lensini, Siena.

festival. The emotional temperature and the level of tension, excitement and expectation steadily increase, thus giving rise to the Sienese description of this period as 'the hot days'. After the Palio, the celebrations of the winning *contrada* not only extend over the days and weeks immediately following the race, but include an official victory supper in September and a final celebratory meal in January or early spring of the next year. Since 1932 they have also always included a special publication, called a *Numero Unico*, celebrating the victory and the life of the victorious *contrada* (Balestracci, 1999; Ancilli *et al.*, 1999a). As one member of a victorious *contrada* reportedly observed, 'the greatest joy is to finish one Palio and start on another', thus illustrating the truth of a popular Sienese saying which affirms that, in reality, the Palio runs all year long (Dundes and Falassi, 1975, chapter 7; Falassi and Catoni, 1982, pp.52 and 76; Falassi, 1996, p.107).[4]

[4] This summary of the Palio and its rituals is derived from a large number of sources in both English and Italian, and also from personal observation of the festival on many occasions. For more detailed accounts, in English, of the Palio and its rituals, see Barzanti (1972); Dundes and Falassi (1975); Hook (1979); Falassi and Catoni (1982); Betti (1995); and Falassi (1998). See also the English versions of two CD-ROMs, both entitled *The Palio of Siena*, published in 1996 and 2000 respectively. Details of the CD-ROMs are provided at the end of the references for this chapter.

Figure 5.8 An assignment of the horses – *contrada* members behind the horse assigned to them as they leave the Campo. Foto Lensini, Siena.

Figure 5.9 The victory supper of the *Contrada della Giraffa*, after winning both the July and August Palii of 1997. Foto Lensini, Siena.

Not surprisingly, it has long been recognized, both by Sienese scholars and others, that the Palio is central to the Sienese sense of identity and self-understanding. It sustains and underpins the Sienese sense of their uniqueness and individuality, their proud recollection of a past history as an independent city state, and their continuing belief in the distinct and special character of Siena and its culture, history and institutions. Thus it has been said that it is impossible to think of Siena without the Palio; that Siena lives perpetually in the atmosphere of the Palio; and that the person who has not seen the Palio does not know Siena. Similarly, the Palio has been called an expression of the soul and spirit of the city; a microcosm and synthesis of Sienese life; and the culminating moment of the city and its culture in which city and festival become one. The Palio and its traditions pervade the everyday life of the Sienese and their consciousness, providing the basis for both proverbial and idiomatic sayings,[5] and the principal source of vitality in modern Sienese civic life. The Palio is thus a twice-yearly restatement and rebirth of the city's civic values, which celebrates traditional Sienese mores, creates a framework and rhythm of life unique to the city, and acts as a metaphor for a specifically Sienese world-view.[6]

If the centrality of the Palio within Sienese life is commonly acknowledged, however, the interpretation of its significance is, by comparison, surprisingly neglected. Despite the many historical studies and numerous popular celebrations of the Palio, there remain surprisingly few attempts to press beyond historical analysis to the question of the meaning and significance of this remarkable festival. The most ambitious attempt to do so remains that of Alan Dundes and Alessandro Falassi. In their seminal study, *La Terra in Piazza*, first published in 1975, they offer an anthropological and psychoanalytical interpretation and explanation of the Palio and its function as an intricate and complex metaphor of the Sienese world-view. Subsequently, alternative anthropological interpretations of the Palio have been proposed. Thus, the Palio has been interpreted as a 'cultural performance' and an 'urban ritual' in which the Sienese

[5] For example, a traditional Sienese encouragement for someone who is sad or downcast is to say that 'soon there will be earth in the piazza', while someone who has failed in an activity or had a misfortune may be described as having 'gone to San Martino' or 'to the mattresses' – a reference to the curve in the Campo where many horses and riders fall in the Palio. For these and other examples, see Dundes and Falassi (1975, pp.156–60).

[6] The judgements summarized in this paragraph appeared in Heywood (1904, p.147); Cecchini and Neri (1958, p.7); Gigli (1960, p.9); Dundes and Falassi (1975, pp.xii–xvi, 153, 160–1, 185, 237); Hook (1979, pp.215–6 and 220); Falassi (1980, p.5); Falassi and Catoni (1982, p.77).

demonstrate, both to themselves and to others, the cultural elements of their identity and the social structures of their city and society (Logan, 1978). Similarly, the Palio has been analysed and interpreted in terms of its role as a 'ritual game', which not only symbolizes and expresses 'the story the Sienese like to tell about themselves', but also performs a crucial politically unifying function in Sienese history (Silverman, 1979; 1989).

It has also been argued, entirely correctly, that a phenomenon as complex as the Palio cannot be reduced to an exhaustive list of meanings or fully explained in terms of any single interpretative approach or academic method. On the contrary, it is recognized that the interpretation of such a subtle and multi-faceted festival requires multiple and complementary approaches and methods (Dundes and Falassi, 1975, pp.xii and 185–6; Silverman, 1979, p.433; 1989, p.236; Falassi, 1980, p.5). Accordingly, by using the concept of civil religion, the present chapter suggests an additional – but certainly not an exclusive or exhaustive – interpretation of the function and meaning of the Palio within Sienese life. In so doing, it proposes a further dimension to the explanation of the enduring vitality of the Palio and its creative contribution to the nurturing of a distinctive Sienese culture and identity.

The Palio and official religion

That the Palio possesses an overtly religious dimension is well known and is immediately obvious to any attentive observer. Both the Palio of 2 July and that of 16 August are run in honour of the Virgin. That of 2 July is run on the feast of the Visitation of the Virgin and in honour of the Madonna of Provenzano (see Chapter 4, p.150). The Palio of 16 August is run in honour of the Assunta, the Virgin of the Assumption. Although designed especially for each race, by long tradition the *drappellone* for each Palio always includes a portrayal of the Virgin as a central feature. The portrayals of the Madonna of Provenzano and the Assunta each have well-established iconographies. That for the Madonna of Provenzano characteristically portrays the head and shoulders of the Virgin – thus evoking the original terracotta bust of this name now housed in the church of Santa Maria di Provenzano. That for the Virgin of the Assumption characteristically depicts the Virgin full-length. In both cases these images normally appear above whatever particular scene is depicted on the rest of the *drappellone*. (See Colour Plates 3, 4, 5 and 6.)

As Chapter 6 will discuss more fully, the other imagery on the *drappelloni* varies considerably – although usually it will involve the depiction or celebration of a particular aspect of Siena, Sienese history, or the relationship between Siena and Italy. Since the early twentieth century, every *drappellone* has also included, somewhere on it, a visual reference to each of the ten *contrade* that will run in the Palio in question, the date of the Palio, the symbols of the Comune of Siena and usually those of the three ancient sections (*terzi*) of the city into which the seventeen *contrade* are still divided. Indeed, the successive editions of the complex and extensive official regulations for the Palio issued in 1906, 1949 and 1982 each included specific articles addressed to the question of what must be included in the design and iconography of the *drappellone* (Falassi and Catoni, 1982, pp.21 and 80). From time to time the Sienese also hold an 'extraordinary' Palio to celebrate a particular event or anniversary. Recent examples include 1969 (the landing on the moon); 1972 (the fifth centenary of the influential Sienese bank, the Monte dei Paschi); 1980 (the sixth centenary of the death of Saint Catherine of Siena); 1986 (the bicentenary of the foundation of the modern Comune of Siena); and 2000 (the new millennium). In these instances, the iconography of the *drappellone* will not necessarily include a reference to the Virgin, but it will certainly refer to the particular event or anniversary that the Palio celebrates (Colour Plates 1, 2 and 7). Other aspects of the iconography of the *drappellone* for an extraordinary Palio will remain standard.

Before each Palio, the *drappellone* is taken in procession from the Palazzo Pubblico – where it has been kept since first being presented to the public – to the church of Santa Maria di Provenzano or to Siena cathedral (depending on whether it is July or August). Accompanied by representatives of the city and by drummers (*tamburini*) and flag-bearers (*alfieri*) from each *contrada*, the *drappellone* is formally blessed at the altar and is then left on display in the church. While processing to the altar, and after the blessing when it is taken to be displayed, the flag-bearers of the competing *contrade* will try to touch the *drappellone* with their flags, while ordinary *contrada* members will wave their *contrada* scarves at the *drappellone* or throw them hoping that scarf and *drappellone* will touch (Falassi and Catoni, 1982, pp.60–1).

On the day of the Palio there are further explicitly religious activities. Early in the morning, at the fourteenth-century chapel in the Campo, the archbishop of Siena celebrates mass for the jockeys who will ride later that day. Later that morning, the archbishop will also preside at a celebration of mass – in Santa Maria di Provenzano in July, or in the cathedral in August – along with the official priests of

Figure 5.10 The *drappellone* for the Palio of September 2000 being blessed by the archbishop. Foto Lensini, Siena.

Figure 5.11 The mass celebrated in the chapel in the Campo on the morning of the Palio. Photo: Gerald Parsons.

each of the *contrade*. In the early afternoon, in each of the *contrade* competing in the race, the horse is taken from its stable into the church (or 'Oratory') of the *contrada*. There, together with the jockey, the horse is blessed by the priest of the *contrada*, in the presence of a large crowd of *contrada* members. The blessing is conducted with great solemnity and concludes with the priest saying, 'Go [name of horse], and return victorious!' (Dundes and Falassi, 1975, pp.94–6; Falassi and Catoni, 1982, p.64; Civai and Toti, 2000, p.283). Once the horse has left the Oratory, the *contrada* members sing a hymn to the Virgin or one of the traditional *contrada* songs, the drums play, and the traditional acclamation of the *contrada*'s name is shouted. The drummers and flag-bearers who will represent the *contrada* in the parade later that afternoon perform a display for their fellow *contrada* members, and then begin a procession around the city. After the Palio, as noted earlier, the winning *contrada* again processes to Santa Maria di Provenzano or the Cathedral, but this time carrying in triumph the *drappellone* which they have won, again to sing a hymn to the Virgin in thanks for their victory. The next day they parade around the city with their drums, flags and newly won *drappellone*, visiting other *contrade* with whom they enjoy friendly relations – and at the Oratory of each of these *contrade* they will, once again, sing the same hymn to the Virgin.

The overtly religious dimension of the Palio is also evident in the life of the *contrade* during the rest of the year. The official Oratory of each *contrada* displays the flag of the *contrada* it serves as well as images of its patron saint and memorials to past members (Ceccherini, 1995) (Colour Plate 9). The Oratories provide the locations for the specifically religious events connected with the annual celebration of each *contrada*'s patron saint – most notably a service ('Solenne Mattutino') held the evening before the day designated for the official celebration of the patronal festival and a mass on the day itself (Falassi, 1996, p.107). The Oratories are also the venues for the annual masses on 2 November, in honour of the dead of the *contrada*. The dead are again honoured each year on the festival of the patron saint of the *contrada*, when the celebrations include an official visit by a delegation from the *contrada* to the two civic cemeteries of Siena to place flowers on the graves of past *contrada* members (Dundes and Falassi, 1975, pp.39–40; Falassi and Catoni, 1982, p.29; Falassi, 1998, p.39).

Indeed, each *contrada* routinely marks the life-cycles and rites of passage of all its members. At the birth of a baby to members of the *contrada*, a flag with a pink (for a girl) or blue (for a boy) ribbon attached will be flown at the 'seat' of the *contrada*, and the official noticeboards of the *contrada* will announce the name of the new *contrada* member. Similarly, at the marriage of a *contrada* member, a page in *contrada* costume will be in formal attendance. Major anniversaries will also be recognized in this way, and the death of a *contrada* member will be marked by a flag flown from the seat of the *contrada*, but now tied back with a black ribbon. The evening before the funeral the coffin may be placed in the Oratory for fellow *contrada* members to pay their respects, and at the funeral the coffin may even be draped with a flag of the *contrada* (Dundes and Falassi, 1975, pp.39–40; Falassi, 1998, p.37). Nor should the intensity of a *contrada*'s remembrance of its dead be underestimated. In the celebrations that followed their victory in the Palio of August 1982, for example, the altars of the Oratory of the Contrada della Chiocciola were covered with hundreds of photographs of past members, both recently deceased and long dead. When asked about this, the present members of the *contrada* explained that, 'in Siena nobody is alone, not even when they are dead' (Ravel, 1992, p.12). Similar examples of the inclusion of deceased *contrada* members in the celebration of a victory in the Palio occurred in July and August 1996. A few days after the victory in July, in accordance with a tradition in their *contrada*, representatives of the Contrada dell'Oca took the horse which had won them the Palio to the public cemeteries to visit the graves of past members (*Corriere di Siena*, 7 July 1996, p.23). Similarly, in August, after winning the Palio for the first time in 41 years, members of the Contrada del Bruco took the *drappellone* that they had won to the cemetery on the Sunday after their victory (*Il Cittadino*, 23 August 1996, p.11). The intense reciprocal relationship that exists between the *contrada* and its individual members is well described by the observation that 'it is not just the individual who participates in the life of the *contrada*; rather it is also the *contrada* that participates in the life of the individual' (Dundes and Falassi, 1975, p.39).

The explicit relationship between the Palio and religion is thus expressed at a variety of levels, from the civic to the personal, and is always mediated through the social institution of the *contrada*. Such a network of religious activities – focused on the twice-yearly Palio and structured to the rhythm of the *anno contradaiolo* – is already suggestive of a number of the characteristic features of a civil religion. For example, it provides a regular cycle of celebrations, both annually and in relation to personal rites of passage; it locates the individual within a wider social group; and it relates such activities to a perception of a transcendent dimension through its celebration of the Virgin, the patron saints of the *contrade*, and the memory of past *contrada* members. The resemblance of the Palio to a civil religion becomes even greater, however, when it is recognized that the explicit relationship between the Palio and religion is deeply rooted within Sienese history.

The modern Palio, run on a circular course (*alla tonda*) around the Campo, dates from the early seventeenth century when, following the fall of the independent Sienese republic and its subjection to Florentine rule, the Sienese self-consciously turned inwards on themselves, their city and its traditions. In particular, the *contrade* steadily assumed an increasingly prominent role in the preservation of Siena's distinctive identity and customs. Within this process, their most crucial contribution was the introduction of the Palio *alla tonda* in the Campo, which at first was an annual event, held every 2 July, in celebration of the festival of the Madonna of Provenzano. Gradually, however, a second annual Palio in the Campo became established, every 16 August, in celebration of the Virgin of the Assumption.

The modern Palio in the Campo also represents a merging of two strands within the traditional festivities and celebrations of medieval, renaissance and early modern Siena. On the one hand, the location of the Palio in the Campo, the intense and combative rivalry between *contrade*, the idea of races with animals, and the association of these activities with elaborate parades, all demonstrate the continuities that exist between the modern Palio and traditional Sienese popular games such as the *elmora, battaglia de' sassi, pugna, pallone, cacce ai tori, asinate* and *bufalate*. All of these games were played in the Campo at various times between the thirteenth and sixteenth centuries (Dundes and Falassi, 1975, pp.2–5; Fiorini, 1986, pp.9–14; Marzucchi, 1998, pp.51–5).[7] On the other hand, the modern Palio is clearly the successor to the much older Palio *alla lunga*, a horse race which was held on a linear course that ran through the streets of Siena and was first recorded in the thirteenth century. Run from a starting point outside the city gates and proceeding on a set route which concluded in the square outside the cathedral, these Palii were held on a variety of occasions, but were closely associated with the celebration of the festivals of particular saints. Thus, there were Palii *alla lunga* in honour of the local thirteenth-century Sienese saint Ambrogio Sansedoni, in honour of Saint Mary Magdalene and, most importantly of all, one every 15 August in honour of the Virgin of the

---

[7] The *elmora* was a jousting game; the *battaglia de' sassi* involved stone-throwing; *pugna* was a fist-fighting game; *pallone* was a kind of football; the *cacce ai tori* was a form of bull-fight; the *asinate* was a race with donkeys; and the *bufalate* a race with buffalo. In the *elmora, battaglia de' sassi, pugna* and *pallone*, the teams represented the three traditional divisions of the city – the *terzi* of Camollia, Città and San Martino. In the *cacce ai tori, asinate* and *bufalate* the competing groups were the *contrade*.

Assumption (Cecchini and Neri, 1958, pp.15–76; Falassi and Catoni, 1982, pp.44–6).[8]

From as early as 1200, the celebration of the feast of the Assumption of the Virgin, in mid-August, was the high point in the annual religious and political life of Siena. The cathedral of the city was already dedicated to the Virgin, and at the annual feast celebrating the tradition of her bodily assumption into heaven, the civic authorities organized an elaborate festival. Central to the festival was the Corteo dei Ceri e dei Censi – 'The Procession of Candles and Tributes' (see Chapter 4, pp.136–7). In this ceremony the Sienese community solemnly processed to the cathedral and the various parts of the community – from civic dignitaries to parishes, *contrade* and even individual citizens – each presented candles of varying value to the Virgin. Moreover, the rituals of this annual act of devotion by the city to the Virgin also included the symbolic resubmission to Siena of the towns, castles, estates and feudal families which together comprised the territory of the medieval Sienese state in southern Tuscany – an act of resubmission symbolized by the presentation to the Virgin of both banners and candles (Norman, 1999, pp.1–3; Civai and Toti, 2000, pp.33 and 70–3).

By requiring that such temporal resubmissions be made directly to the Virgin at the feast of the Assumption, the Sienese also effected an annual symbolic reaffirmation of the heavenly sanction that was claimed for the earthly power and dominion of their city. Not surprisingly, therefore, the Corteo dei Ceri has been described as the highest and most important event in the religious life of the city, and at the same time, the ceremony of greatest political significance (Falassi and Catoni, 1982, p.60; Bonicelli, 1992, p.20). It was also, however, a classic – though by no means unique – example of civil religion in a medieval Italian city state. And on the feast of the Assumption itself, the Sienese Comune in its turn presented a Palio banner for the winner of a Palio *alla lunga* run through the city streets, starting outside the city gate called the Porta Romana and ending in the square outside the cathedral.

If the significance of the festival of the Assumption and the presentation of candles and tributes to the Virgin was thus already well established as part of Sienese civil religion by the middle of the thirteenth century, the events of 1260 nevertheless served to enhance the importance of this annual ritual still further. As explained in

---

[8] The Palio *alla lunga* continued to be run on 15 August until the early 1870s, at which point it was quietly discontinued, the two annual Palii *alla tonda* by then having become the centre and focus of Sienese tradition and popular culture (Heywood, 1899, pp.165–6; Grassi, 1972, vol.2, p.8; Cairola, 1989, p.234).

Chapter 4, in early September 1260, Siena was threatened by the armies of Florence, its powerful northern neighbour and traditional enemy. According to Sienese tradition, the Sienese, facing apparently certain defeat, processed to their cathedral, dedicated their city to the Virgin – even symbolically giving her the keys of the city – and asked for her protection in the coming battle. In the ensuing battle of Montaperti, the Sienese gained a decisive victory over the Florentines. According to legend, moreover, the night before the battle, a white cloud was seen to hover over the Sienese camp – a phenomenon interpreted by the Sienese as the Virgin casting her cloak protectively over them. From 1260 onwards, therefore, the annual celebrations, processions and tributes of the festival of the Assumption inevitably took on an even greater significance in the political life and the civil religion of Siena.

The remarkable sense of continuity that is so characteristic of Sienese culture and history is nowhere more graphically demonstrated than in the continuing tradition of the Corteo dei Ceri and its ongoing relationship with the modern Palio. The Corteo dei Ceri is still celebrated every 14 August, when children from each *contrada*, dressed in *contrada* costumes of medieval style, gather with gifts of candles at the church of San Giorgio in Pantaneto and walk in procession through the streets, via the Campo and the Palazzo Pubblico, to the cathedral. They are accompanied by other children representing the parishes of Siena, grouped according to the three ancient *terzi* of Camollia, San Martino and Città, and by yet more children in medieval costume carrying banners representing the subject towns and castles of the old Sienese state. Representatives of the city also attend – many of them again in medieval costume – bringing, as their medieval predecessors did, a large decorated candle on behalf of the city itself. Officials, drummers and flag-bearers of each *contrada* accompany the procession with the *drappellone* – because in August it is the Corteo dei Ceri that provides the occasion for the transfer of the *drappellone* from the Palazzo Pubblico to the cathedral, to be blessed and displayed amid the emotional acclamation of the assembled *contrada* members.

The Corteo dei Ceri thus provides a compelling affirmation of the underlying continuity that exists between the modern Palio and the civil religion of medieval Siena. This continuity is reinforced by the reports of the annual Corteo dei Ceri in the local papers, which characteristically summarize the history of the event and explicitly relate the modern ceremony to its medieval predecessor. In this way, the intermingling of the ecclesiastical and civil celebrations of the feast of the Assumption in modern Siena – and the connection of both with the Palio – provide a telling illustration of the intimate relationship between the Palio and both 'civil' and 'official' religion.

Figure 5.12 The Corteo dei Ceri – the candle presented by the Comune is lit by the mayor. Foto Lensini, Siena.

Figure 5.13 The Corteo dei Ceri – the candles presented by the Contrada dell'Istrice. Foto Lensini, Siena.

The Palio as civil religion

The argument that the Palio may plausibly be regarded as an example of a civil religion is strengthened by an examination of the rituals of the modern Palio, together with a consideration of the role played by the event in sustaining an overarching Sienese identity above and beyond that of the seventeen individual *contrade*. The appropriate starting point for this is the structure and significance of the Corteo Storico, the two-hour-long historical parade that precedes the running of every Palio.

The roots of the modern Corteo Storico lie in the elaborate allegorical pageants with which the Sienese accompanied their communal games in the Campo from the renaissance onwards (Falassi and Catoni, 1982, pp.67–8; Fiorini, 1987, pp.91–107; Civai and Toti, 2000, pp.74–5; Turrini, 2000, pp.17–34). From the early nineteenth century, however, the Corteo Storico steadily developed an increasingly formalized and historically oriented form, and from 1813 the *contrade* were all required to have the same number of representatives in the parade. From the same date the parade also included a *carroccio*, a large four-wheeled cart, which explicitly recalled the victory of Montaperti and on which the *drappellone* for the Palio was carried into and around the Campo. Until the 1870s, the *contrade* appeared in a variety of styles of costumes, including both evocations of the renaissance era and contemporary styles of military uniform, reflecting the nationalism of the mid-nineteenth century, the era of Italian unification and the foundation of the modern Italian state (Fiorini, 1987, pp.107–8; Cairola, 1989, pp.207–8; Betti, 1995, pp.64–5; Turrini, 2000, pp.34–46; Corsi, 1997, pp.289–303; Civai and Toti, 2000, p.81). In the 1870s, however, the seventeen contrade and the Sienese Comune agreed that the parade would be dressed in medieval and renaissance costumes, thus establishing a custom that has continued to the present day (Corsi, 1997, pp.304–16; Civai and Toti, 1988; 2000, pp.81–6; Brutti, 2000). In 1885, the 'Marcia del Palio' – a march composed for the Palio by the Sienese composer Pietro Formichi – was introduced to the Corteo Storico. It, too, is still used to this day and, in many ways, performs a function analogous to that of a national anthem for the Sienese. The costumes for the Palio were subsequently renewed in 1904, 1928, 1955, 1981 and, most recently, in 2000. At each renewal new designs were commissioned and additional specific historical references were introduced. Similarly, new versions of the *carroccio* were introduced in 1928 and 1955, and the precise order and structure of the Corteo Storico was made increasingly elaborate, detailed and complex. Despite all such modifications and additions, however, there is clearly a direct line of continuity between the Corteo Storico that was established in the late 1870s and that which still occurs today before each Palio.

Since 1981, the contemporary Corteo Storico has consisted of fourteen main sections. Led by representatives of the Comune of Siena and the town band playing the 'Marcia del Palio', the first major section includes 67 standard bearers representing the cities, lands, castles and other territories of the independent Sienese state of the thirteenth to mid-sixteenth centuries. This section is concluded by two larger groups representing two cities to the south-west of Siena which were particularly important to the independent Sienese state. The first, Massa Marittima, had first entered into formal alliance with Siena in 1276. The second, Montalcino, had also been allied with Siena since the late thirteenth century and, after the fall of Siena to Florence in 1555 after a bitter siege, became the location of a continuing Sienese republic in exile for a further four years. The parade then continues with a series of sections representing the three historic *terzi* of Siena, the university and the ancient guilds. These are followed by a group carrying the *masgalano*, a trophy that is awarded each year to the *contrada* whose representatives in the parades for that year's Palii are judged to have presented the most elegant appearance and to have performed most skilfully with their flags and drums – the display of drumming and performance with flags being an integral and ancient part of the parade.[9] (See Colour Plates 12, 13 and 14.)

Then follow the ten groups – called *comparse* – representing the ten *contrade* competing in the Palio, and seven more *comparse* representing the *contrade* not participating in this particular Palio. Each *comparsa* consists of eleven members of the *contrada* in medieval or renaissance costume, comprising one drummer (*tamburino*), two flag-bearers (*alfieri*), three armed men, three pages carrying standards, and two grooms who lead, respectively, the large horse on which the *contrada*'s jockey rides in the parade and the actual horse that he will ride in the Palio. Further sections of the parade represent ancient *contrade* which no longer exist, more civic officials of the ancient Sienese state, and historic Sienese noble families. The climax of the *corteo*, however, is the *carroccio*, drawn

---

[9] On the intricacy, skill and complex symbolism of Sienese flag play and drumming, see Dundes and Falassi (1975, pp.110–20); Falassi and Catoni (1982, pp.12–13 and 71). The two CD-ROMs referred to in footnote 4 include both images of the performances with flags and recordings of the principal drumming patterns. For the history of the *masgalano* that is awarded to the *contrada* judged to have achieved the most elegant performance and appearance, see Fiorini (1987, pp.108–19); and Civai *et al.* (2000).

by four white oxen, evoking the memory of the victory of Montaperti in 1260. On the *carroccio* are seated four civic officials who represent the governing authorities of the ancient Sienese state, together with trumpeters and two attendants, one of whom rings the small bell, the 'Martinella', which recalls the bell of the Florentine *carroccio* captured at Montaperti. Also carried on the *carroccio* is the *drappellone* for which the *contrade* will compete in the now imminent Palio. (See Colour Plate 15.)

Prior to the entry of the *corteo* into the Campo, the *comparse* of each of the seventeen *contrade* will have processed from the territory of its own *contrada* to the assembly point for the *corteo*. Each will have done so via a route through the city which includes a sequence of major civic and cultural institutions: namely, Piazza Salimbeni and the headquarters of the Monte dei Paschi (the 500-year-old Sienese bank which makes a substantial annual contribution to the funding of many aspects of Sienese cultural life, including the Palio); the Casino dei Nobili (the upper-class social club of Siena which overlooks the Campo); the Accademia Musicale Chigiana (a prestigious musical academy housed in the palace of one of Siena's most famous aristocratic families); the cathedral; and the Spedale di Santa Maria della Scala (the ancient hospital of Siena, now a museum complex, which has been a leading force in Sienese cultural and artistic life for

Figure 5.14 *Contrada* scarves being waved towards the *carroccio* as it moves around the Campo at the end of the Corteo Storico. Foto Lensini, Siena.

centuries). At each location, each *comparsa* honours the civic institution in question by performing a complex display with their flags – known as a *sbandierata* – to the accompaniment of the drum. By visiting each of these institutions, each *contrada* symbolically honours the civic life and the culture of the entire city, thus affirming the unity of Siena, above and beyond the seventeen separate *contrade*.

At the appointed time for the parade to begin, the large bell at the top of the Torre del Mangia, next to the town hall, begins to toll, slowly and deeply. Popularly nicknamed the Sunto (in honour of the Assunta, the Virgin of the Assumption), the bell tolls only on ceremonial occasions. The Sunto tolls throughout the parade until just before the horses emerge for the race itself. The drummers of the seventeen *comparse*, on leading their *comparse* into and around the Campo, not only use larger and deeper drums than in other *contrada* parades, but also play a particular pattern of drumbeats known as the *passo della Diana*, used only in the Campo in the parade before the Palio. During the parade, the drummers and flag-bearers of each *contrada* again perform their display several times at a sequence of points around the Campo – and for the *contrada* members gathered in the Campo a highlight of the parade will be the entry into the Campo of their own *comparsa*. For all Sienese present, however, the most emotional moment of all is the entry and progress around the Campo of the *carroccio* carrying the *drappellone*. As the *carroccio* moves slowly around the Campo, successive sections of the huge crowd within the Piazza, each comprised of members of a particular *contrada*, will wave their scarves in unison towards the *drappellone* as it passes – an action which is at once an echo of the earlier attempts to touch the *drappellone* when it is blessed in the cathedral or the church of Santa Maria di Provenzano, and also a moving climax to the Corteo Storico.

Descriptions of the Corteo Storico have frequently resorted to strikingly religious language and terminology in their attempts to convey its ethos and significance, even when the authors in question have been very far from interpreting the Palio in explicitly religious terms. Thus, the Corteo Storico has been described as a 'rite' which embodies and expresses a 'mythic' version of Sienese history during which Siena's 'long history lives again'. Similarly, the period during which the Sunto tolls has been seen as a special time, outside chronological time, during which the Campo is transformed into a 'sacred space'. The parade, specifically designed as a commemoration and celebration of a perceived golden age of Sienese history, reaffirms and reiterates the distinctive values and traditions of the period of Siena's existence as an independent city state (Barzanti,

1972, p.18; Dundes and Falassi, 1975, pp.101–2; Barzanti and Falassi, 1976; Falassi, 1980, pp.23–9). Examples of such 'religious' language also occur in the popular context of the local press. For example, local papers may refer to the 'vigil' of the festival, to the 'rite' of treading on the soil in the 'sacred place' of the Campo, and to the 'liturgy' of both time and place that the Corteo Storico expresses (*Il Campo di Siena*, 3 July 1996, pp.1 and 11).

The use of the Sunto bell and of particular drums and patterns of drumming are, indeed, rituals suggestive of the performance of a 'sacred rite' in a 'sacred place'. Moreover, a closer analysis of the structure of the Corteo Storico also supports such an interpretation. The *corteo* begins with representatives of Siena and the Sienese republic at the height of its power, and ends with the *carroccio*, the symbol of the Sienese victory at Montaperti in 1260. The parade as a whole therefore constitutes a celebration of an idealized 'golden age' of Sienese history. For two hours before each Palio, the ancient Sienese republic – the ideal of which is said to live in the hearts of all Sienese – briefly comes to life again and the ancient republic of Siena is 'reborn'. The hours immediately before the running of every Palio thus provide a dynamic and creative re-presentation of the myth of a free and independent Siena which existed prior to the fall of the republic in the mid-sixteenth century (Dundes and Falassi, 1975, pp.101 and 108–9; Hook, 1979, pp.216 and 230; Betti, 1995, p.65; Mugnai, 1996, pp.31 and 35). The culminating moment of the Corteo Storico, moreover, exhibits this convergence of contemporary 'devotion' and historical 'commemoration' with particular intensity. As the *contrada* members wave their scarves in salute to the *drappellone* as it progresses around the Campo, they are also, simultaneously, saluting the *carroccio*, the symbol above all others of Sienese independence and liberty.[10]

---

[10] The intimate relationship between the *drappellone* and the *carroccio* is also demonstrated in a detail of the ritual associated with the Corteo dei Ceri each August. Attached to the two piers of the cathedral opposite that on which the *drappellone* is displayed after it has been blessed are two immense and evidently ancient wooden masts. By popular tradition these are the masts of the *carroccio* from the battle of Montaperti – although whether of the Sienese or the captured Florentine *carroccio* is a matter of debate. Either way – and regardless of whether they are indeed authentic – the popular association of such 'relics' of Montaperti with contemporary devotion to the Palio is suggestive of the vitality and intricacy of Sienese consciousness and celebration of their history (Heywood, 1899, pp.37–8; Torriti, 1988, p.97; Falassi, 1998, p.10). On the history of the *carroccio* and its symbolic significance for the Sienese, see Barzanti (1995). Significantly, the title of the bimonthly Sienese magazine dedicated to the history, culture and traditions of Siena is also *Il Carroccio*.

Viewed in this way, and within the broader interpretative framework provided by the concept of 'civil religion', the Corteo Storico may plausibly be understood as performing both a 'liturgical' and a 'sacramental' function within the Palio's role as a civil religion. To the extent that the Palio as a whole constitutes a twice-yearly rebirth and reaffirmation of the distinctiveness of Sienese identity and history, the Corteo Storico may be seen as a subtle, complex and effective liturgical celebration and expression of this fact. By a combination of costume, symbol, ritual and re-enactment, the Corteo Storico celebrates and re-presents the 'sacred history' and the 'sacred myths' of Siena. In its emotional and psychological impact, moreover, this 'liturgy' may also be said to constitute a sacramental expression of the devotion of the Sienese to their city and its traditions. For the two hours of 'sacred time' marked out by the tolling of the Sunto, the Corteo Storico brings back to life the long-dead republic. Certainly this act is one of 'remembrance'; but it is also more than this. The sacramental dimension of the Corteo Storico is of such intensity that it is even appropriate to speak of its resulting in a 'real presence' of the spirit of the Sienese republic. Or, to adapt a well-known definition of a sacrament, the Corteo Storico may be said to constitute a striking example of an 'outward and visible sign' of 'an inward and spiritual' reality: indeed, there could hardly be a more telling expression of the relationship between the outward pageantry and ritual of the Corteo Storico and the inward emotion and experience of the Sienese. Similarly, the twice-yearly ritual of laying 'the earth in the Piazza' may plausibly be interpreted not merely as a necessary preparation for the Palio, but also as a regular and ritualized 'reconsecration' of the Campo as the 'sacred space' at the heart of Siena.

The Corteo Storico is, however, by no means the only aspect of the Palio that lends itself to interpretation in terms of civil religion. The race that follows the Corteo Storico replaces the celebration of a historic and collective Sienese identity by the spectacle of intense and fierce rivalry between the Sienese *contrade*. Every Palio is an opportunity for one *contrada* to triumph and thus be reborn. At the end of the race, only one flag, that of the winning *contrada*, will fly on the Palazzo Pubblico. In the coming weeks, only the flags and emblems of that *contrada* will be prominent in Siena. Conversely, while all the other *contrade* will have lost, for the traditional rivals of the winning *contrada*, the losing will be particularly bitter and intense. Indeed, to understand the passion of the Palio it is also necessary to understand the intensity of the allegiance which members feel to their *contrada* – and the depth of rivalry between a given *contrada* and its traditional rivals. *Contrada* members will instinctively identify themselves primarily in terms of their *contrada*.

Outside Siena, they will proudly define themselves as Sienese, but within Siena they will proclaim themselves part of their *contrada,* even to the extent of saying instinctively 'I am from the [name of *contrada*]', or 'I am of the [name of *contrada*]' rather than merely describing themselves as a 'member' of their *contrada* (Dundes and Falassi, 1975, pp.19–20; Falassi and Catoni, 1982, p.9). Again, it is important to understand that such self-identification is deeply embedded within the popular consciousness of the Sienese. Thus, when the local papers refer to a particular local personality they may well indicate that he or she is a devoted member of his/her *contrada.* So, for example, in 1995, one local paper referred to the local historian Roberto Barzanti as a former mayor of Siena, now an MEP, but 'above all' a '*tartuchino*' – that is, a member of the Contrada della Tartuca (*Corriere di Siena*, 1 July 1995).

The rites of passage of *contrada* members now include baptism into the *contrada.* Traditionally, one became a member of a *contrada* by being born within the territorial confines of the *contrada* itself. With the expansion of the population of Siena, however, and with increasing social mobility, especially since the Second World War, the strict requirement of birth within the territory of a *contrada* has been relaxed. This modification in response to changing social trends has resulted in the introduction of an annual rite of baptism in each *contrada.* On the principal day of the *contrada*'s patronal festival, members gather at the official *contrada* fountain or at the Oratory. According to an established ritual – broadly similar in the different *contrade*, but each exhibiting its own specific characteristics – the Prior, the senior figure of the *contrada*, will baptize into the *contrada* babies born to members during the past year. At the same time the Prior will baptize older children and adults who have chosen this *contrada*, demonstrated their commitment and loyalty to it, and been accepted by the *contrada* members as worthy of inclusion. The baptismal rite includes reference to the *contrada*'s patron saint, to the particular traditions and heritage of the *contrada*, and to the special relationship the newly baptized members will now enjoy with their *contrada.* (See Colour Plate 11.) It is, however, a baptismal rite quite separate from that of the Catholic Church. It is the secular figure of the Prior of the *contrada* who baptizes; the 'liturgy' of the baptism relates to the *contrada*, not to the Christian Church; and the rite proclaims inclusion within a specific and privileged group, not membership of the church universal (Dundes and Falassi, 1975, pp.37–9; Falassi and Catoni, 1982, pp.26 and 29; Barzanti *et al.*, 1987).[11]

[11] The significance of *contrada* baptism will be considered in more detail in Chapter 7.

The intensity of commitment to, and identity with, one's *contrada* suggested by such rites of baptism is amply confirmed by the passionate devotion of members to every aspect of their *contrada* and its life. Much of a devoted *contrada* member's social life will focus on the rhythm of the *contrada* year, the functions arranged by the *contrada* social club or 'Society', and, of course, the anticipation of and preparation for the Palio. There are also newspapers and other publications devoted to the contemporary life and the history of each of the *contrade* (Ancilli *et al.*, 1999b). Each *contrada*, moreover, has its own rich heritage of traditions and symbols of identity, and each has a living creature – real or mythical – as its principal symbol. The seventeen *contrade* and their associated symbolic creatures are: Aquila (Eagle); Bruco (Caterpillar); Chiocciola (Snail); Civetta (Owl); Drago (Dragon); Giraffa (Giraffe); Istrice (Porcupine); Lupa (Wolf); Leocorno (Unicorn); Nicchio (Shell); Oca (Goose); Onda (Dolphin); Pantera (Panther); Selva (Rhinoceros); Tartuca (Tortoise); Torre (Elephant); and Valdimontone (Ram).[12] Each *contrada* also has an official flag (*bandiera*) and an official scarf (*fazzoletto*), which will include the symbolic creature as the centre of its design.

The flags fulfil a variety of functions. They are used in the parades around the city that accompany the patronal festival of each *contrada*, and are placed on the buildings of the *contrade* during both the patronal festival and the days of the Palio. They will also figure prominently in the celebration of a victory in the Palio. The scarves, meanwhile, are the principal means by which *contrada* members indicate their identity and allegiance and are prized possessions. At a *contrada* baptism those baptized receive not only a commemorative certificate, but also a personal scarf. Each *contrada* has a coat of arms –which will again include an image of its symbolic creature (Zazzeroni, 1980) – its own motto and colours. All of these appear in the *contrada*'s flags and scarves and in the ceremonial costumes for the Corteo Storico and the parades associated with the patronal festival of the *contrada*.[13]

The confines of each *contrada*'s precisely defined territory within the city are indicated by the symbols of the *contrada* displayed on the buildings that mark their boundaries. Each *contrada* has its own

[12] In most cases, the name of the *contrada* is the same as the symbolic creature. The exceptions are the Onda, Selva, Torre and Valdimontone.

[13] Details of the flags, colours, coats of arms and mottoes of all of the *contrade*, together with other more detailed information about each *contrada*, are available in English, with numerous illustrations, in Fallasi and Catoni (1982) and Betti (1995). The two CD-ROMs referred to in footnote 4 also provide this information, including many additional images.

designated 'entry', square, fountain, and commonly known geo-graphical and topographical designation. Each also has an official 'seat' (which functions as a genuine seat of government, because the *contrade* all enjoy a specific and definable legal and territorial status within Siena), and a museum in which the *contrada* displays its historical memorabilia including all the *drappelloni* won in past Palii (Colour Plate 10). In addition to its flag, scarf, traditional colours and symbolic animal, each *contrada* has a complex and extensive repertoire of songs which celebrate its history, traditions, triumphs and rivalries. These include both songs distinctive to each *contrada*, and individualized versions of songs common, in music and basic form, to all of the seventeen *contrade*. Such songs celebrate the territory of the *contrada* – for example, extolling its particular streets and monuments – its symbolic animal, flag, colours and people. Above all, however, the songs celebrate the Palio, from the assignment of the horses, through the *prove*, to the Palio itself; they celebrate alliances and rivalries, past victories and famous incidents. During the days of the Palio they are sung around the city, and most especially they are sung as *contrada* members escort their horse to the Campo for each of the *prove* and as the assembled crowd awaits the running of each *prova*. The songs are a living tradition. As well as singing traditional verses celebrating past Palii, new verses will be made up in honour of the present festival and its incidents – and they are sung with a passion and emotional intensity that it would be difficult to exaggerate (Dundes and Falassi, 1975, chapter 8; Falassi, 1980; Civai and Toti, 2000, pp.110–40). Each *contrada* also has its own official *inno* (hymn), which functions as the equivalent of a national anthem, celebrates the *contrada* and its history, and is played and sung at *contrada* celebrations (Falassi, 1980, pp.33–59; Mancini, 1993).[14]

Given the precise territorial definition of each *contrada* and the intensity of *contrada* members' devotion to their *contrada*, it is hardly surprising that the *contrade* are often described as 'cities within the city' or 'little countries'. Nor is it surprising that the feelings of *contrada* members for their *contrada* have been compared with the emotions of patriotism and national allegiance to one's country, or that the existence of '*contrada* character' has been compared to

---

[14] The *inni* of the *contrade* are a development of the twentieth century. In some cases *contrade* have replaced their original *inni* with new versions. For the text of the present official *inni* of the *contrade*, together with recordings of them all, plus the 'Marcia del Palio', see the 1997 CD, *Inni delle contrade*, Natali Multimedia srl, Florence. As well as the official *inni*, all of the *contrade* also have a rich tradition of 'sonnets', poems written in celebration of the annual patronal festival of the *contrada*, or in thanks for victory in a Palio (Trabalzini, 1976; Falassi, 1999).

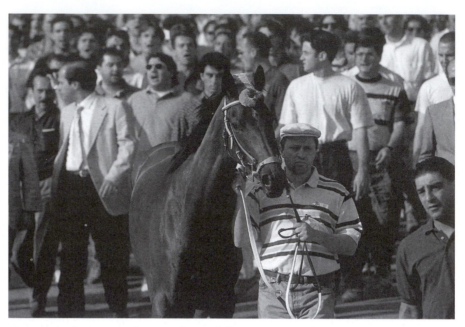

Figure 5.15 *Contrada* members following their horse into the Campo before a *prova*. Foto Lensini, Siena.

the existence of 'national character' (Heywood, 1899, p.197; Dundes and Falassi, 1975, pp.12, 26 and 46; Barzanti, 1980; De Cristofaro, 1988, p.xxvi). Moreover, just as patriotism and national allegiance often lead to rivalries and to the making of alliances, so also rivalry and alliances are part of the life of the Sienese *contrade*. Every *contrada* wishes, above all, to win the Palio for itself. It is also of great importance, however, that the *contrada* that is the traditional rival should *not* win. Thus, even in a Palio in which a particular *contrada* is not competing, there may well be an intense interest in conspiring with other *contrade* that are running, in order to frustrate the ambitions of the traditional rival. An essential part of every Palio, therefore, is the making of secret agreements by which *contrade* agree to help each other or to obstruct rivals (Dundes and Falassi, 1975, pp.72–92; Civai and Toti, 2000, pp.166–7). Nor should the intensity of historic *contrada* rivalries be underestimated. While alliances between *contrade* come and go and are held with varying intensity – often changing over the years from close and formal alliance to informal friendship, or to no official relationship at all – the particular rivalries tend to remain more fixed and intense, often dating back decades or even centuries. Also, while alliances and friendships may exist with several other *contrade* simultaneously, rivalries are essentially one-to-one: thus, a sequence of long-established oppositions criss-crosses the relationships of the seventeen *contrade*. Currently the most firmly established rivalries are those between Aquila and Pantera; Chiocciola and Tartuca; Civetta and Leocorno; Istrice and Lupa; Nicchio and Valdimontone; Onda and Torre; and Oca and Torre. The rivalry between the Oca and the Torre is notoriously intense and is the only one between *contrade* that are not geographically adjacent and who thus do not share a common boundary.[15]

The depth and intensity of such rivalries are considerable. Celebrated in song, instilled into the young from infancy by rhymes and games, and consolidated through the secret agreements and the competition of every Palio, they are essential to the spirit and passion of Sienese life and of the Palio. During the days of the Palio – and especially before each *prova* – *contrada* members both celebrate their own *contrada* in their songs and taunt their traditional rivals. If the rivals are competing directly in the Palio, then there may well be ritualized confrontations in and around the Campo – an echo, clearly, of the old Sienese tradition of fist-fighting in the game of *pugna*. And after a victory, the celebrations of the winning *contrada* will include the mockery of the historic rival, not least through a victory carnival and cartoons posted around the city. By tradition, the losers in the Palio, and especially the rivals of the winning *contrada*, are sent a 'purge' of castor oil by the winners. Many of the jokes and cartoons at rivals' expense are similarly scatological in nature (Dundes and Falassi, 1975, pp.139, 182–3 and 232; Cesarini, 1988, pp.127–8).

It might well be objected that such rivalry between *contrade*, focused on the Palio, constitutes conclusive evidence against the view that the Palio functions as a Sienese civil religion. After all, one of the principal purposes of a civil religion is precisely the unifying of otherwise disparate groups within a given society. In fact, however, despite its celebration – or even 'sacralization' – of the traditional rivalries between the Sienese *contrade*, the Palio nevertheless functions as a unifying force, and one, moreover, whose rituals may again be shown to act as a celebration and re-presentation of centuries-old Sienese traditions. One of the enduring themes of Sienese history – including the history of the independent Sienese state of the thirteenth to mid-sixteenth centuries – is the persistent fear of faction and internal dispute, and, at the same time, the

---

[15] For more detailed accounts of the traditional rivalries, see Dundes and Falassi (1975, pp.40–6); Falassi and Catoni (1982, pp.32–3). These accounts are accurate descriptions of the situation that pertained when they were written and are effective evocations of the ethos of *contrada* rivalry. In the last decade, however, some of the rivalries described in these sources have been resolved. The present position concerning official alliances and rivalries may be explored through the CD-ROMS on the Palio.

recognition that the Sienese were peculiarly prone to such disunity (Hook, 1979, p.144; Caferro, 1998, pp.xix–xx). It is therefore possible to interpret various features of the Palio as evocations of old Sienese traditions. Thus, the fierce rivalries between *contrade* in the Palio may recall those between prominent families and interest groups within medieval and renaissance Siena. The agreements between *contrade* may recall the temporary treaties and alliances that medieval Siena regularly made with neighbouring Tuscan city states. And the fact that the jockeys who ride in the Palio are not members of the *contrade* they represent but are hired for the event may recall the medieval Sienese tradition – shared with other medieval Italian city states – of appointing key civic officials from outside the community and hiring mercenaries to fight for the city in time of war or danger (Dundes and Falassi, 1975, pp.42, 65 and 90–1; Falassi and Catoni, 1982, pp.29–30 and 63). The rivalry and disunity of the Palio may thus be seen as both a recollection and a celebration of the factionalism that figured so largely in Sienese consciousness in the medieval and renaissance periods. But the Palio is not only a celebration of rivalry and factionalism. It is also the means by which such rivalry and factionalism are bound together and subsumed into a greater unity. The Palio unites the seventeen *contrade* of Siena in a manner that transcends the divisions and rivalries of the individual *contrade* and provides the Sienese with a collective identity and a collective sense of their uniqueness in relation to the rest of the world.

The fact that the Campo is the venue for the Palio provides a further powerful symbolic expression and demonstration of the way in which the entire event is an enduring reaffirmation of Sienese 'unity in diversity'. The Campo has been described as 'an essentially sacred place' (Hook, 1979, p.73). Located at the heart of Siena, it was, as we have seen, the location for most of the earlier communal games so beloved by the Sienese in the medieval and renaissance periods. Moreover, from as early as the late twelfth and thirteenth centuries, the Campo had already begun to enjoy a degree and type of protection and regulation more often accorded to religious sites (Cairola, 1963, pp.10–13; Hook, 1979, pp.76–7; Bowsky, 1981, p.294; Waley, 1991, pp.12–13). A popular Sienese metaphor even interprets the shape of the Campo as a representation of the cloak of the Virgin that, according to legend, was cast protectively over the Sienese on the eve of the battle of Montaperti (Dundes and Falassi, 1975, pp.202–3; Hook, 1979, pp.72–3).

After the fall of the independent Sienese republic in 1555, the Campo became the natural focus for the comprehensive turning-inwards that has characterized Sienese self-consciousness ever since. For the Sienese, it has been argued, the world is characteristically seen in terms of a series of oppositions or antinomies, of which, in each case, the first half of the antinomy is always the positive part. Thus, for a Sienese the sequence us/them, Sienese/non-Sienese, inside/outside (especially in the sense of 'inside the walls of Siena, not outside them') will immediately suggest the preferability of the first item in each pair. And at the centre of the 'inside' of Siena itself is the Campo – which is thus understood as the most positive place of all (Falassi, 1980, pp.15–17). The Campo is also the centre of Siena in relation to the seventeen *contrade*, each of which locates and orientates itself within Siena in relation to the Campo. The official entrance to each *contrada* reflects the *contrada*'s relationship with the Campo, not with the world outside Siena. Each *contrada* has a traditional route to the Campo and an acknowledged entrance into and exit from it (Dundes and Falassi, 1975, pp.23–4; Falassi, 1980, pp.9–11; Falassi and Catoni, 1982, p.14). Yet the Campo itself is not part of any *contrada*. It is neutral ground: the place in which all the *contrade* compete for the Palio, but in which none has precedence or priority – save for two occasions: namely the winning of a Palio and the annual day of the patronal festival. On the day of its patronal festival a *contrada* may process around the Campo, its flags dipping and rising around the whole circuit of the piazza, before completing a final celebratory flag display. On the occasion of a victory in the Palio, meanwhile, the winning *contrada* will repeatedly parade the newly won *drappellone* through and around the Campo. But the 'possession' of the Campo is strictly temporary: the next Palio will almost certainly bring a new winner and the 'rebirth' of another *contrada*.

Both the Campo and the Palio thus affirm that the heart of Sienese identity lies, above all, in a paradoxical 'unity in diversity' – a passionate revelling in rivalry and faction which, nevertheless, in and of itself, affirms a greater shared identity and sense of distinctiveness as Sienese. The nature of the paradox is well expressed in the title of the centenary history of the Magistrato delle Contrade, the organization set up by the *contrade* at the end of the nineteenth century to represent and protect their collective interests. The history of the organization, published in 1994, was entitled *Nel Campo in lotta ed al di fuor sorelle* ('In the Campo Conflict, and Outside Allies') (Valacchi, 1994).[16] Similarly, the historical introduction to the new costumes for the Corteo Storico in 1981 concluded with the assertion that, 'Unity in diversity and in division remains one of the fundamental characteristics of the Palio' (Cairola, 1981, p.14).

[16] Literally, 'in the Campo conflict, and outside sisters' – a reflection of the fact that, in Italian, the word '*contrada*' is female and therefore the collective solidarity of the seventeen *contrade* is expressed linguistically in terms of 'sisterhood'.

This sense of a shared identity and shared devotion to Siena, sustained and nurtured by the internal rivalry of the *contrade*, is perhaps nowhere better illustrated than in an incident that occurred in a prisoner-of-war camp in Tunisia in 1943, and has now become a popularly and affectionately remembered Palio anecdote. On 16 August 1943, a group of Sienese among the Italian prisoners proceeded to hold a makeshift Palio, tolling a bell, wearing coloured emblems and marching around an imaginary shell-shaped square. Ten of them finally raced three times around the same imaginary square, and the winner was given a crude 'palio'. When the British guards, alarmed by these unusual events, segregated these prisoners, they proceeded to sing through the night. The song they sang was one of the most popular Sienese tunes, sung in all of the *contrade*. Each *contrada* has its own words to the tune, celebrating its own identity and ridiculing its rival in a variety of verses. Significantly, however, the chosen version in the Tunisian prisoner-of-war camp in 1943 did not celebrate any particular *contrada*. It was, instead, the version of the song that is sung by all Sienese and which celebrates Siena itself, beginning with a reference to the Campo and ending with the affirmation that Siena is the most beautiful of cities (Tailetti, 1967, p.18; 1972, pp.79–80; Dundes and Falassi, 1975, pp.162–4; Falassi, 1980, pp.61–2).[17] Moreover, the popular currency of the anecdote is attested by the retelling of the story from time to time in the local press (as, for example, in *La Voce del Campo*, 13 August 1994, p.10; *Il Cittadino*, 12 August 1996, p.13), while the symbolic importance of the incident for the Sienese is also suggested by the way that it is sometimes referred to as the 'Palio in Africa' or 'the Palio of 1943'. The particular significance of such descriptions lies in the fact that, during both world wars the Palio was suspended for the duration of hostilities – the only periods of sustained interruption to the sequence of races in the history of the modern Palio.

Almost a year after the 'Palio' in the Tunisian prisoner-of-war camp, the events of June 1944 provided a further striking example of the unity of the *contrade* in their devotion to Siena. As Chapter 4 discussed in detail, while the Allied armies advanced towards Siena and the city was threatened with bombardment, the civic authorities again processed to the cathedral and rededicated the city to the Virgin, echoing the actions of their forebears almost seven centuries

---

[17] The title of the version of the song sung in 1943 is 'Nella Piazza del Campo' ('In the Piazza del Campo'). The music and words are reproduced, the latter in both English and Italian, in Dundes and Fallasi (1975, pp.163–4). Like the 'Marcia del Palio', 'Nella Piazza del Campo' has been described as the *inno nazionale* (national anthem) of the Sienese (De Cristofaro, 1988, p.5).

earlier before the battle of Montaperti. They processed from the Palazzo Pubblico to the cathedral, escorted by civic emblems and musicians, by the Rector of the Magistrato delle Contrade, and by the Priors and representatives of the seventeen *contrade*. At the cathedral, in front of a crowd so large that it spilled out of the cathedral and into the square outside, the mayor of Siena renewed the dedication of the city to the Virgin. The Act of Dedication itself is still displayed in the cathedral, next to the Cappella del Voto, the chapel that houses the revered image of the Virgin before which the Sienese had previously rededicated their city in moments of crisis and danger. At the foot of the 1944 Act of Dedication appear the signatures of the mayor, the deputy mayor and the Rector of the Magistrato delle Contrade, followed by the signatures of each of the Priors of the *contrade*. Siena did, in fact, sustain only very limited damage from bombing. With the liberation of the city it again became possible to hold the Palio, and the city celebrated in its customary manner. In 1945, as well as the Palii of 2 July and 16 August, the first extraordinary Palio of the post-war era was run, on 20 August, and officially designated the 'Palio of Peace'.

Conclusion

The argument of this chapter is that the Palio of Siena – together with the rituals and traditions that surround it – constitutes a telling and persuasive example of a civil religion. In conclusion, therefore, it is appropriate to summarize the argument by returning to the definition of a civil religion noted in the introduction and assessing the evidence presented in relation to the Palio against this criterion. According to the definition proposed by Richard Pierard and Robert Linder, such civil religion sustains the widespread acceptance by a people of a shared sense of their nation's history and destiny; it relates their society to a realm of absolute meaning, enables them to look at their society and community as in some sense special, and provides a vision which ties the nation together as an integrated whole; and it promotes a collection of beliefs, values, rites, ceremonies and symbols which, taken together, give sacred meaning to the life of the community and thus provide an overarching sense of unity that transcends internal conflicts and differences.

The Palio, it may reasonably be argued, amply fulfils each of these criteria. Rooted in Siena's centuries-long devotion to the Virgin and in the traditional games and celebrations of the Sienese, the Palio provides a powerful annual re-presentation of Sienese history and self-understanding. Through the traditions and memorabilia of past Palii – not least as preserved in the seventeen *contrada* museums and their archives and in the living traditions of the Palio songs – and through the twice-yearly event of the Corteo Storico before each Palio, the Sienese sense of their own history, identity and destiny is, indeed, facilitated and sustained. It is true that the destiny involved is, in some senses, a tragic one. The *corteo*, after all, celebrates a mythic golden age which, even in its own terms, ended in the mid-sixteenth century with the fall of the Sienese republic. And yet, the Sienese sense of destiny also includes a belief in the continuing distinctiveness of the Sienese spirit and its associated values: the turn inwards after the fall of the republic was also a deliberate strategy for the preservation of the particularity and uniqueness which is Siena and the Sienese world-view. This, too, is annually nurtured and sustained by the Palio and its traditions, rituals, songs and celebrations.

The Palio also enables the Sienese to relate their society to a realm of absolute meaning. Most obviously, it is intimately associated with the long Sienese devotion to the Virgin. The two annual Palii are run in honour of the Virgin and each *drappellone* bears her image – while the continuing vitality of Sienese devotion to the Virgin is attested by the rededication of the city to her in June 1944. Similarly, the Palio relates the Sienese to a realm of absolute meaning in its deeply felt capacity to evoke a sense of rebirth, of the triumph of life over death, and of the bringing of life out of death. For a *contrada*, to win the Palio is to experience the rebirth of the *contrada* itself. For individual *contrada* members, the winning of the Palio will be marked by a personal sense of rebirth, symbolized by the wearing of a baby's dummy, or the drinking of wine from a baby's bottle, while parading through the streets with the newly won *drappellone* – itself now called *il neonato*, 'the newborn'. The Palio thus allows the Sienese the possibility of briefly transcending historical time and the limits of a human lifetime. The old hope to live to see their *contrada* win the Palio one more time, and when a *contrada* wins the Palio there is a palpable sense of the old growing young again in their celebration and joy (Dundes and Falassi, 1975, pp.187 and 236; Falassi, 1980, p.13). Similarly, the members of a *contrada* live in the certainty that their *contrada* will continue after their passing; that their children will maintain family and *contrada* traditions; that they will confront the traditional rival in the Campo; and, above all, that the Palio itself will continue. For Siena as a whole, meanwhile, the Corteo Storico provides a twice-yearly rebirth of the republic: for two hours before each Palio the Sienese republic is once more alive, liturgically re-presented to the contemporary Sienese.

Equally clearly, the Palio, together with its values, ceremonies, rites and symbols, provides a vision that ties together otherwise disparate elements and thus creates an overarching unity that transcends the internal rivalries and divisions within Siena. Both the concept and the reality of 'unity in diversity' are fundamental to Sienese consciousness and experience. A relatively small city and society is subdivided into no less than seventeen separate entities, each of which possesses a territory, history and social structure amounting to a city within the city; each of which commands a loyalty of such intensity that it is commonly compared to patriotism; and between which there exist a series of fierce and passionate rivalries. Yet, out of such division, the Palio creates a formidable unity, focusing the internal rivalries in which the Sienese – by long tradition – take such delight, and forging from them a common identity and pride as citizens of a unique city. It is hard to see how one of the most fundamental functions of a civil religion might be fulfilled more successfully.

Finally, the interpretation of the Palio in terms of its role as a civil religion may also help to explain the frequently posed question as to why this phenomenon has continued to flourish – and indeed to dominate the life of the city – in Siena, while elsewhere in Italy similar civic festivals have frequently either ceased to exist, have survived into the twentieth century as little more than tourist attractions, or have been revived only after long periods in abeyance.[18] As the Sienese rightly insist, the Palio is neither a revival nor a mere survival. It is not a revival because it has a continuous history stretching back, in its modern form alone, to the early seventeenth century, to say nothing of its continuity with, and summation of, earlier Sienese traditions and festivities dating back to the thirteenth century. It is not a mere survival because it is not an event kept going by a minority of enthusiasts or principally for the benefit of Sienese tourism (Dundes and Falassi, 1975, p.185; Hook, 1979, p.218; Barzanti, 1988, p.xx; Silverman, 1989, p.224; Civai and Toti, 2000, p.68). On the contrary, it is a pervasive influence on Sienese life, nurturing and sustaining both the personal and the corporate identity of the Sienese.

It has been suggested that while no one explanation of the enduring vitality of the Palio is likely to be sufficient – precisely because the complexity and intricacy of the Palio defies any single interpretative approach – at least a part of the explanation of its endurance may be found in its close association with religion

[18] For a survey of such festivals in Tuscany, which confirms the distinctive nature of the Palio precisely because of its continuity, see Artusi and Gabbrielli (1978). For a broader survey of popular festivals in the various regions of modern Italy, see Falassi (1988). This survey also confirms the distinctiveness of the Sienese Palio.

(Dundes and Falassi, 1975, pp.5–6). The point is well made for, as has also been observed, the Palio is at once both a corporate game and a corporate act of worship (Hook, 1979, p.224). Such judgements, however, have hitherto been based principally on readings of the Palio in terms of its relationship with 'official' religion, and its incorporation within its rituals of overtly religious activities such as the association with the Virgin, the blessing of the *drappellone* and the horses, and the singing of a hymn to the Virgin in thanks for victory. How much more pertinent are these judgements if the Palio, in all its complexity and richness – and in addition to its many other undoubted meanings and significances – is recognized to be, in itself, a modern expression of the 'civil religion' of the Sienese?

References

Ancilli, L., Borghi, L. and Nencini, R. (1999a) 'Numeri Unici 1932–1999', in *Caratteri di Contrada: numeri unici e giornali delle Contrade di Siena*, Siena: Protagon Editore Toscani/Biblioteca Comunale degli Intronati, pp.39–104.

Ancilli, L., Borghi, L. and Nencini, R. (1999b) 'Giornali di Contrada', in *Caratteri di Contrada: numeri unici e giornali delle Contrade di Siena*, Siena: Protagon Editore Toscani/Biblioteca Comunale degli Intronati, pp.105–14.

Artusi, L. and Gabbrielli, S. (1978) *Gioco, Giostra, Palio in Toscana*, Florence: Libreria SP 44.

Balestracci, D. (1999) 'Quando le Contrade cominciarono a dare i numeri', in *Caratteri di Contrada: numeri unici e giornali delle Contrade di Siena*, Siena: Protagon Editore Toscani/Biblioteca Comunale degli Intronati, pp.9–20.

Barzanti, R. (1972) *Siena: A Territory, a History, a Festival*, Siena: Monte dei Paschi.

Barzanti, R. (1980) 'Contrada Città-Stato', in A. Pecchioli (ed.) (1980) *Il Palio di Siena*, Rome: Editalia, pp.77–82.

Barzanti, R. (1988) 'Tra mito e storia', in J. Hook, *Siena: una città e la sua storia*, Siena: Nuova Immagine Editrice, pp.xi–xxiv.

Barzanti, R. (1995) 'C'è Carroccio e carroccio!', *Il Carroccio*, 57, pp.4–6.

Barzanti, R. (1996) 'Il Palio', in R. Barzanti, G. Catoni and M. De Gregorio (eds) *Storia di Siena II*, pp.109–22.

Barzanti, R., Catoni, G. and De Gregorio, M. (eds) (1995) *Storia di Siena I: dalle origini alla fine della repubblica*; (1996) *Storia di Siena II: dal granducato all'unità*; (1997) *Storia di Siena III: l'età contemporanea*, Siena: Edizioni Alsaba.

Barzanti, R. and Falassi, A. (1976) 'Il corteo da allegoria a metafora', *Nuovo Corriere Senese*, 10, p.9.

Barzanti, R., Falassi, A. and Crispolti, E. (1987) *Le fontane di Contrada*, Siena: Il Leccio.

Betti, L. (ed.) (1995) *A Guide to the Palio*, Siena: Betti Editrice.

Bonicelli, G. (1992) 'La Madonna, Siena e il Palio' in L. Betti (ed.) (1992–3) *Pallium: evoluzione del drappellone dalle origini ad oggi*, 4 volumes, Siena: Betti Editrice, vol.2, pp.19–22.

Bowsky, W. (1981) *A Medieval Italian Commune: Siena under the Nine, 1287–1355*, Berkeley: University of California Press.

Brutti, M. (2000) 'I rinnovi dei costumi dal 1878 al 2000: aspetti storici ed istituzionali', in *Le Comparse della Torre dal cinquecento al Duemila*, Siena: Carlo Cambi Editore, pp.47–68.

Caferro, W. (1998) *Mercenary Companies and the Decline of Siena*, Baltimore: Johns Hopkins University Press.

Cairola, A. (1963) 'L'Architettura', in A. Cairola and E. Carli, *Il Palazzo Pubblico di Siena*, Rome: Editalia.

Cairola, A. (1981) *The New Municipal Costumes in the Historical Procession Preceding the Palio of Siena*, Siena: Editalia.

Cairola, A. (1989) *Siena – le contrade: storia, feste, territorio, aggregazione*, Siena: Edizioni Il Leccio.

Cannon, J. and Vauchez, A. (1999) *Margherita of Cortona and the Lorenzetti: Sienese Art and the Cult of a Holy Woman in Medieval Tuscany*, University Park Pennsylvania: Penn State Press.

Cannon, J. and Williamson, B. (eds) (2000) *Art, Politics, and Civic Religion in Central Italy 1261–1352*, Aldershot: Ashgate.

Ceccherini, D. (1995) *Gli oratori delle contrade di Siena: storia, architettura, arte*, Siena: Betti Editrice.

Cecchini, G. and Neri, D. (1958) *The Palio of Siena*, Siena: Monte dei Paschi.

Cesarini, P. (1988) *Il Palio*, Siena: Lombardi.

Chittolini, G. (1990) 'Civic religion and the countryside in late medieval Italy', in T. Dean and C. Wickham (eds) *City and Countryside in Late Medieval and Renaissance Italy*, London: The Hambledon Press, pp.69–80.

Civai, M. and Toti, E. (1988) *Il rinnuovo del Corteo Storico del Palio di Siena*, Siena: Alsaba.

Civai, M. and Toti, E. (1992) *Siena: The Gothic Dream*, Siena: Edizioni Alsaba.

Civai, M. and Toti, E. (2000) *Palio: la corsa dell'anima*, Siena: Edizioni Alsaba.

Civai, M. *et al.* (2000) *Cinquanta Anni di Masgalani delle Contrade di Siena (1950–2000)*, Siena: Monte dei Paschi.

Corsi, S. (1997) 'Le origini del corteo storico a le prime comparse del Nicchio', in M. Ciampolini (ed.) *Il museo e l'oratorio della Nobile Contrada del Nicchio*, Siena: Edizioni Alsaba, pp.289–316.

De Cristofaro, R. (1988) *Siena: I canti del popolo*, Siena: Edizioni Cantagalli.

De Gregorio, M. (1999) 'Notizie dal Territorio', in *Caratteri di Contrada: numeri unici e giornali delle Contrade di Siena*, Siena: Protagon Editore Toscani/Biblioteca Comunale degli Intronati, pp.21–32.

Dickson, G. (1998) 'The 115 cults of the saints in later medieval and renaissance Perugia: a demographic overview of a civic pantheon', *Renaissance Studies*, 12, pp.6–25.

Dundes, A. and Falassi, A. (1975) *La Terra in Piazza: An Interpretation of the Palio of Siena*, Berkeley: University of California Press.

Falassi, A. (1980) *Per forza e per amore: i canti popolare del Palio di Siena*, Milan: Bompiani.

Falassi, A. (ed.) (1988) *Le Tradizioni Popolari in Italia: le feste, le terre, i giorni*, Milan: Electa.

Falassi, A. (1996) 'Le Contrade', in R. Barzanti, G. Catoni and M. De Gregorio (eds) *Storia di Siena II*, pp.95–108.

Falassi, A. (1998) *Palio: The Colors of Siena*, Siena: Comune of Siena.

Falassi, A. (1999) 'I Sonetti delle Contrade', in *Caratteri di Contrada: numeri unici e giornali delle Contrade di Siena*, Siena: Protagon Editore Toscani/ Biblioteca Comunale degli Intronati, pp.33–8.

Falassi, A. and Catoni, G. (1982) *Palio*, Milan: Electa Editrice.

Fiorini, A. (1986) *Metamorfosi di una festa: dalle 'Pugna' al 'Palio alla tonda'*, Siena: Supplemento al Nuovo Corriere Senese.

Fiorini, A. (1987) 'Masgalano', in *Palio e Contrade tra Ottocento e Novecento*, Siena: Edizioni Alsaba, pp.91–110.

Gigli, S. (1960) *The Palio of Siena*, Siena: Stefano Venturini Editore.

Grassi, V. (1972) *Le contrade di Siena e le loro feste – il Palio attuale*, 2 volumes, Siena: Edizioni Periccioli.

Heywood, W. (1899) *Our Lady of August and the Palio of Siena*, Siena: Enrico Torrini.

Heywood, W. (1904) *Palio and Ponte: An Account of the Sports of Central Italy from the Age of Dante to the XXth Century*, London: Methuen.

Hook, J. (1979) *Siena: A City and Its History*, London: Hamish Hamilton.

Kempers, B. (1994) 'Icons, altarpieces, and civic ritual in Siena cathedral, 1150–1530', in B. Hanawalt and K. Reyerson (eds) *City and Spectacle in Medieval Europe*, Minneapolis: University of Minnesota Press, pp.89–136.

Logan, A. (1978) 'The Palio of Siena: performance and process', *Urban Anthropology*, 7, pp.45–65.

Luchini, L. (1987) *Palio XX secolo: una città fra realtà e leggenda*, Siena: Tipografia Senese Editrice.

Mancini, C. (1993) 'Le Contrade inno per inno', *Il Carroccio*, 44, pp.32–5; 45, pp.19–22.

Marzucchi, M. (1998) *Le Contrade di Siena: evoluzione storica e attualità*, Siena: Betti Editrice.

Mugnai, A. (1996) *Siena trionfa immortale: Silvio Gigli, il Palio, la radio*, Siena: Becocci Editore.

Norman, D. (1999) *Siena and the Virgin: Art and Politics in a Late Medieval City State*, New Haven and London: Yale.

Pierard, R. and Linder, R. (1988) *Civil Religion and the American Presidency*, Grand Rapids, Michigan: Zondervan.

Ravel, E. (1992) 'The mysteries of Siena', in M. Civai and E. Toti, pp.11–16.

Silverman, S. (1979) 'On the uses of history in anthropology: the Palio of Siena', *American Ethnologist*, 6, pp.413–36.

Silverman, S. (1989) 'The Palio of Siena: game, ritual, or politics', in S. Zimmerman and R. Weissman (eds) *Urban Life in the Renaissance*, Newark: University of Delaware Press, pp.224–39.

Tailetti, A. (1967) *Anedotti Contradaiolo*, Rome: Olimpia.

Tailetti, A. (1972) 'Cronistoria del Palio dal 1938 al 1972', in V. Grassi, vol.2, pp.67–134.

Torriti, P. (1988) *Tutta Siena: contrada per contrada*, Florence: Bonechi.

Trabalzini, G. (1976) *I Sonetti della Vittoria: le poesie celebrative del Palio di Siena dal 1900 al 1976*, Siena: Edizioni Periccioli.

Turrini, P. (2000) 'Dal Rinascimento all'Unità d'Italia: comparse, stemmi e bandiere della Contrada della Torre', in *Le Comparse della Torre dal cinquecento al Duemila*, Siena: Carlo Cambi Editore, pp.17–46.

Valacchi, F. (1994) *Nel Campo in lotta ed al di fuor sorelle: il Magistrato delle Contrade 1894–1994*, Siena: Edizioni Cantagalli.

Vauchez, A. (1993) *The Laity in the Middle Ages: Religious Beliefs and Devotional Practices*, Notre Dame, Indiana: University of Notre Dame Press.

Waley, D. (1991) *Siena and the Sienese in the Thirteenth Century*, Cambridge: Cambridge University Press.

Webb, D. (1993) 'Saints and cities in medieval Italy', *History Today*, 43, pp.15–21.

Webb, D. (1996) *Patrons and Defenders: The Saints in the Italian City-states*, London: Taurus.

Zazzeroni, A. (1980) *L'araldica delle contrade di Siena*, Florence: Scala.

Other media

CD (1997) *Inni delle Contrade*, Florence: Natali MultiMedia.

CD-ROM (1996) *The Palio of Siena*, Siena/Monteriggioni: Betti Editrice/Zeus MultiMedia.

CD-ROM (2000) *The Palio of Siena*, Milan: More Interactive/2001 Production.

CHAPTER 6

Images of civic devotion: Palio *drappelloni* and Sienese civil religion

The large rectangular banner of painted silk, known as the *drappellone*, which is the prize awarded to the *contrada* that wins the Palio of Siena, is an artefact that, simultaneously, performs many separate functions, and can be analysed and studied in many different ways. Each *drappellone* is an original work of art, painted by an artist who is officially appointed by the Sienese civic authorities. The painter may be Sienese, from another part of Italy, or from abroad, but in each case will have an established and respected reputation. Each *drappellone* is a carefully regulated expression of the particular Palio for which it is created. It must include a reference to the date of the Palio concerned, as well as a number of other specific details and historical references. It will make its own distinctive contribution to the history of the Palio and to the long development of the *drappellone* as a particular type of artefact. And it will also be an object of intense desire and devotion, both before and after the Palio for which it is the prize.

Before the Palio, the *drappellone* will be the object of ritual acts by members of the ten *contrade* who will compete, such as the throwing against it of *contrada* scarves as an expression of hope that their *contrada* will win. The *drappellone* will be analysed for clues or omens in the colours, design, imagery, organization or iconography chosen by the artist, which may suggest that a particular *contrada* is destined to win it. After the Palio, members of the winning *contrada* will be desperate to touch the prized *drappellone* as it is carried from the Campo, paraded through the streets and taken back to their own part of the city. It will be placed in the Oratory of the *contrada* next to the altar, where it will be admired, repeatedly and at length, apart from the many times in the following days and weeks when it will again be taken in procession through the city. It will appear in a place of honour at the victory parade and at the official victory supper held by the winning *contrada*. And then it will receive a permanent place of honour in the Sala della Vittoria (the 'Room of Victory') in the *contrada*'s museum, taking its place alongside the other *drappelloni* won by the *contrada* throughout its history. At this point it will also, thereby, become part of the historic artistic patrimony and heritage not only of the particular *contrada*, but of Siena as a whole – the latest addition to a set of seventeen collections of Palio *drappelloni* kept in the seventeen *contrada* museums of the city.

Drappelloni may be studied as works of art, and assessed according to various aesthetic and art historical criteria, or as historical texts, and analysed for what they reveal about the preoccupations and concerns of the Sienese at particular moments in their history. Or they may be studied as objects of popular culture, or from an anthropological perspective and in terms of their symbolic or social significance. They may also be studied from a specifically theological standpoint and assessed primarily in terms of their depiction and celebration of the Virgin and other saints. This chapter will not adopt any one of these particular approaches, although it will draw on insights derived from all of them. Instead, the chapter will focus on the *drappelloni* as expressions of, and vehicles for, the articulation of Sienese civil religion. It will do so in three stages. First, it will briefly examine the history of the evolution of the *drappelloni*, from the eighteenth to the beginning of the twenty-first century. Second, it will consider a number of particular *drappelloni* in some detail. Finally, it will explore various ways in which these *drappelloni* express and celebrate Sienese civil religion.

The evolution of the *drappelloni*

In 1906, the official regulations for the Palio issued in that year included an article that defined certain iconographical details that must be included within the overall design of the *drappellone* for each Palio. Thus, article 80 of the 1906 regulations stipulated that the *drappellone* must have, at the top, the image of Santa Maria di Provenzano (a revered bust of the Virgin housed in the Sienese church of the same name) for the Palio of 2 July, and the image of Maria Assunta in Cielo (the Virgin ascending to heaven) for the Palio of 16 August. In addition, each *drappellone* must include the date of the Palio, the emblems of the Comune of Siena and of the individuals responsible for the administration of the Palio, and the symbols of the *contrade* that were to compete in the Palio (Comune di Siena, 1906, pp.24–5).

In requiring the inclusion of these details, the regulations of 1906 did not introduce entirely new features to the design of the *drappellone*. For example, the inclusion of either the Madonna of Provenzano or the Virgin of the Assumption had been a feature of Palio *drappelloni* ever since the seventeenth century – as even a cursory examination of the surviving *drappelloni* from the seventeenth, eighteenth and nineteenth centuries will quickly confirm (Betti, 1992–3, volumes 1 and 2).[1] Similarly, the inclusion of civic emblems and symbols and of the coats of arms of prominent Sienese families had also been common on earlier *drappelloni*. From the 1870s, meanwhile, the emblems and symbols of the *contrade* competing in a particular Palio were more and more frequently included in the *drappellone*. Indeed, by the 1890s, this had become a feature of the majority of the *drappelloni* of that era – although exceptions to this pattern continued to occur (Betti, 1992–3, vol.2, pp.64–89).

Nevertheless, despite such substantial continuities with earlier examples, article 80 of the regulations of 1906 represented an important moment in the history and development of the *drappelloni* painted for the Palio. From then on, all of the elements defined in these regulations were to become established features of the iconography of Palio *drappelloni*. The only exceptions – and they were only partial exceptions – were to be the *drappelloni* for extraordinary Palii, run in honour and celebration of particular events or anniversaries. These did not require the portrayal of the Virgin – although in some cases, as Colour Plate 1 illustrates, the Virgin might still be a central element of the design. The requirement to include the date of the Palio, civic emblems and clear reference to the *contrade* competing, remained. Moreover, the imagery of a *drappellone* for an extraordinary Palio was – and still is – required to refer explicitly to the event in honour of which the extraordinary Palio was to be run. Thus, in the most recent edition of the regulations for the Palio, issued in 1982, article 93 repeats substantially the same requirements as those of 1906, though it is even more specific in its definition of the precise civic emblems and symbols that are to be included, citing by name the *balzana* (the black and white shield that is the principal civic symbol of Siena), the other two emblems of the

---

[1] The four volumes in this series contain reproductions of all surviving *drappelloni* from the seventeenth century until the early 1990s. The two CD-ROMS listed under references to other media at the end of Chapter 5 also contain information on the history of the *drappellone* and a number of images of particular *drappelloni*.

Comune (a red shield displaying a lion rampant and representing the people, and a blue shield bearing the word 'liberty'), and possibly – although not necessarily – the emblems of the three ancient *terzi* into which Siena is still divided, and the coat of arms of the mayor who is currently in office ('Regolamento del Palio', in Civai and Toti, 2000, p.329).

From the mid-1890s it had also become increasingly common for the *drappelloni* to include either an allegorical figure representing Siena or an aspect of Sienese tradition, or a depiction of a well-known view or architectural feature of the city. Thus, for example, a *drappellone* of 1894 showed Saint Francis and the church of San Francesco in Siena. *Drappelloni* for 1895, 1896 and 1904 showed views of the Sienese skyline, with well-known buildings clearly visible. Others for 1895, 1900, 1903 and 1904 showed particular locations within Siena, such as the piazza outside the cathedral, or the fourteenth-century chapel in the Campo. Others again, for 1902, 1903 and 1904, showed the Campo and the Palazzo Pubblico during the Palio itself (Betti, 1992–3, vol.2, pp.74–88). After 1906, this tendency – together with a further trend towards celebrating Siena and its history within the broader context of Italian history – became an even more common element of Palio *drappelloni* and has remained so to this day.

The particular form that such visual celebration of Siena might take in any particular case varied greatly, but the trend itself was consistent. Indeed, it is no exaggeration to say that, during the first four decades of the twentieth century, the self-conscious visual celebration of Siena and its history became a firmly established and, indeed, predominant feature of the majority of Palio *drappelloni*. At the same time, particular *drappelloni* were notable for the way in which they linked Siena to a broader Italian context. Thus, during the period of Fascist rule in Italy in the later 1920s and the 1930s, in addition to the emblems and symbols of Siena, Palio *drappelloni* also regularly included the 'fasces' (a bundle of bound rods with an axe at the centre), which was one of the principal symbols of Italian Fascism. Similarly, during this period, *drappelloni* included not only the conventional date (such as 1927 or 1933), but also the official year of the Fascist era, as defined by the Fascist regime (for example, year 'V' in 1927, or year 'XI' in 1933). Even more strikingly, both of the *drappelloni* for 1936 explicitly celebrated the political and military values of the Fascist regime, including the Italian conquest of Ethiopia, while the *drappellone* for July 1939 celebrated the Italian conquest of Albania (Betti, 1992–3, vol.2, pp.112–13, 126 and 129). The *drappellone* for the Palio of August 1939 – the last before the suspension of the Palio for the duration of the Second World War –

celebrated both Siena and Italy, depicting Saint Catherine of Siena (who had been proclaimed patron saint of Italy on 18 June that year) casting her cloak protectively over a city. On close examination, this can be seen to be an idealized version of an Italian city containing within its walls representations of famous buildings from a number of Italian cities, including Rome, Naples, Perugia, Florence, Milan, Bologna and Venice, as well as Siena itself (Betti, 1992–3, vol.2, p.129).

After the Second World War, the habit of celebrating Siena and its history – while locating this within the broader context of Italian history – continued, as the *drappelloni* illustrated in this volume clearly demonstrate. From the 1970s onwards, moreover, non-Sienese artists have increasingly been invited to paint *drappelloni*, in addition to a continuing tradition of Sienese artists, while the first non-Italian was appointed in 1975. This precedent has since been followed on many other occasions, although the original decision to broaden the range of artists invited to paint *drappelloni* was not uncontroversial (Fallasi and Catoni, 1982, pp.22 and 80; Mazzoni della Stella, 1993; Zetti, 1999, p.155). The tension between the expression of Sienese traditions and the use of contemporary artistic styles sometimes prompts sharp disagreements among the Sienese concerning the merits of a particular *drappellone*. Nor are the Sienese public at all reticent about expressing their disapproval if they do not like a *drappellone*. For example, in both 1996 and 1997, the *drappellone* for the July Palio prompted a hostile response from the majority of Sienese, both when it was presented to the public and in subsequent discussion in the press. In each case, the *drappellone* was thought to lack adequate or sufficiently traditional reference to Siena. By contrast, the *drappelloni* for the August Palii in those years received widespread acclaim for the way in which they evoked aspects of the history and spirit of Siena and the Palio.[2] Such approval or disapproval did not, however, turn simply, or even primarily, on the identity or nationality of the painter. Thus, in 1996 the *drappellone* for August (Colour Plate 4), which received great acclaim and approval, was painted by a well-known British pop-artist.

Similarly, in 2000, when three Palii were run – the extraordinary one being to celebrate the new millennium – the relative enthusiasm of the Sienese for the different *drappelloni* was not determined by the identity of the painter. The most popular of the three *drappelloni* in 2000 was probably that for the August Palio (Colour Plate 6), which

---

[2] Accounts of the receptions given to these *drappelloni* appeared in the Sienese newspapers *Il Cittadino* and *Corriere di Siena* (27 June and 11 August 1996; 26 June and 11 August 1997).

was painted by an artist from Rome – who had, however, lived and worked in Siena for some years. The second most popular *drappellone* was arguably that for the July Palio (Colour Plate 5), which was painted by an acclaimed American pop-artist. The *drappellone* for the extraordinary Palio in September (Colour Plate 7) was the only one painted by someone of Sienese descent, although he now works as an artist in Milan. Although not unpopular in the way that some *drappelloni* have been, it would be true to say that this *drappellone* prompted a more ambiguous response than either of the other two – not least because it was not, in fact, painted but digitally created, photographic images having been manipulated using computer technology.[3]

In the end, the determining factor in Sienese attitudes towards any particular *drappellone* will not be who painted it, or even necessarily its particular stylistic features. The crucial issue in each case will be whether the *drappellone* in question possesses *Senesità*; whether, that is to say, it embodies, expresses and celebrates what it is to be Sienese. The next section of this chapter will examine a number of examples of *drappelloni* which, in one way or another, express *Senesità*.

Drappelloni and *Senesità*

The eleven Palio *drappelloni* considered here are all taken from the period since the Second World War. They have been chosen because, in different ways, they demonstrate many of the characteristic features of the design and iconography of Palio *drappelloni* during this period, and also because of their potential significance and function as expressions of Sienese civil religion. Five have been chosen from the period 1996–2000, including all three of the *drappelloni* for the year 2000 – thus ensuring that the consideration of Palio *drappelloni* as expressions of civil religion does not depend solely on older examples of such works. The analysis of these *drappelloni* will deliberately focus on the detailed yet essential task of establishing what, exactly, is portrayed on each one. The final section of the chapter will then present a discussion of the ways in which these particular *drappelloni* relate to, and express, Sienese civil religion.

---

[3] For accounts of reactions to these three *drappelloni*, see the editions of the local newspapers *Corriere di Siena* (27 June, 11 August and 4 September 2000) and *Siena Oggi* (27 June, 11 August and 5 September 2000).

September 1954

The *drappellone* for the extraordinary Palio of 5 September 1954 combined traditional imagery with an overt and explicit concern with civil religion. This Palio was run as part of the Sienese acknowledgement and celebration of the fact that 1954 had been proclaimed by the Pope as a Marian year – a year of special devotion to the Virgin. The *drappellone* (Colour Plate 1) portrays the Virgin standing with her cloak spread protectively over Siena. The depiction of the city includes four clearly identifiable buildings, the most prominent of which is the cathedral, portrayed at the centre of Siena, with its tall campanile pointing directly towards the Virgin. The dome of the cathedral – just in front and to the right of the campanile – and the top of the front face of the cathedral are also clearly visible. To the left of the cathedral appears the tall tower called the Torre del Mangia, which stands next to the town hall and dominates the Campo, which is itself the central civic space at the heart of Siena. On the far right of the city there appears another tall campanile, square in shape and with a series of symmetrically located windows. This is clearly a representation of the campanile of the church of San Giorgio in Pantaneto – a church closely associated with the victory of Montaperti in 1260 and from which, each August, the Corteo dei Ceri processes to the cathedral. The large building with a campanile, on the far left of the city, meanwhile, is a representation of the church of San Domenico. This church is included because of its close association with Saint Catherine of Siena. Her shrine is located near San Domenico, and a chapel in the church houses her head, which is one of the most highly prized relics possessed by the Catholic Church in Siena. Moreover, 1954 was the fifteenth anniversary of the proclamation of Saint Catherine as patron saint of Italy in June 1939.

Above the city, and on either side of the Virgin, appear two small scenes, each clearly identified by a date. On the left-hand side, the scene depicts details from the events of early September 1260 and the myth of Montaperti. In the foreground, the keys of the city are presented to the Virgin. Just above this presentation, the *carroccio* or war cart of the Sienese is portrayed, carrying a huge black and white banner – the principal traditional symbol, the *balzana*, of Siena – and a large wooden crucifix. Above this appears the hill of Montaperti, ringed by a circle of cypress trees. The scene to the right of the Virgin portrays the events of June 1944, when the Sienese rededicated their city to the Virgin as the front between the German and Allied armies drew closer and closer to Siena. In the foreground a page kneels with the black and white *balzana* of Siena, above which are visible the banner of the Magistrato delle Contrade and the Italian flag. Behind him is a black and white striped building, which is clearly intended to be the cathedral of Siena where the rededication of 1944 took place, and which, indeed, displays such 'stripes' of black and white marble. In the sky above the flags appear aircraft – a reference to the fact that, in 1944, the Sienese were particularly afraid that their city would suffer aerial bombardment.

At the top of the *drappellone* are the words SENA VETUS CIVITAS VIRGINIS ('Ancient Siena, City of the Virgin') which were introduced to Sienese coins minted after the victory of Montaperti. In the lower half of the *drappellone*, below the portrayal of the city, appears a female wolf suckling two small children. This is a reference to the classical myth of the foundation of the city of Rome by Romulus and Remus, twins who had been abandoned and suckled by a she-wolf. As part of their own attempt, in the fifteenth century, to construct a prestigious myth concerning the origins of their own city, the Sienese also adopted the symbol of the she-wolf suckling the twins, in recognition of a legend that Siena was originally founded by Ascanius and Senus, the sons of Remus (Ciacci, 1995, pp.9–10). Below the wolf on the *drappellone* appear the date of the Palio (together with an explanation that this was for an extraordinary Palio for the Marian year) and sixteen shields of different sizes. The three largest show, from left to right, the word LIBERTAS (liberty) against a blue background, the black and white *balzana* of Siena, and a lion rampant against a red background – the three civic emblems of Siena. Three more shields show the emblems of the three large sections, or *terzi*, into which Siena is divided, namely Camollia (represented by a large 'K', referring to the old spelling of this *terzo*); Città (represented by a white cross on a red background); and San Martino (represented by an image of Saint Martin giving half of his cloak to a beggar). The remaining ten shields show the symbolic creatures associated with each of the ten *contrade* that competed in this Palio.

July 1955

At the top of this *drappellone* (Figure 6.1) there appears a highly conventional version of the image of the Madonna of Provenzano, below the words AVVOCATA NOSTRA ('Our Advocate'). At the bottom of the *drappellone* appear, as in the previous example considered, the wolf suckling two children, the date of the Palio, and the emblems of Siena, the *terzi*, the then current mayor of Siena, and the competing *contrade*.

In the scene that occupies the central section of the *drappellone*, Siena is once again depicted, with the cathedral and the Torre del Mangia again dominating the portrayal of the city. As with the

Figure 6.1 The drappellone for the Palio
of 2 July 1955. Foto Lensini, Siena.

drappellone for September 1954, the scenes portrayed present a
double narrative. To the left of Siena are scenes of conflict, clearly of a
past era given the armour worn by many of those involved. The walls
of the city are manned by soldiers. In the foreground figures are
fighting. In the background, meanwhile, a line of figures travels
towards another city, high on a hill. These narrative details evoke the
events of 1555, precisely 400 years before the Palio for which the

drappellone was painted. The scenes portray the final siege that ended the existence of the independent Sienese republic. The figures in the background travelling to a hilltop city represent those Sienese who, after defeat in 1555, set up a continuing republic in exile at Montalcino, and continued to resist for four more years. Behind the wolf, the two flags that point towards these scenes are the Sienese *balzana* and the *fleur-de-lis* of the French forces who fought with the Sienese during the siege of 1554–5. The scene to the right of the city on the *drappellone* refers to the events of 1944. With the flags of modern Italy and France prominent, it shows the Sienese rejoicing at the arrival of French troops in Siena, to liberate the city, on the morning of 3 July 1944.

September 1960

This *drappellone* (Colour Plate 2) was again painted for an extraordinary Palio, held to celebrate the seventh centenary of the battle of Montaperti – as the painted inscription beneath the central figure of Saint George clearly indicates. Although the Sienese victory at Montaperti was attributed primarily to the aid of the Virgin, Saint George was also associated with it because he had been the favoured saint of the German mercenary cavalry who had fought with the Sienese in the battle. Hence the figure of Saint George, a dead dragon behind him, dominates this *drappellone* – in which the Virgin, in this instance, does not appear. To the left of Saint George is a series of scenes based on the chronicle narratives of Montaperti. In the foreground the Sienese and the Florentines clash in battle. Above them a figure appears on a tower, drumming – a representation of Cerretto Ceccolini who, according to the fully developed version of the myth of Montaperti, viewed the battle from the tower of the Saracini palace in Siena and relayed its progress to the Sienese, announcing each report of the battle by a burst of drumming. Above this detail are portrayals of the Sienese forces, carrying the banners of the three *terzi*, and the Sienese *carroccio*, on which the Sienese *balzana* is being flown. And above this appears the city of Siena, on a hill (which is correct, though the hill portrayed here is far steeper than that on which Siena actually exists). To the right of Saint George the hill of Montaperti is shown, with its characteristic cypress trees. In this case, the three civic shields and the emblem of the current mayor are placed at the top of the *drappellone*, while the symbols of the three *terzi* are located at the bottom. The ten *contrade* that competed in this Palio are represented by their symbolic creatures, each within a rectangle. In the middle of the symbols of the ten *contrade* is a symbolic tribute to the Olympic games of September 1960, held in Rome.

July 1962

This *drappellone* (Colour Plate 3) combines celebration of a July Palio with celebration of the fifth centenary of Catherine of Siena being made a saint by Pope Pius II, who was a member of a prominent Sienese family. At the top of the *drappellone* the Madonna of Provenzano is shown, surrounded by the symbols of the ten competing *contrade*. At the bottom, along with the date, appear the customary symbols of Siena, its *terzi* and the mayor. In between, in the central section of the *drappellone*, the city of Siena is shown, with the familiar landmarks of the cathedral and the Torre del Mangia 'framing' the figure of Saint Catherine. Immediately in front of Saint Catherine, situated beneath her left hand, is depicted the distinctive double loggia of the Sanctuary of Saint Catherine. This is the principal shrine to her in the city and, since her proclamation as patron saint of Italy, the site of an annual ceremony during her patronal festival in April, which is attended not only by the Sienese civic authorities, but also by representatives of the Vatican, the Italian state, and other Italian cities.

July 1980

Like the *drappellone* for July 1962, the *drappellone* for the Palio of July 1980 (Figure 6.2) celebrated both the Madonna of Provenzano (portrayed at the top of the banner) and an anniversary of another Sienese saint – in this case the sixth centenary of the birth of Saint Bernardino, a popular Sienese saint of the first half of the fifteenth century who was born at Massa Marittima in 1380. Massa Marittima was one of the principal subject cities of the independent Sienese republic, located to the south-west of Siena. The figure of Saint Bernardino, at the centre of the *drappellone*, is set against a background of an idealized representation of the Sienese territories, with Siena itself on the hill near the horizon. Saint Bernardino is shown holding an image of the sun, on which are superimposed a cross and the letters 'IHS' – the symbols that Bernardino used, in his preaching, to encourage popular devotion to the name of Jesus.[4] In front of Bernardino, the ten *contrade* competing in this Palio are represented by the ten jockeys, mounted on their horses.

Each jockey wears a costume in the colours of the *contrada* that he will represent, and carries the symbol of the *contrada* on his back – just as the actual jockeys who ride in the Palio do. Each jockey salutes

[4] The letters IHS are a traditional monogram, created by taking the first three letters of Jesus' name as spelt in the Greek script used between the fourth and eighth centuries.

Saint Bernardino by holding aloft a nerbo (a kind of leather whip), which he will carry in the Palio and may use against rival jockeys during the race. Again, the act of saluting the saint in this way accurately mirrors a moment that occurs immediately before the Palio. As the jockeys ride from the Sienese town hall to the point in the Campo at which the race starts, each salutes members of the *contrada* for whom he rides by this same gesture. In the foreground appear a crowd of spectators, many of whom are shown wearing the colourful *fazzoletti* (scarves) that *contrada* members wear to indicate their identity and allegiance. At the bottom of the *drappellone* are, as usual, the date of the Palio, a statement of its special celebration of the sixth centenary of the birth of Saint Bernardino, and the heraldic symbols of Siena, its three *terzi*, and the mayor.

July 1982

Once again, this *drappellone* (Figure 6.3) celebrated both the Madonna of Provenzano, portrayed among the clouds at the top of the *drappellone*, and a centenary. On this occasion, however, the centenary in question was not one connected with a Sienese saint or a particular moment in Sienese history. The *drappellone* marks the centenary of the death of Giuseppe Garibaldi, one of the leading figures in the unification of Italy in the nineteenth century and a popular hero of the Sienese, who had been enthusiastic supporters of the movement for Italian unification and independence. Thus, the central feature of this *drappellone* is an extremely accurate representation of the statue of Garibaldi that was erected by the Sienese in 1896, and which still stands in the public gardens known as the Lizza. The statue is flanked by views of the city showing the Torre del Mangia of the Palazzo Publico to the left, and Siena cathedral to the right. The date of the Palio and its dedication to the centenary of Garibaldi's death are indicated on the poster that is portrayed as if fixed to the base of the statue. In the bottom quarter of the *drappellone* there appear the customary symbols of the city, its *terzi*, the mayor, and the *contrade* competing in the Palio. Both the painted fabric against which these symbols appear and the particular portrayal of the *balzana* are copied from actual artefacts owned by the Comune (Falassi, 1982, p.245).

August 1996

The *drappellone* for the Palio of August 1996 (Colour Plate 4) portrays the Virgin of the Assumption in traditional manner, dressed in blue and placed above the city of Siena. Immediately below the Virgin and behind the city appear two hills, with bare earth towards their

Figure 6.2 The drappellone for the Palio of 2 July 1980. Foto Lensini, Siena.

Figure 6.3 The drappellone for the Palio of 2 July 1982. Foto Lensini, Siena.

summits, which are highly reminiscent of the hills – known as the *crete* – that are a famous feature of the landscape of the countryside to the south-east of Siena. The city itself is portrayed in idealized yet immediately recognizable form. The depictions of both the Palazzo Pubblico and the cathedral are highly realistic, although their spatial relationship in the *drappellone* is not topographically accurate. Below the Virgin and the city, the symbols of the ten *contrade* competing in the Palio are assigned an unusually large amount of space and are depicted through a combination of the creatures that are representative of the *contrade* and the vivid use of the colours of the *contrade*. This combination of creatures and colours within a series of squares results in a representation of the symbols of the *contrade* which evokes a sense of the scarves and flags that are central to *contrada* identity. At the bottom of the *drappellone* appear, as usual, the date and the symbols of the city, the three *terzi*, and the mayor.

On this occasion, the artist, Joe Tilson – a renowned British exponent of pop-art – also painted the reverse side of the *drappellone*. The back of the *drappellone* carried the word 'Siena', the black and white *balzana* of the city, the date, the artist's name, and a series of black and red triangles, arranged in sharply geometrical patterns. It was the front of this *drappellone*, however, that prompted a particularly enthusiastic reception from the Sienese. They praised it for the way in which this example of the work of a British, and self-consciously modern, artist nevertheless drew on authentically Sienese traditions and imagery. In the portrayal both of the Virgin and of Siena and its surrounding countryside, the Sienese saw echoes of the portrayals of these subjects in the work of Sienese artists of the fourteenth and fifteenth centuries, such as Duccio di Buoninsegna, Simone Martini, Ambrogio Lorenzetti, Sano di Pietro and Sassetta. The portrayal of the *contrade* was similarly seen as embodying Sienese characteristics that were both highly traditional and genuinely popular in nature. This *drappellone*, it was even suggested, represented the entire city through its evocation of Sienese religious devotion, history, art and landscape (Calabrese, 1996, p.6; Piersimoni, 1996, pp.13–14; Falassi, 1999, pp.13–14; Zetti, 1999, p.155).

August 1998

In contrast to the *drappellone* for August 1996 considered above, in some respects the *drappellone* for the Palio of August 1998 (Figure 6.4) broke with tradition in its design and iconography. Nevertheless, it is significant that it was well received by the Sienese. This *drappellone* is dominated by the figure of a horse, which stands on the left-hand side of the *drappellone* with its hooves placed within a representation of Siena – with the cathedral and the Palazzo Pubblico again clearly identifiable. The bridle of the horse, which snakes down the centre of the *drappellone*, contains ten rectangles, representing the competing *contrade* by means of their traditional colours. Close to the upturned end of the bridle (on which appears the date of the Palio), are four balls, three of which represent the standard symbols of Siena, the fourth representing the emblem of the mayor. In the top right-hand corner is the face of the Virgin, modelled in relief. Across the whole of the background of the *drappellone*, there is a painted

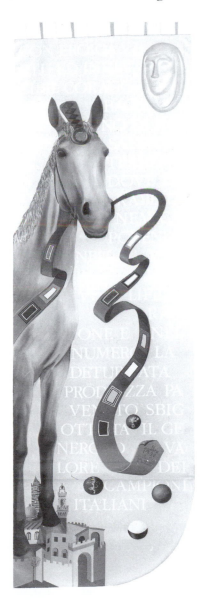

Figure 6.4 The drappellone for the Palio of 16 August 1998. Foto Lensini, Siena.

inscription in honour of the Sienese students who, in 1848, took part in the early stages of the struggle for Italian independence and fought in the battles of Curtatone and Montanara. This *drappellone* is, therefore, far from conventional. The Madonna is not in the customary pose for the Virgin of the Assumption. There is no explicit representation of the three *terzi* of Siena – although it might be argued that the city in the lower foreground performs this function in a highly symbolic manner. In addition, the inscription on the *drappellone* focuses firmly on the 150th anniversary of a significant event in nineteenth-century Sienese history.

Why, then, was this *drappellone* broadly popular and well received, despite such departures from tradition? Several reasons may be suggested. For example, it retains some very traditional elements, such as the depiction of Siena, the colours of the *contrade*, the symbols of the city and the clear – if unconventional – presence of the image of the Virgin. It also celebrates a historical episode of which the Sienese continue to be proud. In the courtyard behind the entrance to the University of Siena there is a monument to the Sienese students who fought in the campaign of 1848. The monument was erected in 1893, during a series of celebrations that included an extraordinary Palio (Catoni, 1993). On 25 April each year, when Italians celebrate the anniversary of the end of the Second World War, the Sienese civic authorities and the local military honour three particular monuments in the city: that to the Sienese dead of the First World War; that to the Sienese students of 1848; and that to those members of the Jewish community of Siena who were deported to concentration camps during the Second World War.

In addition, this *drappellone* is full of other details that are expressions of, and references to, the Palio and its culture. For example, the hooves of the horse are painted gold, just as the hooves of the horse that wins the Palio will be painted gold when it is led through the streets in celebration in the days after the Palio. Similarly, the horse wears an ornamental headpiece attached to its bridle, just as all the horses who participate in the Palio will do – the headpiece being in the colours of the *contrada* that the horse represents. Moreover, the very prominence given to the horse on the *drappellone* was itself pleasing to the Sienese, whose passion for the horses that compete in the Palio is profound. The balls, which represent the civic symbols of Siena and its mayor, are very similar to the coloured balls that are used to determine – by chance – the sequence by which the horses will line up at the start of the race. Finally, the background on which the inscription is painted is a sandy colour – immediately associated by the Sienese with the colour of the earth that makes the track for the Palio. In other words, although unconventional in its design and iconography, this *drappellone* is nevertheless an intense and detailed expression of *Senesità*.

July 2000

The *drappellone* for the July Palio of 2000 combines the traditional and the innovative (Colour Plate 5). Painted by Jim Dine, a well-known American pop-artist, the civic emblems of Siena and its mayor appear at the top of the *drappellone*, immediately above the Madonna of Provenzano, while the date of the Palio is placed in front of the very traditionally conceived depiction of this image. Below this, and occupying fully half of the *drappellone*, are ten squares, each containing a freely drawn image in charcoal of the creature associated with one of the *contrade* competing in the Palio. Along the side of each image appear the colours of the relevant *contrada*. The *contrada* symbols are innovative in that they portray life-like examples of the creatures concerned, rather than the traditional imagery that is commonly found on *contrada* scarves and flags. On the other hand, the overall effect of the *drappellone* is traditionally Sienese: the Madonna and the *contrade* predominate. Thus, this *drappellone* provides another example of Sienese enthusiasm for a *drappellone* painted by a non-Sienese, and non-Italian, artist, which nevertheless respects and draws on authentically Sienese themes, images and traditions.

August 2000

Although none of the *drappelloni* for the three Palii of 2000 generated negative reactions from the Sienese, it was the one painted for the August Palio that prompted the most enthusiastic response (Colour Plate 6). Unquestionably the most traditional of the three *drappelloni* of 2000, it portrays both the Virgin of the Assumption and Saint Catherine of Siena. Saint Catherine stands at the centre of the *drappellone* gesturing outwards towards the viewer, while behind her stands the Virgin, with her arms raised upwards. Immediately behind the Virgin appears a fan-like sequence of nine segments in shades of brown – a highly stylized representation of the Campo of Siena which is, indeed, of this shape and divided into nine segments by the patterning of the bricks that make up its surface. Above the Virgin's upraised hands is a dark blue area decorated with twelve small stars. These represent the emblem of the European Union. As the words on the bottom section of the *drappellone* make clear, the *drappellone* celebrates the fact that, in addition to being patron saint of Italy, in October 1999, Saint Catherine was officially accorded the status of co-patron saint of Europe (along with saints Bridget of Sweden and Edith

Stein). The European theme is also represented on the *drappellone* by the figure of Saint Catherine being depicted standing on a stylized map of Europe. In the bottom section of the *drappellone* there appear the customary civic and mayoral emblems and those of the competing *contrade*. To the right and left of the figures of Saint Catherine and the Virgin are a number of small details and scenes, which evoke either incidents from the life and legend of Saint Catherine, or characteristic moments of the Palio.

September 2000

The third and final *drappellone* from the year 2000 was for the extraordinary Palio run on 9 September in celebration of the year 2000 (Colour Plate 7). Generated by computer graphics and the digital manipulation of photographic images, this *drappellone* is notable for the absence of any representation of either the Virgin or a Sienese saint. Indeed, the only explicit reference to official religion appears in the inscription in the centre of the bottom section of the *drappellone*. This reads, in translation, 'Siena 9 September 2000. Year of the Jubilee. Extraordinary Palio of the Millennium'. The brief reference to the 'Year of the Jubilee' acknowledges that the Catholic Church had so designated the year 2000. But, at the same time, the designation of the Palio as the 'Extraordinary Palio of the Millennium' subtly but significantly places the principal emphasis on the more general celebration of the new millennium rather than on the more specific claims of the Catholic Church. This emphasis is maintained in the rest of the *drappellone*, which is essentially a celebration of Siena, the *contrade* and the Palio. Thus, the top third of the *drappellone* consists of a computer-generated representation of the Palazzo Pubblico, with the Torre del Mangia next to it. Significantly, however, the cathedral – which so often appears with the Palazzo Pubblico – is not included on this *drappellone*. The middle section of the *drappellone* is dominated by the figures of two horses running across a sandy surface. For anyone who has seen the Palio, the sandy surface is immediately recognizable as the earth that is laid in the Campo for the Palio. The two horses are not only in a pose that is characteristic of the moment in the Palio when horses make the turn around the corner known as San Martino, but are, in fact, a digitally adjusted version of a photograph from exactly this moment in an actual Palio. In the final section of the *drappellone*, on either side of the date, inscription and civic and mayoral symbols, appear the symbols of the ten competing *contrade*, on this occasion represented by computer-generated images of the scarves of the ten *contrade* concerned.

Palio *drappelloni* and Sienese civil religion

The *drappelloni* examined in the preceding section are no more than a few examples of the almost 500 such artefacts that are preserved and displayed in the museums of the seventeen *contrade* of Siena – an overall number that increases year by year. Although they are only a fraction of the total number of surviving *drappelloni*, however, it is fair to say that the examples considered here nevertheless embody many of the characteristic features of this highly traditional Sienese phenomenon, especially as it has developed since the late nineteenth and early twentieth centuries. In the present context, however, it is the way in which these particular examples of Palio *drappelloni* relate to Sienese civil religion that is the principal concern.

It will be helpful, at this point, to recall several of the main arguments of the preceding two chapters concerning Sienese civil religion. In Chapter 4, it was argued that the continuing devotion of the Sienese to the Virgin – a devotion dramatically demonstrated in the rededication of the city to the Virgin in 1944, and popularly sustained by the Palio and the Sienese *contrade* – can only be understood adequately if it is located within a long historical perspective, stretching back to the late thirteenth century. Thus, the modern expression of Sienese devotion to the Virgin repeatedly and insistently draws on, and refers back to, themes, incidents and details from the history of Sienese civil religion and devotion to the Virgin from the thirteenth century onwards. Whatever the precise historical truth of the myth of Montaperti, or of other moments when the Virgin is deemed to have saved Siena, and however much popular recollection of details of particular events may become vague or hazy as it is mixed with local traditions and folk memories, modern and contemporary Sienese civil religion is inescapably orientated towards Sienese history and, in particular, to the history of Sienese civic religion and devotion.

In Chapter 5, it was argued that, as well as having a close relationship with 'official' religion – most obviously through the association of the Palio with the traditional Sienese devotion to the Virgin – the Palio of Siena and its culture and traditions amounts, in itself, to a modern expression of Sienese civil religion. Thus, using the definition of 'civil religion' provided by the American scholars Richard Pierard and Robert Linder, it was argued that the Palio and its rituals help the Sienese to sustain a collective sense of their shared history and destiny, and enable them to look at their society and community as in some sense special. In particular, it was suggested, the Palio provides the Sienese with a collection of beliefs, values, rites, ceremonies and symbols which, taken together, give sacred meaning to the life of their city and community, and thus provide an overarching sense of unity which transcends internal conflicts and differences.

How do the *drappelloni* considered in this chapter relate to such civil religion? There are at least four important points that may be made about the relationship between them and Sienese civil religion. First, and most obviously, as a group they demonstrate the continuing importance of the Virgin in Sienese culture and tradition. With only two exceptions (the *drappelloni* for the extraordinary Palii of September 1960 and September 2000), all of the *drappelloni* considered here portray an image of the Virgin – as, indeed, they are required to do by the regulations that govern the Palio. The fact that such images are required should not, however, obscure the cumulative and ongoing effect of the twice – and sometimes more than twice – yearly reaffirmation, in an original work of art, of the traditional Sienese devotion to the Virgin. Moreover, in the majority of cases, the particular image of the Virgin that is portrayed is one that is intimately connected with Sienese history. Thus, the images of the Virgin on *drappelloni* for July Palii show the Virgin in the form of the Madonna of Provenzano. These images of the Virgin are thereby directly associated both with the specific terracotta bust of the Virgin still housed in the Sienese church of Santa Maria di Provenzano, and with earlier representations of this particular bust of the Virgin on, for example, the painted covers of civic account books, or the *drappelloni* painted for the July Palii of the seventeenth, eighteenth or early nineteenth centuries.[5] The *drappelloni* for August Palii celebrate the Virgin of the Assumption, and therefore celebrate the annual religious festival that has been at the centre of Sienese civil religion since the thirteenth century. Although the *drappellone* for the extraordinary Palio of September 1954 celebrated the Marian year proclaimed by the Pope, it also firmly located this recognition of the official celebration of the Virgin by the Catholic Church within the particular and specific context of Sienese civic devotion to the Virgin. In this case, the Virgin was shown on the *drappellone* in the traditional manner, with her cloak spread protectively over Siena. Above her appeared the Latin version of the assertion that Siena is 'the city of the Virgin' – a text that was placed on Sienese coins after the victory of Montaperti.

---

[5] For examples of the portrayal of the Madonna of Provenzano on the covers of civic accounts, see the illustrations in Chapter 4 (p.151).

Second, the examples considered in this chapter also show how *drappelloni* self-consciously celebrate the history of Siena itself. For example, the *drappellone* for the Palio of September 1954 portrayed the events of both 1260 and 1944, the first and last occasions on which Siena was formally dedicated to the Virgin. A year later, the *drappellone* for July 1955 recalled and portrayed the fall of Siena in 1555, and the setting up of a final independent Sienese republic in exile at Montalcino. The *drappellone* for 1960 celebrated the seventh centenary of the victory of Montaperti, complete with representations of many details of the myth associated with it. The *drappelloni* for July 1962 and July 1980 each celebrated centeneries associated, respectively, with the Sienese saints Catherine and Bernardino. The *drappelloni* for July 1982 and August 1998 celebrated anniversaries connected with Sienese support for the struggle for Italian independence and unity in the nineteenth century. Finally, one of the most recent *drappellone* considered here – for August 2000 – again celebrated Saint Catherine of Siena, but this time placed the celebration of this Sienese saint within the wider context, not just of Italy, but of Europe at the start of the third millenium. Thus, in the majority of the *drappelloni* considered here, Siena itself – in the form of its history – is celebrated as much as the Virgin in whose honour the Palio is traditionally run. Nor is this a peculiar or unusual characteristic of the *drappelloni* chosen for particular consideration here. In the period since 1945 alone, many other *drappelloni* have celebrated particular moments or anniversaries in Sienese history, in Italian history, or in connection with Sienese saints (Betti, 1992–3, volumes 3 and 4).

The third point that may be made about Palio *drappelloni* and Sienese civil religion is that *drappelloni* not only celebrate particular moments or figures in Sienese history, but also the very fabric of Siena and its history and traditions, and most especially the traditions of the Palio and the *contrade*. Indeed, it may be argued that the celebration of Siena itself, through such means, is the most constant element of all, encompassing both the *drappelloni* for the annual Palii of July and August and also those for extraordinary Palii. The city of Siena appears in many *drappelloni*, depicted either as a whole or through representative buildings – centrally placed or as a detail in one part of the *drappellone*, realistically rendered or evoked schematically. The civic symbols of Siena and its *terzi* are always present, as are those of the *contrade*, and the latter sometimes assume a highly prominent role within the *drappellone* as a whole – as, for example, in the *drappelloni* for the Palii of August 1996 and July 2000. References to the Palio are also common – whether through the presence on a *drappellone* of a representation of a horse or horses, the use of colour to evoke the earth that is laid in the Campo for the Palio, the evocation of the shape of the Campo where the Palio will be run, or evocations of the scarves or flags of the *contrade*. Towards the end of her book on Siena and its history, the English historian Judith Hook suggested that, for those trying to understand Siena and its culture, 'Palio-*contrade*-Siena' composed a 'virtually inter-dependent trinity' (Hook, 1979, p.225). Subsequently, the official guide to the Palio issued to visiting journalists by the Comune of Siena quoted her judgement with approval (Falassi, 1998, p.47). The same interdependence between Siena, its *contrade* and the Palio is also found in the imagery, colours and symbolism that are characteristic of Palio *drappelloni*.

Finally, a fourth point may be made about the relationship between Palio *drappelloni* and Sienese civil religion. *Drappelloni* do not only evoke and portray such civil religion. They are themselves an expression of it. When a *drappellone* is presented to the public it becomes, in itself, an object of devotion. *Contrada* members will stand in front of it and wish it to become theirs. They will throw their *contrada* scarves at it in the hope of securing victory in the Palio. When it enters the Campo on the day of the Palio, carried on the Sienese *carroccio*, it will be the climax of the historical parade before the Palio. And as the *drappellone* moves slowly around the Campo it will receive the adulation of thousands of *contrada* members as they wave their scarves in unison as it passes. The *drappellone* is also a symbol of the new life and the sense of rebirth that will come to the *contrada* that wins the Palio – and therefore it will itself become known as *il cittino* or *il neonato* ('the little citizen' or 'the newborn') as it is carried in triumph around the city by the winners in the days after the Palio. Finally, it will be placed in the winning *contrada*'s museum, where it will become valued and revered in a manner reminiscent of the devotion and affection that might be given to a conventional religious relic (Falassi, 1982; Betti, 1994; Petti, 1997; Fattorini, 1999a; 1999b; Torriti, 1999).

At the end of Chapter 5, it was suggested that the Palio of Siena was not merely related to the religious history and life of the Sienese, but was itself a modern and contemporary expression of Sienese 'civil religion'. The consideration of Palio *drappelloni* in this chapter suggests a similar conclusion concerning the interpretation of these symbols of Sienese identity. In August 1997, the *drappellone* for the Palio was painted on both sides. On the front, the Virgin appeared, holding in her hands a scarf composed of the colours of all of the *contrade* of Siena. On the back appeared a tumultuous crowd of Sienese, their *contrada* flags waving above them, as they received the *drappellone* at the end of the Palio. In the speech in honour of this *drappellone* when it was presented to the Sienese by the civic authorities, it was suggested that its two sides represented a remarkable understanding of two moments at the heart of the Sienese passion for the Palio, one 'religious' and the other 'civic' (Santi, 1997, p.6). It was an appropriate and accurate summary of the *drappellone* in question. But it would also, surely, be true to say that in most *drappelloni* there is not merely a presence of the 'religious' and the 'civic', but rather a fusion of the two, which makes these artefacts powerful symbols and expressions of a deeply-rooted 'civil religion'.

References

Barzanti, R., Catoni, G. and De Gregorio, M. (eds) (1995) *Storia di Siena I: dalle origini alla fine della repubblica*, Siena: Edizioni Alsaba.

Betti, L. (ed.) (1992–3) *Pallium: evoluzione del drappellone dalle origine ad oggi. vol.1 dalle origini ai moti risorgimentali; vol.2 dall'unità d'Italia all'ultimo conflitto mondiale; vol.3 dal dopoguerra alla conquista della luna; vol.4 il drappellone verso il XXI secolo*, Siena: Betti Editrice.

Betti, L. (1994) 'L'oggetto del desiderio', in *La Chiesa dei Santi Pietro e Paolo ed il Museo della Contrada della Chiocciola*, Siena: Betti Editrice, pp.254–77.

Calabrese, O. (1996) 'Figure pianamente senesi', in *Palio: I giorni della festa, Numero Unico edito in occasione del Palio del 16 agosto 1996*, Siena: Alsaba, p.6.

Capperucci, M., Torriti, P. and Manganelli, G. (eds) (1999) *Nobile Contrada dell'Aquila Testimonianze del Secondo Millennio: Storia – Arte – Architettura*, Siena: Terre de Sienne Editrice.

Catoni, G. (1993) *I Goliardi Senesi e il Risorgimento: dalla guerra del Quarantotto al monumento del Novantatré*, Siena: Università degli Studi.

Ciacci, A. (1995) 'Le origine tra mito e archeologia', in R. Barzanti, G. Catoni and M. De Gregorio (eds) *Storia di Siena I*, pp.9–26.

Civai, M. (ed.) (1999) *Tilson: Conjunctions*, Siena: Comune di Siena.

Civai, M. and Toti, E. (2000) *Palio: la corsa del'anima*, Siena: Edizioni Alsaba.

Comune di Siena (1906) *Regolamento per l'esecuzione delle tradizionali Corse del Palio*, Siena, Tipografia Cooperativa (reprinted by Betti Editrice, Siena, 1995).

Falassi, A. (1982) 'Ottanta anni di Palii. Note iconografiche', in *Bisogna Credeci, Numero Unico della Contrada di Valdimontone*, Siena: Il Leccio, pp.227–45.

Falassi, A. (1998) *Palio: The Colors of Siena*, Siena: Comune of Siena.

Falassi, A. (1999) 'The false and the real Tilson', in M. Civai (ed.) pp.13–18.

Falassi, A. and Catoni, G. (1982) *Palio*, Milan: Electa Editrice.

Fattorini, G. (1999a) 'Sala Emilia Griccioli Brandolini d'Adda', in M. Capperucci, P. Torriti and G. Manganelli (eds) pp.102–13.

Fattorini, G. (1999b) 'Sala Silvio Griccioli', in M. Capperucci, P. Torriti and G. Manganelli (eds) pp.153–63.

Hook, J. (1979) *Siena: A City and Its History*, London: Hamish Hamilton.

Mazzoni della Stella, V. (1993) 'Ma il "problema" è qualità o residenza?"', in L. Betti, Volume 4, pp.9–10.

Petti, R. (1997) 'I Drappelloni della Contrada: Premi, Documenti Storici, Oggetti d'Arte', in M. Capperucci, P. Torriti and G. Manganelli (eds) pp.360–401.

Pierard, R. and Linder, R. (1988) *Civil Religion and the American Presidency*, Grand Rapids: Zondervan.

Piersimoni, C. (1996) 'Tradizione a ritmo pop', *Il Carroccio*, 65, pp.13–15.

Santi, B. (1997) 'Due fasi, due facce: per forza e per amore ...', in *Palio: I giorni della festa, Numero Unico edito in occasione del Palio del 16 agosto 1997*, Siena: Alsaba, pp.5–6.

Torriti, M. (1999) 'Sala Giovanni Antonio Pecci', in M. Capperucci, P. Torriti and G. Manganelli (eds) pp.164–79.

Zetti, M. (1999) '"Sena Vetus Civitas Virginis". Evoluzione dell'iconografia mariana nei drappelloni del Palio di Siena (1930–1996). Analisi e confronti', in S. Bruschelli (ed.) *Ianua Coeli: dalla Porta del tempio all'Immagine di Maria, Leggere l'arte della Chiesa, Quaderni dell'Opera*, 3, pp.77–163.

CHAPTER 7

'Sacred and profane': popular rituals in Sienese civil religion

In their influential study and interpretation of the Palio of Siena, *La Terra in Piazza*, the American anthropologist Alan Dundes and the Sienese anthropologist Alessandro Falassi suggested that 'the Palio like so many festivals provides a special time of license, an opportunity for reversing reality'. In particular, they noted, the blessing of the horses that will run in the Palio, together with other aspects of the behaviour of *contrada* members, can be interpreted as moments when the 'sacred' status of a *contrada*'s church is ignored or deliberately set aside by the performance of 'profane' actions (Dundes and Falassi, 1975, pp.96–8). The contrast between the 'sacred' and the 'profane' to which Dundes and Falassi drew attention is one that also appears regularly in popular Sienese discussion of the Palio, as well as in scholarly studies of this festival. During the days of the Palio, and the weeks before and after it, references will often be found in the Sienese daily and weekly newspapers to the contrast or tension between the sacred and the profane in the Palio and its rituals and traditions. Often, reference to this tension is conveyed by the single 'shorthand' term *sacra/profana* (sacred/profane). Similarly, the local television station, Canale 3 Toscana, which runs a rolling sequence of programmes devoted to the Palio and its history throughout the period of each Palio, regularly includes studio discussions and interviews exploring aspects of the issue of *sacra/ profana*.

The aim of this chapter is to explore, briefly, this proposed contrast between the 'sacred' and the 'profane' in the Palio of Siena and its rituals. The first section of the chapter will describe a number of examples of actions that might be regarded as evidence of the 'profane' – or, more exactly, of the 'profanation of the sacred' – in the rituals and traditions of the Palio. The second section will then question whether the description of these actions as 'profane' is an entirely appropriate or adequate characterization of their nature and significance. A brief conclusion will consider the potential significance of this chapter for the argument that the Palio constitutes a modern expression of Sienese civil religion.

Profaning the sacred?

There are a number of moments within the rituals and traditions associated with the Palio and the life of the *contrade* of Siena that might easily be described in terms of a tension between the sacred and the profane. The most obvious examples – and the ones usually cited in discussions of this theme – are the blessing of the horses that run in each Palio, together with the singing, shouting and drumming within church buildings which are associated with both the preparation for the Palio and the celebration of victory after it.

The blessing of the horses takes place in the early afternoon of every Palio. In each *contrada* that is running in the Palio, the horse that will represent it is taken from its stable to the church of the *contrada*. There, together with the jockey who will ride it, and in the presence of a large crowd of *contrada* members, both the horse and the jockey will be blessed. This blessing is the climax of a short religious service. The horse will be sprinkled with holy water and, perhaps, also have a crucifix or reliquary pressed to its forehead, while the official priest of the *contrada* exhorts it to 'go and return victorious' (Dundes and Falassi, 1975, pp.94–6; Falassi and Catoni, 1982, p.64; Civai and Toti, 2000, pp.282–3). The event takes place in strict silence, apart from the words of the short service and of the blessing by the priest. Should the horse defecate during the ceremony it will be taken as a sign of good fortune. After the blessing, the horse is led from the church. Once the horse has left, the assembled *contrada* members will shout loudly the name of their *contrada* using a traditional three-stage chant, such as 'Ci-Ci-vetta' (for the Contrada della Civetta), 'Lu-Lu-Lupa' (for the Contrada della Lupa), or 'Se-Se-Selva' (for the Contrada della Selva). At this point they may well also sing, probably choosing either the short hymn to the Virgin called 'Maria, Mater Gratiae', or their *contrada*'s particular version of the Palio song 'Per forza e per amore' ('By strength and by love') that is used by all of the *contrade*.[1] Then the drummers who will accompany the representatives of the *contrada* in the historic parade

---

[1] This is the *contrada* song that is discussed in Chapter 5 (p.210).

before the Palio may well begin to drum, still within the church. The effect and impact of the entire sequence is apt to be both surprising and intense. It is also, certainly, strikingly different from the type of behaviour normally associated with presence in Christian Churches.

A similar combination of emotions will be likely to accompany an observer's first experience of other moments when *contrada* members attend churches either before or after the Palio. Before the Palio, when the *drappellone* is taken to be blessed, either in the church of Santa Maria di Provenzano (for the Palio of 2 July), or in Siena cathedral (for the Palio of 16 August), shouting and drumming within church will also occur. As the *drappellone* enters the church and is taken to the altar to be blessed, the drums of the *contrade* will fill the church in question with a crescendo of noise, while the flags of the *contrade* will wave in salute to the *drappellone* and in the attempt to touch it as it passes. After the *drappellone* has been blessed, the drums will again roll, as they will when the *contrade* leave the church in sequence at the end of the ceremony. In August, as members of each *contrada* enter the cathedral for this ceremony, they may well, again, shout the name of their *contrada* in its three-stage form. These

Figure 7.1 Blessing of a horse before the Palio. Foto Lensini, Siena.

moments are very far from conforming to the usual norms of behaviour in churches.[2]

Even more contrary to such behavioural norms are the celebrations that take place in the church of Santa Maria di Provenzano and the cathedral after the Palio has been won. The members of the winning *contrada* carry their newly-won *drappellone* from the Campo, where the Palio has been run, to the appropriate church. By the time they reach the church it will already contain many *contrada* members, most of whom will have gathered at or near the altar which will already be surrounded by waving flags, while the church will resound to drumming. As other *contrada* members arrive, they will also head towards the altar. As the main groups arrive from the Campo, the numbers in the church will swell and the altar will be completely surrounded by the crowd. The winning jockey will be carried in on the shoulders of *contrada* members. He will be taken to the altar and will kneel in front of it, and he may even stand on the altar with the captain of the winning *contrada*. The greatest wave of emotion, drumming and swirling of flags will be as the *drappellone* itself enters the church and is carried to the altar. Hands and arms will be stretched towards it. Those who can do so will touch it, holding it tightly and kissing it if possible. All around, *contrada* members will embrace one another, many of them in tears because of the sheer emotion and joy of the moment. They will then sing the hymn to the Virgin, 'Maria, Mater Gratiae', and quite possibly 'Per forza e per amore' as well. Then they will leave the church to carry their new *drappellone* to their own *contrada*. (See Figures 7.3, 7.4, 7.5 and 7.6; Colour Plates 1 and 19.)

Again, the contrast with 'normal' behaviour in church is striking and, for those concerned to preserve the proprieties and decorum that are customarily associated with such places, it is not difficult to see how and why such moments might be regarded as profane. Thus, from time to time, the ecclesiastical authorities in Siena criticize the 'excesses' of *contrada* members in their celebrations and behaviour in the cathedral or Santa Maria di Provenzano, and will call for an

---

[2] The descriptions presented here, and in other parts of this chapter, are based not only on accounts in standard works on the Palio (for example, Dundes and Falassi, 1975, p.136; Falassi and Catoni, 1982, p.75; Civai and Toti, 2000, pp.310–12), but also on personal observation on numerous occasions. In addition to registering my own reactions to such moments, I have witnessed the sheer surprise and shock that is sometimes evident in the reactions of non-Sienese who are encountering these ceremonies for the first time. Such shock does not necessarily imply disapproval. It is, rather, evidence of the unexpectedly unconventional behaviour in church and the sheer intensity and emotion that is generated among both participants and observers.

Figure 7.2 A scene in Provenzano after victory in the Palio. Foto Lensini, Siena.

Figure 7.3 A scene in Provenzano after victory in the Palio. Foto Lensini, Siena.

Figure 7.4 A scene in Provenzano after victory in the Palio. Foto Lensini, Siena.

appropriate restraint and respect in the manner in which *contrada* members express themselves. In August 2000, for example, the official notice for the Corteo dei Ceri (see Chapter 4) contained two severely worded sentences, printed in bold type, requesting respect for the sacred nature of the ceremony. Participants in the procession were to maintain proper behaviour and were specifically asked not to express *contrada* allegiance through acts or words for which there were other appropriate times and places during the Palio. Significantly, however, such pleas from the church authorities are apt to fall on deaf ears and to make little impact on the traditional celebrations of *contrada* members.[3]

If the phenomena discussed above are the most striking and dramatic examples of moments at which the rituals associated with the Palio might be described as 'profane', they are not, however, by any means the only such moments. The very intensity of the way in which *contrada* members regard the *drappellone* might be regarded as one such example. As previous chapters have explained, when the *drappellone* is blessed and displayed in either the cathedral or Santa Maria di Provenzano, *contrada* members seek to touch it with their *contrada* scarves – an act that is clearly an expression of both the desire and the hope that the *drappellone* will become theirs after the Palio. The *drappellone* is thus itself, in practice, the central object of devotion during these ceremonies. This is confirmed by observation of the mood or rhythm of the ceremonies when the *drappellone* is blessed. Although, in theory, the focal point of the event is the blessing of the *drappellone*, in practice the emotional and psychological climaxes of the ceremonies are the moments when the *drappellone* enters the church or cathedral and is carried to the high altar, and when it is then carried from the high altar to be displayed on a pillar – in each case passing through the flags of the *contrade*. It is at these moments that the sense of devotion and collective participation peaks. It is then that a sense of worship is most intense. A similar intensity then recurs when the *drappellone* enters and passes around the Campo, just before the Palio itself, and is evident again in the desire of members of the winning *contrada* to touch and kiss it. From the perspective of the church authorities, such intense devotion to a particular object and, in the context of the services of blessing, the priority given to it, rather than to the actual act of blessing the

---

[3] They are also apt to prompt statements in the press in defence of the traditional modes of celebration, as well as statements of support for the church authorities, as, for example, in the *Corriere di Siena* (27 June 1999, p.22 and 1 July 1999, p.25). For the request to respect the sacred nature of the Corteo dei Ceri in 2000, see the 'Ordinamento del Corteo del Cero 14 Agosto 2000', published by the cathedral authorities.

drappellone, might easily be described as 'profane', or even 'idolatrous'.

A further aspect of the Palio and its traditions that invites description in terms of the contrast between the sacred and profane is the Sienese enthusiasm for discerning omens and esoteric patterns of significance in, for example, the colours, design, organization or symbolism of a *drappellone*, or in the numerological patterns and historical precedents that may be identified in the complex organization of each Palio. Thus, each *contrada* is associated with a particular number (Dundes and Falassi, 1975, pp.32–3), and *contrada* members may see significance in the relationship between this number and other sequences that may be identified in the history and statistics of the Palio. There is great enthusiasm for the identification of numerological patterns, sequences and omens of good luck within such statistics and, during the period of the Palio, the local newspapers regularly carry whole pages devoted to this subject. Moreover there are many aspects of each Palio that are deliberately left to luck in the form of the drawing of lots – for the three *contrade* that do not run 'by right' in a particular Palio, for the horse that is assigned to each *contrada*, and for the order in which the horses will start the Palio itself. This accentuates the element of chance and the fascination with esoteric patterns of significance, whether these are numerological or connected with other aspects of the rituals of the Palio or the history of particular *contrade* (Luchini, 1987, pp.285–91). Despite – or perhaps because of – this deeply-rooted instinct to attempt to discern signs of good or bad fortune, and to seek to manipulate such fortune to the advantage of a particular *contrada*, there is a proverbial acceptance that, in the end, sheer chance remains an essential element of the Palio. Indeed, according to a popular Sienese saying, 'Fortune is the Queen of the Palio' (Dundes and Falassi, 1975, p.238; Hook, 1979, p.220).

Interest in astrological interpretations of the likely fortunes of the different *contrade* is also high and, again, will feature in both the newspapers and on television programmes devoted to the Palio. Similar patterns of interpretation and seeking for signs of good fortune are applied to the *drappellone* for each Palio. *Contrada* members may interpret the prominence of their *contrada*'s colours on a *drappellone* as a sign that their *contrada* will win this Palio. Or the particular positioning of the symbol of their *contrada* may be interpreted in this way – if, perhaps, the Virgin or a saint portrayed on the *drappellone* may be said to be looking or gesturing towards the *contrada* symbol in question. Other signs of good fortune are associated with the order in which the flags of the *contrade* are placed – again by chance – on the pillars in the centre of the cathedral for various religious festivals. Others again relate to being the first to touch the *drappellone*, to aspects of the behaviour of the horse at the *contrada* stable, or to particular details of the historic parade (Luchini, 1987, pp.284–5; Civai and Toti, 2000, pp.182–3). The local press routinely refer to such speculation as the '*cabbala*' of Palio, thus associating it – though in a loose and colloquial way – with the esoteric and mystical traditions of 'Kabbalah' found in medieval and early modern Judaism, and which also flourished in Florence during the late fifteenth century. Speculation of this sort by the Sienese is also sometimes described in terms of a distinction between 'religion' and mere 'superstition' – with the implication that the *cabbala* of Palio is much closer to the latter. Thus, it has been argued by one well-informed contemporary Sienese author, Luca Luchini, that it is sometimes difficult to distinguish clearly between, on the one hand, popular requests to the Virgin and the saints in respect of the Palio, and on the other hand, invocations of fortune and strategies to secure good luck. In recent times, moreover, in Luchini's judgement, there are signs that the delicate balance between religion and superstition in relation to the Palio is tilting in the direction of superstition (Luchini, 1987, pp.273–300; 1999, p.45).

Three further examples of the possible tension between the sacred and the profane within the traditions of the Palio merit brief consideration. The first is the carnival-style parade that a victorious *contrada* will hold to celebrate its victory. Usually held on the Sunday evening following the Palio victory, the parade will assemble in the public gardens in Siena known as the 'Lizza', and will progress through the streets to the Campo and then return to the territory of the winning *contrada*. Most of the jokes in the parade will be designed to poke fun at the *contrada*'s principal rival, and to a lesser extent will mock the efforts of the other *contrade* who ran in the Palio but failed to win. Satire on religion is, however, often a significant element of such parades. Thus, for example, when in 1994 the Contrada della Tartuca won the August Palio, the *drappellone* included a celebration of the fact that the Pope had honoured Siena earlier that year. The victory parade then included a mock 'Pope' travelling in a mock 'pope-mobile', satirizing the vehicle in which Pope John Paul II habitually travels through the streets of cities that he visits. And in August 1995, when the Contrada del Leocorno won the Palio, black-edged notices appeared in the streets the following Sunday in the form of the traditional Sienese announce-ment of a death, but announcing, complete with cartoon owl, the death and burial of the Civetta – the rival *contrada* whose symbolic creature is an owl. That night, in the Campo, a 'funeral cortege',

Figure 7.5 The mock 'pope-mobile' in the victory parade of the Contrada della Tartuca after the August Palio of 1994. Foto Lensini, Siena.

Figure 7.6 The memorial notice posted by the Contrada del Leocorno after victory in the Palio of August 1995. Photo: Gerald Parsons.

Figure 7.7 The 'gravestone' for the Civetta placed over the main drain of the Campo by members of the Contrada del Leocorno after their victory of August 1995. Photo: Gerald Parsons.

dressed like a religious lay confraternity, duly 'buried' the Civetta, placing a mock gravestone over the main drain of the Campo.

The final two examples of a possible tension between sacred and profane are somewhat different and concern the popular use and adaptation of 'official' Catholic forms and ceremonies, not the deliberate mocking of them. As Chapter 4 (pp.157–73) explained, the traditional Sienese hymn to the Virgin, entitled 'Maria, Mater Gratiae', is an integral part of the rituals of the *contrade*. It is sung by *contrada* members not only when they celebrate victory after the Palio in the cathedral or the church of Santa Maria di Provenzano, but also in the churches of other *contrade* when they visit them the day afterwards and, again, by all *contrade* during the annual festival of their patron saint. During these patronal festivals *contrada* members will sing this hymn as part of the celebrations in their own *contrade* church (Pepi, 1984, p.40; Falassi, 1996, p.107). But they also sing it in the churches of other *contrade* that they visit as part of their celebrations – and on these occasions the hymn is not only sung with great vigour and enthusiasm, but is also preceded and followed by the drumming that characteristically accompanies the festivals, parades and celebrations of the Sienese *contrade*. The version of the hymn that is sung so enthusiastically by *contrada* members on such occasions is, however, very much a popularized – or even, it might be said, a vulgarized –

version of the original Latin hymn on which it is based. Thus, this version of the original hymn has been described as 'mangled' or 'spoiled', while the style of singing deployed is not one normally associated with religious praise or worship (Sensi, 1995). Rather than being measured, disciplined and devotional, the ethos is determinedly relaxed, popular and enthusiastic. The informal and imprecise nature of the use of this hymn by the *contrade* – when such use is seen from a conventionally religious perspective – is also indicated by the fact that it is popularly referred to as a 'Te Deum', when this is not the case. A 'Te Deum' is a Latin hymn directed to God, whereas 'Maria, Mater Gratiae', in both its original and popular forms, is most definitely a Latin hymn to the Virgin (Falassi, 1980, p.193; De Cristofaro, 1988, pp.7 and 24–5; Bonicelli, 1992, p.19; Sensi, 1995, p.10).

Such popular use and adaptation of a traditional hymn to the Virgin could, again, be cited as an example of the tendency for the rituals of the Palio to include elements of the 'profane', in this case because of the disregard of the origins and 'proper' use of the hymn concerned. A similar point might also be made about the ritual of the *contrada* baptism, for here also a traditional Christian ceremony – indeed, the fundamental rite of initiation into the Christian faith in most branches of the Christian Church – is adopted and adapted by the Sienese *contrade* as a rite of initiation into their distinct communities. Although the *contrada* baptism does not make any claim that conflicts with, or contradicts, the claims made in baptism into the Christian Church, the ceremony is certainly modelled on the Christian rite. The Prior of the *contrada* recites a formal and ritual statement welcoming each person presented for baptism into the *contrada* and its traditions – a statement that will include reference to the patron saint of the *contrada*. The Prior then baptizes the individual using water drawn from the official *contrada* fountain (Colour Plate 11). The ritual, moreover, is intended to signify a lifetime commitment and allegiance to the *contrada* – just as Christian baptism is intended to signify such commitment to the Christian faith (Dundes and Falassi, 1975, pp.37–9; Falassi and Catoni, 1982, pp.26 and 29; Barzanti, Crispolti and Falassi, 1987).

Simply profane, or differently sacred?

When viewed or interpreted from the perspective of official Catholic Christianity, various rituals, actions and modes of behaviour that are part of the Palio and its traditions might be regarded as 'profane', or as a mixture of the sacred and the profane. The sacred will be represented by those moments and elements of the Palio when the festival interacts with, and participates in, 'official' religion. The profane, by contrast, will be represented by those moments and elements when the customary decorum and disciplines of official religion are set aside, and popular, unconventional or unorthodox behaviour and rituals predominate. But is this the only, or even the most appropriate, way of interpreting the traditional tension between 'sacred' and 'profane' in the Palio and the life of the Sienese *contrade*? What if the rituals and customs of the Palio and the *contrade* are interpreted not simply from the perspective of the authorities and standards of the Catholic Church, but as part of the rituals of Sienese civil religion? Interpreted from this standpoint, many of the rituals and actions that might be described as 'profane' in conventional terms appear, rather, as important and integral parts of the 'sacred' content of Sienese civil religion. A reconsideration of several of the particular rituals examined in the preceding section of the chapter may serve to demonstrate the case for this alternative reading.

For all its unconventionality and novelty value – especially for many tourists to Siena, who are habitually intrigued by the ritual – the blessing of the horse before the Palio, is, in fact, a moment of immense solemnity, intensity, devotion and emotion. The church will be crowded to overflowing. As the horse arrives at the church an utter silence will be required – and if necessary strictly enforced. The brief service will take place in this silence, broken only by the priest's words and the responses of the *contrada* members – responses which will themselves be restrained and calm. The climax of the service will be the blessing – administered by the official priest of the *contrada* who will probably wear both a liturgical stole and a *contrada* scarf – and the invocation to return victorious. Still in complete silence, the horse will be led out. And only then will the tension be broken by the ritual shouting of the *contrada*'s name, by passionate singing, and by drumming. At the end of the nineteenth century, William Heywood, an Englishman who lived in Siena for many years and wrote a series of books about the city and its history, commented about the blessing of the horses before the Palio:

> And hither is led the horse which is about to compete for the Palio to receive the priestly benediction. Does the idea shock you? It need not do so. The service is a reverent one enough ... To my mind, I confess, the irreverence, if any there be, is to be found in the mental attitude of those foreigners – English and Americans, for the most part – who, entering God's house, make no attempt to understand the prayers offered up, and, prejudging the whole ceremony, regard it merely as a

curious instance of puerile superstition, forming part of the afternoon's entertainment.

(Heywood, 1899, pp.217 and 220)

Heywood's writings on the Palio are still highly thought of in Siena
and are regarded as a rare example of a non-Sienese demonstrating a
genuine understanding and feeling for the festival and its traditions –
so much so that his classic study of the Palio, which was originally
published only in English, was translated into Italian and republished
in Siena in 1993. In the same year, the passage from Heywood's work
quoted above was cited approvingly in a brief Sienese article devoted
to the ceremony of the blessing of the horse (Falassi, 1993, p.17).
Moreover, Heywood's point remains well made. To witness the
blessing of a horse before the Palio is still to observe a ritual
conducted with great reverence and solemnity. If there is profanity to
be seen at the event then, as in Heywood's day, so also in ours, it is
most likely to be found in the behaviour of some tourists whose
insistence on attempting flash photography might very well be
thought to constitute a profanation of a moment that is deeply sacred
to the Sienese.

The potential clash between the sacred and the profane in the
blessing of the *drappellone* in the cathedral or in the church of Santa
Maria di Provenzano is similarly apt to become less clear-cut if the
ritual is considered as a mixing and intermingling of the sacred in
both official Catholicism and Sienese civil religion. The testimony of
Joe Tilson, the British pop-artist who painted the *drappellone* for the
Palio of August 1996 (Colour Plate 4) may help to illustrate the point.
Tilson was subsequently both thrilled and moved to see his work
receive public acclaim and then assume 'a sacred significance as it
became a holy icon' during the blessing in the cathedral (Falassi,
1999, p.15). In his own words:

> The most moving thing was to walk arm in arm with mayor Piccini in
> the Cathedral like a forest of black and white pillars with drums and
> flags on either side of us. And then the Archbishop looks at you, looks
> beyond you, above you, at the Madonna. In that very moment your
> work changes from the secular to the sacred. The only moment this
> happens for a contemporary artist ...

(Quoted in Falassi, 1999, p.15)

At first sight, Tilson's words might be taken as support for the view
that it is precisely in the act of blessing that the sacred is involved –
thus endorsing the contrast of sacred and profane. A more careful
reading, however, would suggest that Tilson's perception of the
transition of his work from 'secular' to 'sacred' involved not just the
blessing, but rather the blessing as the climax of the act of walking

between the pillars, the flags and the drums. Rather than a clash between elements of the sacred and the profane, it may be more profitable to see the blessing of the *drappellone*, and the enthusiasm of *contrada* members that accompanies it, as a meeting of two impulses to the sacred. Officially blessed and made sacred by the actions of the church, the *drappellone* is also treated and confirmed as a sacred object by the actions and devotion of the *contrada* members present.

The exuberant celebrations in the cathedral and in Santa Maria di Provenzano after victory in the Palio are also susceptible to similar reinterpretation in terms of an alternative version of the sacred, rather than an example of the profane. These celebrations, it has been observed, are 'as devout as they are disorderly' (Falassi and Catoni, 1982, p.75). This description, once again, suggests that the stark contrast of sacred and profane is too simple and unsubtle. The behaviour of *contrada* members is certainly exuberant, loud, emotional and ecstatic. It is not the behaviour that is customary in church. It does not conform to the usual decorum associated with being in a church. But neither is it intentionally disrespectful to the church or its beliefs. The noisy and boisterous behaviour is not designed to repudiate or mock the religious environment in which it occurs. It is an instinctive response to victory in the Palio, an explosion of emotion which the Sienese authors of the most recent study of the Palio call simply '*il tripudio*' – a word that may be translated equally well as 'rejoicing', 'jubilation' or 'exultation' (Civai and Toti, 2000, p.310). Significantly, the first place to which victorious *contrada* members go after winning the Palio is the church in which the just-won *drappellone* was blessed only days earlier. The 'rejoicing', 'jubilation' and 'exultation' of the victorious *contrada* members might thus be interpreted as an unconventional, but nonetheless sincere, response to a deeply sacred moment in the life of their *contrada*. Indeed, in a letter to a Sienese daily newspaper in 1999, in response to a call by the archbishop of Siena for greater decorum in the celebration of victory in the Palio, one *contrada* member put this point with even greater force. The songs, clamour and drumming in victory, she argued, contain nothing that might offend God. They are, rather, a way of 'reconsecrating' two places that are central to Sienese worship and where, twice a year, a thousand years of history, tradition and popular devotion converge. Sometimes, she concluded, a 'thanks' shouted through tears and from the sheer joy of life might be worth more than a hundred more formal prayers (Losi, 1999). Again, therefore, the blending of official Catholicism and popular devotion to the traditions and rituals of the Palio appears to be at least as valid a way of describing this moment as the contrast between sacred and profane.

A similar point may also be made about the popular manner in which the Marian hymn, 'Maria, Mater Gratiae' is sung in *contrada* celebrations, and about the adoption and adaptation of the rite of baptism within the *contrade*. Again, in both of these cases there is a coexistence between two types of devotion, two forms of the sacred, rather than an opposition. Thus, for example, the same author who noted that the version of 'Maria, Mater Gratiae' that is regularly sung by *contrada* members is in fact a 'spoiled' or 'mangled' version of the original Latin hymn from which it is derived, also argued that the popular transformation of this hymn did not make it, or the prayer contained in it, either blasphemous or profane. What the singing of the *contrada* version of this traditional hymn may lack in precision, accuracy and conventional decorum, it may be said to gain in terms of heartfelt devotion and instinctive enthusiasm – thus becoming a popular symbol and expression of traditional Sienese affection for, and gratitude towards, the Virgin (Sensi, 1995, p.12). It is also a popular expression of Sienese affection for the Virgin that is completely embedded in the annual rituals of the Palio and of the *contrade*. Thus such singing sustains and regularly re-emphasizes the relationship between contemporary Sienese customs and rituals and the particular Sienese devotion to the Virgin that has endured for over seven centuries – and it does so, moreover, in the collective, communal context of *contrada* life.

The institution of the rite of *contrada* baptism in the period after the Second World War similarly affirms the importance of the community of the *contrada*. As modern Siena increasingly expanded beyond the walls of the medieval and renaissance city, so the direct, physical link between *contrada* members and their *contrada* was reduced. More and more, *contrada* members did not actually live within the territory of their *contrada*. It was out of this experience and the need to devise a symbolic and ritual means of reaffirming the closeness and commitment of membership of a *contrada* that the *contrada* baptism was born. As one historian of the institution of *contrada* baptism has observed, at one time the introduction of a separate *contrada* baptism, distinct from that of the Catholic Church, would have been unthinkable. This was not least because, in earlier periods, when the population of Siena was smaller and the majority of *contrada* members still lived within the territory of their *contrada*, the Catholic baptism of most *contrada* members would have taken place within the church of the *contrada*, thus providing a ritual in which Christian initiation was also firmly located within the community and territory of the *contrada* (Barzanti, 1987, p.17).

With new patterns of social mobility and the expansion of the suburbs of Siena, however, this intimate relationship between *contrada*, *contrada* church, Christian baptism and *contrada* community inevitably weakened. Thus, the *contrade* introduced a new 'civil-religious ritual', which celebrated and affirmed the relationship between individuals and their *contrada*, even if they were born and lived outside its territorial confines. As a sentence in a special publication to celebrate the fiftieth anniversary of one *contrada*'s children's group proudly affirmed, *contrada* baptism anoints with the spirit of the *contrada* the children of *contrada* members who, increasingly, are born and raised in Petriccio, Vico Alto, San Miniato or other modern suburbs of Siena (cited in Barzanti, 1987, pp.17–18).[4]

The ritual of *contrada* baptism is carried out each year during the festival of the patron saint of the *contrada*. It is an immensely joyful, celebratory ritual in which entire families – and the extended 'family' of the *contrada* itself – participate. Each baptism is accompanied by the roll of the drums and the salute of the flags of the *contrada*. Those baptized receive a certificate and their baptismal *contrada* scarf. Most of those baptized will be babies born during the last year, since the last *contrada* baptism. But there will also be others. These may include older children who have not already been baptized for one reason or another – perhaps their family, although Sienese by origin, now lives elsewhere in Italy or abroad and has not previously been able to attend a *contrada* baptism – and young people or, indeed, adults who have chosen to give their allegiance and commitment to this particular *contrada* and have been accepted by the *contrada* as worthy of such formal and yet intimate inclusion within the community. Although often described as a 'lay' or 'secular' ceremony (Dundes and Falassi, 1975, p.38; Civai, 2000, p.331), this is true only in the sense that it is not a ceremony of the Christian Church. As the reference to *contrada* baptism as a 'civil-religious ritual' suggests, it is also a deeply 'religious' and 'sacred' moment in the life of each *contrada* – an interpretation that is also suggested by the description of *contrada* baptism as 'ritual consecration' of those who wish to become members of a *contrada* (Pepi, 1984, p.154).

At the same, there is no clash or tension between this civil-religious ritual and the Christian rite of baptism on which it is modelled. The *contrada* baptism makes no claim that conflicts with or contradicts the Christian rite of baptism. The two ceremonies coexist in the life of

---

[4] The term 'civil-religious ritual' is one used in the original Italian version of this source. The children's group in question was that of the Contrada della Chiocciola, the Sezione Piccoli Chioccolini.

the *contrade* – a fact that was well illustrated in 1999 when the Contrada dell'Onda celebrated the renovation of its *contrada* fountain. The fountain of the Contrada dell'Onda is situated immediately outside the church of the *contrada*. On the occasion of the *contrada* baptism in 1999, the baptismal ceremonies were preceded by a ceremony to bless the restored fountain. The blessing of the fountain was conducted by the official Catholic priest of the *contrada*, using the traditional Christian forms of blessing. After the blessing, however, the priest left the fountain and went about other business, leaving the Prior of the *contrada* to baptize new members.[5] The incident, although small and highly localized, provides an extremely effective symbol of the subtle relationship that exists between official Catholic religion and civil religion in Siena as a whole. In the blessing of the restored fountain, Catholic religion and civil religion are completely intertwined. In the subsequent *contrada* baptism, civil religion takes over, but borrows the forms and rituals of Catholic religion. It is a basic pattern which is often repeated within Sienese life and in the rituals and traditions of the Palio and the *contrade*.

Conclusion: *sacra/profana* and Sienese civil religion

It has been the argument of this chapter that the traditional contrast and opposition between the sacred and the profane that is said to characterize many of the popular rituals of the Palio of Siena is, on closer examination, only partly valid and appropriate. It is valid and appropriate if the rituals of the Palio and the *contrade* of Siena are viewed from the perspective of traditional Catholic belief and the norms of conventional religious behaviour. From such a perspective, various elements in the rituals and traditions of the Palio and the *contrade* may well appear not merely popular and unconventional but profane. It is valid and appropriate also in respect of some of the deliberately irreverent and carnival-like victory celebrations in which the winners of a Palio will often indulge. And it may even be valid and appropriate in respect of some of the more esoteric and superstitious customs associated with signs and portents of good fortune associated with the Palio.

It is less valid and appropriate, however, if the rituals of the Palio and the *contrade* are interpreted from the perspective of civil religion

---

[5] The description here is based on personal observation of the event.

and in terms of the intricate interrelationship between official Catholicism and Sienese civil religion. Once viewed from this perspective, many of the actions, rituals and modes of behaviour that are often described as profane appear, rather, as highly religious expressions of the devotion and fervour that lies at the heart of Sienese civil religion. Rather than being profane, they appear, instead, as alternative expressions and experiences of the sacred – but the sacred conceived and perceived primarily in terms of the history, culture and traditions of Siena. Inevitably, because Siena, by centuries-long tradition, is a Catholic culture in which the Catholic version of Christianity has long been the predominant religious influence, Sienese civil religion is expressed predominantly through Catholic forms and rituals. The Virgin is central; images of her, hymns to her, and processions in her honour are regular and essential elements; patron saints are prominent; the churches of the *contrade* are Catholic in ritual, ethos and worship. And in the past, when Siena has been formally dedicated to the Virgin, it has been the cathedral of Siena that has been the traditional location for such acts.

At the same time, however, Sienese civil religion is also much more than simply Catholicism in a Sienese context. Thus, although it interacts with the calendar of Catholic Christianity (most obviously in the relationship of the July Palio to the feast of the Visitation, of the annual August Palio to the feast of the Assumption, and in the dates of the festivals of the patron saints of the seventeen *contrade*), Sienese civil religion has its own annual cycle and rhythm. It begins its year on 1 December – the festival of Saint Ansano. The highpoints of its year, meanwhile, are not the principal festivals of the Christian year such as Easter, Pentecost or Christmas, but the two Palii of July and August. It is the rhythm of the Palio – its anticipation, its preparation, its celebration and its recollection – that is the defining rhythm of Sienese civil religion. Moreover, Sienese civil religion may be said to be devoted to Siena itself as well as to the Virgin – and its devotion to the Virgin is very much to the Virgin precisely as patron, protectress and historic 'saviour' of Siena. Thus the bronze door that commemorates the last formal dedication of Siena to the Virgin does so precisely by celebrating the history of Sienese devotion to particular revered images of the Virgin and their perceived role in the repeated protection of the city. The discussion in Chapter 6 provided a series of examples of the way in which such simultaneous devotion to Siena and to the Virgin is regularly explored and expressed in Palio *drappellone*. The present chapter has also explored this theme, but in a somewhat different way. When the exuberance of *contrada* members threatens to exceed the bounds of reasonable decorum in church, when hymns to the Virgin are sung in popular and unconventional forms, when the *drappellone* for the Palio is treated like a sacred object meriting devotion, and when the official rites of the church are adapted to celebrate initiation into *contrada* membership, what is happening is not the undermining of the sacred by the profane. Rather, it is the response to – and the expression of – the sacred in a civil religion.

References

Barzanti, R. (1987) 'I luoghi della fonte', in R. Barzanti, E. Crispolti and A. Falassi, pp.17–25.

Barzanti, R., Crispolti, E. and Falassi, A. (1987) *Le Fontane di Contrade*, Siena: Il Leccio.

Bonicelli, G. (1992) 'La Madonna, Siena e il Palio', in L. Betti (ed.) *Pallium: evoluzione del drappellone dalle origini ad oggi. Volume 2: Dall'unità d'Italia all'ultimo conflitto mondiale*, Siena: Betti Editrice, pp.19–22.

Civai, E. (2000) 'Il Palio in cento parole', in M. Civai and E. Toti, pp.331–6.

Civai, M. and Toti, E. (2000) *Palio: la corsa dell'anima*, Siena: Alsaba.

De Cristofaro, R. (1988) *Siena: I canti del popolo*, Siena: Edizioni Cantagalli.

Dundes, A. and Falassi, A. (1975) *La Terra in Piazza: An Interpretation of the Palio of Siena*, Berkeley: University of California Press.

Falassi, A. (1980) *Per forza e per amore: I canti popolare del Palio di Siena*, Milan: Bompiani.

Falassi, A. (1993) 'Benedetto quel barbero', in *Palio: I giorni della festa, Numero Unico edito in occasione del Palio del 16 agosto 1993*, Siena: Alsaba, pp.16–17.

Falassi, A. (1996) 'Le Contrade', in R. Barzanti, G. Catoni and M. De Gregorio (eds) *Storia di Siena II: dal granducato all'unità*, Siena: Edizioni Alsaba.

Falassi, A. (1999) 'The false and the real Tilson', in M. Civai (ed.) *Tilson: Conjunctions*, Siena: Comune di Siena, pp.13–18.

Falassi, A. and Catoni, G. (1982) *Palio*, Milan: Electca Editrice.

Heywood, W. (1899) *Our Lady of August and the Palio of Siena*, Siena: Enrico Torrini.

Heywood, W. (1993) *Nostra Donna d'Agosto e il Palio di Siena*, edited by A. Falassi, Siena: Protagon Editori Toscani.

Hook, J. (1979) *Siena: A City and Its History*, London: Hamish Hamilton.

Losi, S. (1999) 'Perché soffocare il "Te Deum"', *Corriere di Siena*, 27 June 1999, p.22.

Luchini, L. (1987) *Palio XX Secolo: una città fra realtà e leggenda*, Siena: Tipografia Senese Editrice.

Luchini, L. (1999) 'Religione e superstizione', *Il Carroccio*, 80, pp.44–7.

Pepi, G. (1984) *Siena: Il Palio*, Siena: Azienda Autonoma di Turismo.

Sensi, S. (1995) 'Un canto storpiato', *Il Carroccio*, 56, pp.10–12.

Conclusion: civil religion reconsidered

The seven chapters in this book have examined the value of the concept of 'civil religion'. Using the five-stage definition of civil religion proposed by Richard Pierard and Robert Linder, they have explored the potential of this concept and definition in relation to two particular areas. The first three chapters did so in relation to the national rituals and traditions of remembrance of those killed in war that are characteristic of the modern and contemporary USA and UK. The following four chapters did so in relation to the local traditions, culture and rituals of the Italian city of Siena. This conclusion now seeks to reflect, briefly, on the argument and evidence presented in the preceding chapters, and to identify some of the continuing questions concerning civil religion that are prompted by these case studies.

Each of the case studies suggests that the concept of civil religion, as defined by Pierard and Linder, is indeed a useful analytical tool for interpreting and seeking to understand the significance of the rituals and traditions considered. At the national level, in terms of remembrance of those killed in war, the first three chapters showed how, in both the USA and UK, a variety of rituals, ceremonies and traditions of remembrance and commemoration have functioned as a means of transcending divisions and unifying what might otherwise be deeply divided national communities. Thus, in the USA, rituals and traditions of remembrance and commemoration initially emerged from the traumatic experience of the Civil War in the mid-nineteenth century, and were intimately linked to an ideology of reconciliation between the victorious North and the defeated South. In the first half of the twentieth century, the experience of two world wars consolidated and reinforced those rituals and traditions, while in the final quarter of the twentieth century the Vietnam Veterans Memorial proved to be an innovative and powerful means of transcending at least some of the deep divisions in American society caused by the Vietnam War.

In the UK, meanwhile, the 'invention' of an entire set of 'traditions' of remembrance after the First World War provided an enduring expression of collective recollection and memorial of those killed. In the British case, the annual Remembrance Day, and subsequently Remembrance Sunday, rituals – held simultaneously at the Cenotaph and at literally thousands of local memorials – provide a compelling example of a civil religious ritual that unites diverse elements of the community and emphasizes a sense of a shared history and destiny. At the same time, as Chapters 2 and 3 demonstrated, the capacity of war memorials and cemeteries to evoke reflection on questions of 'absolute meaning' is nowhere more evident than in their impact on individuals who visit such sites, either as self-conscious 'pilgrims', or as tourists or casual visitors who are then surprised into profound but unexpected reflection.

In applying the concept of civil religion and Pierard and Linder's five-stage definition to Siena, the four subsequent chapters of the book move decisively below the level of the nation state and focus instead at the determinedly local level of a single city. The resulting analysis of Sienese customs, traditions and rituals suggests that 'civil religion' is, indeed, a highly effective analytical tool for the interpretation of the distinctive culture and history of this city. Although the history of Siena, and in particular the significance of the festival of the Palio within that history, are open to – and indeed require – interpretation and explanation from a variety of intellectual standpoints and perspectives, the particular perspective provided by the concept of 'civil religion' offers important and persuasive insights. In particular, this perspective shows how the rituals and culture of the Palio draw on much older traditions of Sienese civil religion in order to sustain a distinctive contemporary Sienese world-view, and in order to unite a society which, despite its distinctive world-view, nevertheless revels in diversity, rivalry and division. The detailed examination of the example of Siena also provides an opportunity to explore, in some detail, the subtle relationship that exists between Sienese 'civil religion' and the rituals and norms of 'official' Catholic religion in Siena. Finally, but importantly, the Sienese case clearly demonstrates that, in principle, the concept of civil religion can be deployed in a highly specific and precise way. As the Sienese example shows, the concept of civil religion can be given detailed and precise content.

At the same time, the case studies in this book pose a variety of questions about the concept of civil religion and its application. For example, although the analysis of rituals and traditions of remembrance in the USA and UK demonstrated that these phenomena do perform the unifying function that is an essential aim of a civil religion, yet these rituals and traditions were also shown to be less than entirely successful in that role. Indeed, as Chapter 1 showed, the rituals and traditions of remembrance can themselves prove to be the sources of disunity and conflict. Thus, the ideology of reconciliation after the American Civil War bought unity between North and South only at the price of the continued exclusion of black Americans from the history of the war and the subsequent processes of reconciliation. Likewise, the memorialization of the battle of the Little Bighorn still sharply divides Americans and reveals the continuing tension and conflict that surrounds the history of the confrontation between Native Americans and those who conquered them. In the UK, meanwhile, the annual rituals of remembrance can still give rise to conflict, whether because of the perceived tension between regular Christian worship and the particular rituals of Remembrance Sunday; because of the questioning of the relevance of remembrance as the generations that fought in both world wars pass; or because of the attempt to include religious traditions other than Christianity within the traditional ceremonies of remembrance. Even more strikingly and profoundly, in Northern Ireland, the rituals and traditions of remembrance are themselves a potential focus for continuing division and conflict, in which contested versions of the past continue to sustain and foster separate and opposing civil religions, representing distinct communities within both Northern Ireland as a whole and within particular cities in Northern Ireland.

Moreover, even to the extent that rituals and traditions of remembrance in the USA and UK were shown to be successful in performing the unifying function of a civil religion, it was also clear from the case studies that, in both national contexts, they achieved this only by the extensive deployment of strategies of reticence and studied ambiguity. Thus, in the USA, the ideology of reconciliation between North and South deliberately avoided detailed discussion of the causes of the Civil War, the morality of the issues involved, or the significance of the racial issue. In the UK, unity in remembrance and commemoration were founded on the agreement that the dead should be honoured and their sacrifice valued, but the precise meanings of those sacrifices were frequently left deliberately unspecified and unproclaimed. The symbols and rituals of remembrance that were most effective – such as the Cenotaph and the two minutes' silence – were precisely those that left space for individuals to supply their own personal and specific meanings. And in the USA, in the last quarter of the twentieth century, the Vietnam Veterans Memorial was widely understood to be successful as a memorial to the experience of those who fought – and especially those who died – in Vietnam precisely because it was so formidably and deliberately ambiguous: it did not tell the visitor what to think.

Conversely, Sienese civil religion is not characterized by reticence, lack of specificity or ambiguity. On the contrary, Sienese civil religion, in its modern expression in the Palio and the life of the Sienese *contrade*, is apt to permeate and dominate the life of the city, providing an alternative calendar, sustaining a distinctive world-view, and embodying the meaning of *Senesità* – 'Sieneseness'. Sienese civil religion is thus detailed – often minutely so – in its expression through artefacts such as *contrada* scarves, flags and songs, or the imagery and symbolism of the *drappelloni* for successive Palii. Certainly the Sienese will argue – often fiercely – about the qualities of a particular *drappellone* or the rights of their *contrada* and its merits, in contrast to the perceived faults and shortcomings of its rival. But such argument thrives precisely on detail, not on ambiguity; on assertive expression, not on reticence. And, in the wider context of Siena as a whole, it is precisely this 'unity in diversity' that lies at the heart of Sienese civil religion.

Does this perhaps suggest, therefore, that the effectiveness of civil religion will be greater where the society concerned is smaller and more compact? Despite the fact that most discussion of modern civil religion has focused on the nation state, does this suggest that civil religion is likely to be more effective and more substantial at the level of a smaller community, such as a single city, than at the national level? Does it mean that civil religion, by its very nature, necessarily possesses a limited, particular, local significance – thus placing it in some tension with the contemporary emphasis on globalization?

These are all questions that merit further and closer consideration. They cannot be answered here – although the case studies in this book suggest their relevance. The case studies here also suggest, however, that the answers to these questions are unlikely to be clear-cut or straightforward. For example, the chapters on Sienese civil religion point to the possibility that a more local context is likely to foster a closer, more specific form of civil religion which genuinely unifies a particular local society. Yet even the very brief reference to the example of Northern Ireland in Chapter 1 indicates that not all local contexts will tend to this end. In Northern Ireland, civil religions are designed to affirm particular and specific communal identities and unities, while dividing the wider civil and civic society as a whole. This, in turn, suggests another important characteristic of civil religions: namely that, however much they may exhibit similar characteristics, they will also, in every case, be given specific shape and colour by their local circumstances. Beyond a general definition such as that offered by Pierard and Linder, civil religions will be characterized by the specific empirical contexts in which they exist and out of which they have emerged.

To this extent they may well also stand as something of an exception to the commonly proposed rule that modern life will increasingly be characterized by globalization and by the diminution of the enduring significance of the local and the particular. Sienese civil religion is so specific and so detailed precisely because it is so fiercely local, particular and – in one sense – exclusive. Sienese civil religion is not exclusive in an aggressive, militant sense. Visitors to Siena are welcome to watch its rituals and – if sensitive to the traditions and feelings of the Sienese – may well be invited to share in the closer and more intimate moments of *contrada* life. The outsider who makes her or his home in Siena and demonstrates an appropriate involvement and commitment will be able to join a *contrada*. But in the end, in order to participate in Sienese civil religion as more than a spectator or a guest, one must be Sienese – preferably by birth, but at the very least by adoption.

In one sense this is also true of American or British civil religion. To be in any real sense a participant in such civil religion one must be American or British – although once again, a sympathetic observer might be deeply moved, perhaps even to tears, by witnessing a particular expression of American or British civil religion, such as a visit to the Vietnam Veterans Memorial, perhaps, or a trip to a Commonwealth War Graves Cemetery. However, full participation in American or British civil religion will require a personal sense of being 'American' or 'British', and therefore of sharing, in some way, in a common heritage of traditions and values. But, in contrast to the particularity and detail of the Sienese example, the very diversity of ways of being American or British at the start of the twenty-first century means that the content of American and British civil religion must inevitably tend to be more generalized, more attenuated and less specific. Or at least this must tend to be the case unless one particular group seeks to impose its particular version of civil religion on American or British society as a whole – at which point the unifying function of civil religion itself begins to break down as rival versions of civil religion compete.[1] Hence the tendency for American and British rituals of remembrance to rely on reticence and studied ambiguity, thereby providing civil religious symbols and traditions that can unite different groups and opinions precisely because they remain imprecise and open to a variety of specific interpretations.

In this respect, civil religions are affected by globalization, even as they remain, in other ways, a testament to the continuing relevance of locality and particularity. For example, as both American and British societies become increasingly culturally and religiously diverse, the range of traditions that need to be encompassed by American or British civil religion – if such civil religions are genuinely to perform a

---

[1] See, for example, the brief discussion of this phenomenon in the context of the recent and contemporary USA in the introduction (pp.3–4), and the references to relevant literature cited there.

unifying function – requires, and will continue to require, the continued avoidance of over-specific civil religious symbols. At the same time, the diversity of the traditions that are accommodated within American and British civil religion can enrich the civil religion in question. Thus, the consideration of rituals of remembrance in this book suggests that, in both the British and American cases, at the level of the popular and the personal, remembrance of those killed in war has come to include elements that are not traditionally part of the predominant religious heritage of these societies. As noted in the introduction to this book, historically both the USA and the UK are predominantly Protestant cultures and societies; yet two of the most striking aspects of personal involvement in the rituals of remembrance in both countries are the sense of 'pilgrimage' to memorials, cemeteries or particular graves, and the stubborn insistence that, in some way, there is communication with the dead. These, however, are forms of behaviour that, in the Christian tradition, would normally be seen as characteristic of Catholic rather than Protestant belief and practice.

The development of the Internet also brings the impact of globalization to bear on civil religion, including the particular examples of civil religion considered here. In both the American and British cases, the Internet has brought new dimensions and possibilities to the processes of remembrance and memorialization of those killed in war. The Commonwealth War Graves Commission web site receives thousands of hits each week, and offers the possibility of tracing the records and the place of burial or memorial of individual service personnel. It also facilitates the possibility of visiting such locations by supplying information about the sites concerned. In the American context, meanwhile, the Internet offers the possibility of visiting the Virtual Wall, of locating particular names, of taking electronic rubbings of names, and of leaving electronic messages at the Virtual Wall.

The Internet also affects Siena and its traditions. Since the last quarter of the twentieth century, one of the major challenges facing the Sienese has been the impact of mass tourism, of the mass media, and of popular journalism, on Siena and the Palio. While proud of their city and its traditions, and while economically dependent on tourism, the Sienese are also only too aware of the acute tension that exists between increasing interest in the Palio – which is evident not least through a variety of web sites – and the preservation of the distinctively Sienese character and significance of this civil religious festival. The protection of the nature and the reputation of the Palio is a prominent preoccupation of the Sienese, and the globalizing effect of the Internet offers both opportunity and risk in this respect. On the one hand, the civic authorities may use the Internet to present accurate and officially approved information and up-to-date news of the Palio and its traditions. Similarly, the *contrade* can exploit the Internet as a further means of self-expression and communication – especially with, and for, *contrada* members not resident in Siena. But on the other hand, the Internet provides the opportunity for anyone to write about the Palio and its rituals, sympathetically or unsympathetically, accurately or inaccurately, in an informed manner or from a position of ignorance. Sienese civil religion – which is so local, so minutely detailed and so particular – is thus subjected to increasingly widespread, though not necessarily well-informed, scrutiny by the non-Sienese. It is hardly surprising, therefore, that the Sienese regard the preservation and protection of the authentic spirit and traditions of the Palio as a major concern.

The Sienese case is not the only evidence to suggest that the preservation of such local expressions of civil religion may be a significant phenomenon despite – or perhaps because of – the pressures of globalization. It is also possible to cite other examples of local communities asserting their distinctiveness through religious festivals that celebrate local identity and affirm the distinctiveness of local culture, even as many of the centralizing tendencies of modern life militate against the preservation of a sense of locality. It has been pointed out that in Spain, in recent decades, while there has been a marked decline in conventional religious practice, there has been a growing commitment to local festivals, the religious element of which is frequently focused on devotion to a local saint or to a local representation of the Virgin (Davie, 2000, pp.152–3). In such festivals, the overtly religious element is often central to the assertion of the unity of the local community – as, for example, in the particular case of the annual festival of the Virgin des Desemparats in Valencia. In terms that might, indeed, be applied with little or no adaptation to Siena, it has been argued that these local Spanish festivals should be regarded as genuinely religious, though not an expression of conventional Catholicism. Thus, there are many examples of:

> ... local dignitaries who do not 'believe' in any credal sense, but who see no incompatibility between their participation in the local festivities (including the religious aspects of this) and their formal stance *vis-à-vis* the church. This is not a question of religion versus non-religion, but of different manifestations of the sacred.
>
> (Davie, 2000, p.153, drawing on Albert-Llorca, 1996)

Such observations at once indicate both the importance and the limitations of the case studies of Sienese civil religion presented here. They suggest their importance because they point to the probability that the application of the concept of civil religion to other cities and local contexts would result in further fruitful studies of the interaction of locality, 'official' religion and 'civil' religion. They also suggest that Siena and Sienese civil religion may indeed represent a particularly highly developed and historically deeply-rooted example of civil religion in a local context. Conversely, they point to the limitations of the Sienese example precisely because they confirm that the phenomenon of local civil religion is by no means unique to Siena. Thus, in order to understand both the genuine distinctiveness of Sienese civil religion and its conformity to broader patterns and forms of local civil religion, it would be necessary to examine a variety of expressions of civil religion in other cities in Italy, Spain, elsewhere in Europe, and indeed in other parts of the world.

Consideration of some of the implications of globalization, and its complex relationship to locality, for the expression of the civil religions examined in this volume also raises the question of the wider relationship between civil religions and the broader themes of tradition, modernity and change that are addressed in the series of which this book is a part. Each of the expressions of civil religion considered here engages with the concept of tradition, and each also demonstrates that tradition itself is a fluid, developing phenomenon. In the case of the rituals of remembrance considered in Chapters 1–3, it was shown how traditions of remembrance were invented in both the USA and UK – in the American case primarily in the context of the Civil War, in the British case primarily in response to the First World War. It was also shown, however, that these traditions were not static, but developed during the twentieth century, and continue to develop in the present. In Chapters 4–7, meanwhile, it was shown that modern and contemporary Sienese civil religion self-consciously draws on traditions that date back several centuries. In Siena, therefore, it is less the invention of tradition that characterizes modern and contemporary Sienese civil religion, but rather the reinvention of tradition. Thus, for example, in the late nineteenth century, it was established that the historic parade before the Palio was to dress in medieval and renaissance style – a decision subsequently reaffirmed and defined more precisely at successive renewals of the costumes for the parade. Similarly, the procession to the cathedral carrying candles on the eve of the feast of the Assumption was reintroduced in 1924 after several decades in abeyance. However, modern Sienese civil religion has also involved the 'invention' of new traditions, such as commemorative publications to celebrate victory in the Palio, a practice only begun in the 1930s, and the introduction of *contrada* baptisms in the second half of the twentieth century.

The role of modernity in relation to the expressions of civil religion considered here is similarly clear. Thus, it was the distinctive character of modern warfare and its large-scale destruction of life that prompted the invention of both American and British rituals of remembrance. And at the beginning of the twenty-first century, it is the aggressively modern medium of the Internet that is responsible for some of the more innovative personal engagements with remembrance which are now possible, as individuals search records and memorials electronically. In the Sienese context, modernity is similarly significant in respect of the Palio and Sienese civil religion. Modern tourism, television, and now the Internet, have all obliged the Sienese to devise innovative strategies to promote knowledge and informed awareness of the Palio and the way in which it expresses and sustains Sienese traditions. Yet at the same time, these strategies must also protect the Palio from uninformed and inaccurate misrepresentation and preserve its rituals and rhythms from being swamped by the impact of modern mass culture and globalized communication. More positively, the Sienese experience of becoming part of the modern Italian nation state in the mid-nineteenth century gave rise to the reassertion of the distinctiveness of Sienese history, culture and civil religion even as Siena took its place within modern Italy. The development of Palio *drappelloni* from the mid-nineteenth century onwards offers an example of this process at work. As supporters of Italian unification, the Sienese celebrated the new nation on a number of the *drappelloni* of the years following Italian unification. Similarly, in the twentieth century, many *drappelloni* explicitly located Siena and Sienese civil religion within the wider Italian context. At the same time, however, the predominant theme of the imagery of Palio *drappelloni* of the twentieth century proved to be the self-conscious celebration of Siena itself and its rituals and traditions – a reassertion of *Senesità* that was itself prompted, in part at least, by the Sienese desire to reassert their continuing distinctiveness as Sienese even as they accepted and affirmed their identity as modern Italians.

As to change, again both the rituals of American and British remembrance and those of Sienese civil religion exhibit a dynamic and flexible capacity that enables them to adapt to new situations as well as to preserve and affirm continuity with the past. While older aspects of American rituals of remembrance – such as Veterans Day or Memorial Day – have been retained, the range of American rituals of remembrance has been expanded. The Vietnam Veterans Memorial has inspired renewed reflection on remembrance – leading to the creation of new memorials, such as the Korean War memorial and the memorial to black Americans who served in the Civil War, which itself uses the powerful symbol of listing the names of all the individuals it seeks to remember. And at the same time, the Vietnam Veterans Memorial has given rise to a whole variety of innovative rituals of remembrance inspired by the power of the monument itself. In the UK, the principal feature of rituals of remembrance would arguably be their preservation of 'traditions' first 'invented' following the First World War. Yet here too there are also signs of attempts to develop and change some emphases of British rituals of remembrance, whether by introducing increasing representation of religious traditions other than Christianity to official ceremonies, or by seeking to orientate remembrance to younger generations. In the Sienese case, the creative tension between preserving continuity and accommodating innovation is nowhere better exemplified than in the institution of *contrada* baptism. In order to preserve and sustain a sense of identity with particular geographical sections of the city at a time when social mobility was causing the dispersal of previously compact communities, the Sienese invented a new ritual of initiation. Within 50 years, however, that 'invented tradition' had become an integral and essential feature of the life of the *contrade*, and a central moment in the annual patronal festival of each of Siena's seventeen 'cities within the city'.

The examples examined in this book thus suggest that civil religion – whether national or local – shares with other, more familiar forms of religion a capacity to maintain distinct traditions, while engaging with modernity, and accommodating, and even at times initiating, change. As Robert Bellah observed over 30 years ago, in his seminal and still influential article on American civil religion, it would seem that, whatever the definitional controversies that may continue to surround it, civil religion 'has its own seriousness and integrity and requires the same care in understanding that any other religion does' (Bellah, 1967, p.1).

References

Albert-Llorca, M. (1996) 'Renouveau de la religion locale en Espagne', in G. Davie and D. Hervieu-Leger (eds) *Identités religieuses en Europe*, Paris: La Découverte, pp.235–52.

Bellah, R. (1967) 'Civil religion in America', *Daedalus*, 96, pp.1–21.

Davie, G. (2000) *Religion in Modern Europe: A Memory Mutates*, Oxford: Oxford University Press.

Glossary of Sienese words

In several cases, the Sienese words listed below appear in the text of Chapters 4–7 in both singular and plural form. Where two versions of a word appear in this glossary, the first is the singular version, and the second, in brackets, is the plural.

alfiere (*alfieri*) a member of a ***contrada*** who carries the *contrada* flag, with which he performs ritual displays of flag-play.

anno contradaiolo the ***contrada*** member's year, an alternative annual calendar, beginning on 1 December, and geared to the rhythm of the **Palio**.

balzana the black and white coat of arms that is the principal civic symbol of Siena, comprised of a shield, the top half of which is white and the bootom half of which is black.

bandiera (*bandiere*) the official flag of a ***contrada***.

Campo the central piazza of Siena, regarded as the heart of the city, where the **Palio** is run.

carroccio the huge cart on which the battle-standards of Italian cities were displayed in the medieval era. In the parade before each **Palio**, the modern version of the Sienese *carroccio* carries the ***drappellone*** for the Palio around the *Campo*.

cencio Sienese slang – literally meaning 'the rag' – for the ***drappellone***.

comparsa (*comparse*) a group in medieval or renaissance costume representing a ***contrada***.

contrada (*contrade*) one of the seventeen precisely defined districts within Siena into which the city is divided, and which compete in the **Palio**.

Corteo dei Ceri e dei Censi the annual procession each August, dating back to the thirteenth century, in which the Sienese process to Siena cathedral on the eve of the Feast of the Assumption, carrying candles as tributes to the Virgin.

Corteo Storico the two-hour historical parade before the **Palio**.

drappellone (*drappelloni*) the painted silk banner that is the prize for the ***contrada*** that wins the **Palio**.

fazzoletto (*fazzoletti*) the scarf, in the colours and displaying the symbols of a ***contrada***, worn by *contrada* members when they wish to display their *contrada* identity, especially during the **Palio** and the patronal festival of the *contrada*.

inno (*inni*) the official song, amounting to a 'national anthem', of a ***contrada***.

Magistrato delle Contrade the organization that represents the collective interests and concerns of the seventeen *contrade* of Siena.

Marcia del Palio the march that is played by the civic band during the historic parade before the **Palio**.

'Maria Mater Gratiae' the Marian hymn in Latin that is sung by *contrada* members at their patronal festival, when they visit the churches of other *contrade*, and when they win the **Palio**.

masgalano the prize awarded to the *contrada* whose *comparsa* presents the most elegant appearance in the historic parades before the **Palii** in a particular year.

nerbo the leather whip given to jockeys who ride in the **Palio** and which they may use against each other during the race.

Palazzo Pubblico the Sienese town hall that faces the **Campo**.

Palio (Palii) the twice-yearly festival that culminates in a horse race around the **Campo**.

prova (*prove*) the six 'trial' races that precede each **Palio** and take place in the three days preceding the Palio.

sbandierata an intricate and complex display performed with the flag of a *contrada*.

Sala della Vittoria the room in each *contrada* museum in which the *contrada* displays the *drappelloni* that it has won throughout the history of the **Palio**.

Senesità the quality and characteristics of being Sienese, what it is to be Sienese, 'Sieneseness'.

Solenne Mattutino the religious service in the church of the *contrada* that formally opens the celebration of the patronal festival of the *contrada*.

Sunto the large bell at the top of the **Torre del Mangia** that tolls throughout the historical parade before each **Palio**.

tamburino (*tamburini*) a member of a *contrada* who is a drummer in *contrada* parades.

Torre del Mangia the tall tower of the **Palazzo Pubblico**.

Index